London Serial Killers

London Serial Killers

Jonathan Oates

An imprint of
Pen & Sword Books Ltd
Yorkshire - Philadelphia

First published in Great Britain in 2022 by
PEN & SWORD CRIME
An imprint of
Pen & Sword Books Ltd
Yorkshire – Philadelphia

Copyright © Jonathan Oates 2022

ISBN 9781399003698

The right of Jonathan Oates to be identified as Author of this work has been asserted by him in accordance with the Copyright, Designs and Patents Act 1988.

A CIP catalogue record for this book is available from the British Library

All rights reserved. No part of this book may be reproduced or transmitted in any form or by any means, electronic or mechanical including photocopying, recording or by any information storage and retrieval system, without permission from the Publisher in writing.

Typeset in Chennai, India
by Lapiz Digital Services.

Printed and bound by CPI Group (UK) Ltd, Croydon CR0 4YY

Pen & Sword Books Ltd incorporates the imprints of Pen & Sword
Archaeology, Atlas, Aviation, Battleground, Discovery, Family History, History, Maritime, Military, Naval, Politics, Social History, Transport, True Crime, Claymore Press,
Frontline Books, Praetorian Press, Seaforth Publishing and White Owl
For a complete list of Pen & Sword titles please contact

PEN & SWORD BOOKS LTD
47 Church Street, Barnsley, South Yorkshire, S70 2AS, England
E-mail: enquiries@pen-and-sword.co.uk
Website: www.pen-and-sword.co.uk

Or

PEN AND SWORD BOOKS
1950 Lawrence Rd, Havertown, PA 19083, USA
E-mail: Uspen-and-sword@casematepublishers.com
Website: www.penandswordbooks.com

Contents

Acknowledgements vi

    Introduction 1

    Chapter 1: Jack the Ripper, 1888 3

    Chapter 2: The Deptford Poisonings, 1885–89. 28

    Chapter 3: The Lambeth Poisoner, 1891–92 46

    Chapter 4: The Southwark Poisoner, 1897–1902 64

    Chapter 5: The Brides in the Bath, 1912–14. 81

    Chapter 6: The Black Out Ripper, 1942 101

    Chapter 7: The Acid Bath Murders, 1944–49. 119

    Chapter 8: John Christie, 1943–53 137

    Chapter 9: The Thames Nudes Murders, 1964–65 156

    Chapter 10: Other serial killings? 1881–1948. 174

    Conclusion 191

Notes 197
Bibliography. 212
Index 215

Acknowledgements

This book has been greatly assisted by a number of the author's friends. Foremost among these is Lindsay Siviter, for loaning crucial texts, for commenting on this book's chapters and for help and encouragement. John Gauss has, as always, been kind enough to correct the author's grammar and English. John Curnow corrected parts of Chapter 8. Lindsay Siviter, John Coulter, Gareth Long and Paul Lang helped with the supply of pictures. Ros Seton has also provided advice.

This book is dedicated to Nikki Norris who prefers fact to fiction.

Introduction

In the last two decades there have been many books about serial killers. Many focus on those in the USA and Britain and provide fairly limited and poorly researched information on numerous cases. Many others study just one case. In Britain it is Jack the Ripper who has inspired a mini-industry of books, of varying quality, and although most set out to name the killer, none has yet done so satisfactorily. This book looks at London serial killers from the nineteenth to the later twentieth century (1888–1965). Some are well known, such as the Ripper killings and those by John Christie and John Haigh. Recently there has been a limited renaissance of books on the Nudes murders of the 1960s. Others are less known. There has never been a book dedicated to the Deptford poisonings of the 1880s, for instance. The Black Out Ripper is also relatively little known. Then there were a number of prostitute slayings in London in the 1930s and 1940s in Soho, which may have been the work of one man.

Each chapter does not aim to replicate the better books on the better-known cases (some, but by no means all, of which are listed in the bibliography), but will use contemporary sources throughout to produce a concise history of each. The police, prison and Home Office files from The National Archives are a major source used in this book, though there are none available for the some of the cases detailed here. Contemporary newspapers have also been used, as well as trial transcripts, and to a lesser extent the memoirs of police officers, pathologists and genealogical sources.

It is important to state what a serial killing is. The term itself became widely used at the end of the twentieth century to describe the relatively rare pattern of murders that has been occurring since at least the nineteenth century (Agatha Christie has a policeman use the term 'series murders' in 1936). It is well to remember that the crimes detailed in this book were not designated serial killings at the time; it is a much later term.

A serial killer is generally described as someone, usually a man, who kills at least three people over a period of time, with 'cooling off' stages between each crime. Method and motive are usually the same, and many are geographically limited. Motives are usually impersonal and sometimes there is little or no prior acquaintanceship between killer and victim. Often sexual and/or sadistic motivations are crucial. Serial killers can be divided into the organised and the disorganised, with the former going out prepared to kill and taking more precautions than the latter. They are often more difficult to apprehend than the majority of killers, and are liable to create a reign of terror in a district because it is impossible to predict who will be the next victim. Serial killers usually carry on killing until they are caught, or are imprisoned or die or are otherwise incapable of further slaughter, but not always.

This book is, then, a study of individual serial killers and their victims, in chronological order. It seeks to discuss the motivation and methods of the killers and how they escaped detection for so long, or did so wholly in some cases. It will also cast a light on changing methods of policing and detection and on those unfortunate people who suffered at their hands (to which we should add grieving family and friends). The last chapter covers a number of murders which may or may not have been serial killings.

Policing altered dramatically in the century and a half covered by this book. In 1829 the Metropolitan Police Force was established in what we would now call inner London by the then Home Secretary Robert Peel. London was divided into a number of divisions, each with its own police force headed by a superintendent, but responsible to the Commissioner of Police, who in turn took his orders from the Home Secretary; unlike later county forces, there was no Watch Committee, made up of councillors and magistrates, to oversee the police.

Initially the police were uniformed and were there to deter crime as much as to solve it, by means of regular patrols on foot. As the century progressed, a detective force was instituted, of plain-clothes men whose work was to investigate crime. Each London division had a detective force.

London had the biggest and best crime fighting force in Britain; so much so that county forces, lacking their expertise, would often call on Scotland Yard to send an experienced detective to lead a murder enquiry. Increasingly, in the twentieth century, science was used to assist the investigator. In 1905 fingerprints were first used to convict murderers. Pathologists such as doctors Bernard Spilsbury, Keith Simpson and Francis Camps brought their medical expertise to bear in the solving of crimes, as we shall see. A Police Laboratory was established in London in the 1930s to process evidence found at the scene of the crime, and thus killers who might have escaped in earlier decades were sometimes brought to justice. However, the new methods were not infallible and one of the unsolved cases featured in this book occurred in more recent times.

London itself changed radically in the period covered by this book. Already a populous city of over four million inhabitants in 1888, as well as being a centre of government, commerce and industry, it became more so by the mid-twentieth century, with a population of almost nine million by 1939. It had always been ethnically diverse, but had become more so with waves of immigration, from Eastern Europe in the late nineteenth century and from the Commonwealth in the 1950s and 1960s. The population was also transient, with some Londoners moving away from the capital in the post-1945 years. Many from other parts of Britain arrived to take their homes in London; many were very poor. London was and still is a city of great contrasts.

In the years covered by this book, the currency used in Britain was pre-decimal. Twelve pence made up a shilling and 20 shillings made up a pound. A guinea was 21 shillings. Cash values changed considerably and there is no attempt here to convert these into twenty-first century equivalents.

Chapter 1

Jack the Ripper, 1888

So much has been written about every aspect of the killings associated with this man and every scrap of known evidence has been pored over in minute detail. As with all major historical events, the story has been encrusted with a great deal of mythology that loses nothing in its repetition. It has spawned fantastic theories about the killer's identity which have been portrayed in books and films and so have gained much popular credence. Hundreds of men have been identified as the killer, yet in all cases on the scantiest of evidence, which would never have held up in court even if it got that far. A chapter of about 13,000 words cannot hope to rival the best of what has already been written on the case. Instead it aims to present in a concise format the salient facts of the case, with a minimum of theorising.

The murders took place in Whitechapel and Spitalfields, which was a poor district in London's East End. In 1888, the population of the district of the Whitechapel Board of Health was estimated to be 74,500. It was extremely crowded. The poorest lived in the 149 registered lodging houses existing there in that year, if they could afford them. Poverty, drunkenness, crime and vice were commonplace, but murder was not. Indeed, in the two decades prior to the Ripper's killings there was only one murder there per year on average. People died far more commonly from natural causes, as the medical officer of health noted: 'we suffer somewhat more from constitutional and respiratory diseases' than from violent crime; there were 24 deaths in 1888 from measles, for example. The death rate was 21.1 per 1,000 residents and 2,607 residents had died in 1888 (less than 1 percent were murdered). It was also a very ethnically diverse neighbourhood, with a large influx of refugees from eastern Europe, mostly Jewish, fleeing persecution, as well as a large number of Irish.[1]

There were two murders in Whitechapel in 1888 that are sometimes linked to the Ripper. The first occurred in the early hours of Tuesday 3 April 1888, when Emma Smith was brutally attacked in Osborne Street by Taylor's cocoa factory. She told how three men, including a youth, had set upon her and gave her injuries which were to prove fatal. She died in hospital on the following day. Most commentators do not believe she was a Ripper victim as her killer was not one man, but three.

Then there was the death of Martha Tabram or Turner, whose body was found in George Yard Buildings, just off Wentworth Street (now the very atmospheric Gunthorpe Street), on 7 August 1888. She was last seen by a friend with a soldier, but the man could not be identified in line-ups and a later client was probably her killer. She had been stabbed 39 times by a long knife or bayonet. Some consider her to be the first Ripper victim, but this is a far from universal view. Both women were prostitutes and had been killed savagely in the same district.

The first unquestioned Ripper murder was that of Mary Ann Nichols on 31 August 1888. She was born in London in 1845 and her father was Edward Walker. She married William Nichols, a printer, in London in 1864 and they had five children together, born between 1867 and 1880, and by 1888 four of them lived with their father and one with their grandfather. The pair had separated in about 1880 due to Mary's drinking habits and her husband's affair with Rosetta Walls, a neighbour whom he later married. Mary was living in south London.[2] Her husband had not seen her for three years. Mary had certainly fallen on hard times and had had to spend time in Southwark Workhouse in 1880, and the Holborn and Lambeth Union workhouses in 1888. More recently she had had lodgings in Thrawl Street, Whitechapel.[3]

Late on 30 August 1888 Mary was seen on Whitechapel Road and just after midnight was in the Frying Pan pub on Brick Lane. In the early hours of the next morning she was in a lodging house on Thrawl Street but was bereft of money. Confident she could earn it soon enough, she asserted 'I'll soon get my doss money. See what a jolly bonnet I've got now' and strolled out. She was last seen alive walking down Osborne Street at about half past two, by Emily Holland, with whom she had a brief conversation about having earned her doss money three times over but then spent it all on drink.[4]

It was in the early hours of Friday morning, 31 August, that Charles Lechmere Cross, a carman, was coming home from work. Shortly after 3.30am he saw something lying by a gateway in Bucks Row. Thinking it was a tarpaulin, he went over to inspect it and found himself looking at the body of a motionless woman. Seeing another man coming from the same direction as himself, he urged him to join with him in investigating. They touched the body and believed that the woman was either dead or dying. They then left the scene. They saw Constable Mizen and told him of their findings.[5]

The first policeman on the scene, however, was PC John Neil, who was on his beat when he saw a figure lying in the street, near the gateway to stables. It was about 3.45am (he had walked up the same street at 3.15 and had seen nothing untoward then). Blood was oozing from a wound in the woman's throat. The constable saw a colleague, probably PC Thain, in Brady Street and asked him to summon Dr Rees Ralph Llewellyn, who lived nearby, immediately. He asked another constable to fetch an ambulance. The doctor arrived at about 4am and had the body moved to the mortuary for an examination. PC Neil found a piece of comb, a bit of a looking glass and a handkerchief on the body. He had heard nothing suspicious and neither had two slaughtermen who were working nearby. There were no marks of any horse-drawn vehicle having been nearby (so much for the cinematic and TV treatments showing one being used by the killers).[6]

Dr Llewellyn examined the body at the scene of the crime and believed the woman had died at about 3.30 that morning, as the body was still warm. When he examined the body, which, to his annoyance, had been stripped of its clothing by two inmates of the workhouse, later that morning he noted that the 'abdomen was cut very extensively'. There was also bruising to each side of the face. The wounds that had killed her were the incisions across the neck made by a long knife 'moderately sharp and used with great violence'. What were more shocking were the very deep wounds to the lower abdomen, inflicted by the knife striking downwards. If murder was rare, mutilation was even rarer.[7]

Initial police investigations were led by Inspector Spratling, who learnt of the murder at about half past four that morning. There had been a bloodstain by the body, but there were no other signs of blood in nearby Brady Street and Bakers' Row. Enquiries were made with a railwayman whose signal box was 50 yards from where the body had been found, but he had 'heard nothing particular on the night of the murder'. Mrs Purkiss, a neighbour, had been awake at the time of the murder but her husband said that she had heard nothing and another neighbour, Mrs Green, had looked out on the scene but had seen nothing unusual. Nor had the slaughtermen, whose work was quiet enough, heard any vehicles or screams during the early hours.[8]

The inquest was held at the Working Lads' Institute on Whitechapel Road on Saturday 1 September and continued on Monday 3 September. The coroner was Mr Wynn E. Baxter, whose district was south-east Middlesex. The inquest was then adjourned for two weeks and then again. Evidence was given by police, witnesses and Dr Llewellyn. There was discussion over whether a reward should be offered, and that there had been other foul murders in the locality in recent times. The inquest concluded on 22 September. It is interesting to note that there was an element of class conflict, with a juryman raising the issue that the case would have been treated differently had the victim been a rich woman not a poor one. Mr Baxter gave a summing up. The murder had taken place shortly before 3.45 on the morning of 31 August, on Buck's Row. The abdominal injuries occurred when the body was on the ground.[9]

Baxter then turned to the identity of the murderer:

> It seems astonishing at first thought that the culprit should have escaped detection, for there surely must have been marks of blood

about his person. If, however, blood was principally on his hands, the presence of so many slaughter-houses in the neighbourhood would make the frequenters of this spot familiar with blood stained clothes and hands and his appearance in that way might have escaped attention…and was lost sight of in the morning market's traffic.[10]

The coroner commented on the dissimilarity between the weapon used in this case and those used in the murders of Emma Smith and Martha Tabram. Robbery and jealousy were ruled out as motives. A degree of anatomical knowledge was probably possessed by the killer, he said. He also noted of the crime that 'the audacity and daring is equal to its maniacal fanaticism and abhorrent wickedness'. The jury then brought in the inevitable verdict of murder by persons unknown.[11]

Baxter had also suggested that the killer had been disturbed before he could do all that he wanted to do to the body, and that the murder had many similarities with the next one, which occurred before the inquest on Mary had been completed.[12]

John Pizer of 22 Mulberry Street was a Polish shoemaker, known as 'Leather Apron'. He was arrested by PS Thicke on 9 September, on suspicion of being the murderer, but was released shortly after due to a lack of evidence and a cast-iron alibi. He then went into hiding.[13]

While the inquest into Mary's death was in progress, another murder occurred. John Davies was a carman employed at the Leadenhall Market who lodged at 29 Hanbury Street, Spitalfields. Shortly before 6am on 8 September he went out into the back yard and 'saw a woman lying down in the left hand recess, between the stone steps and the fence. She was on her back with her head towards the house and her legs towards the wood shed. The clothes were up to her groins'. There would have been no difficulty in anyone gaining access to the yard as the entrances to it were not locked.[14]

Davies also noticed two employees of Mr Bailey's, a packing-case maker located in Hanbury Street, standing nearby at the workshop. Davies knew them by sight and drew their attention to the body. They then went for the police. Davies went to the police station on Commercial Street and reported what he had seen to the inspector there.[15]

One of the men Davies saw was James Kent and he took a look at the body, later giving a description of what he had seen. It was shocking:

> I could see that the woman was dead. She had some kind of handkerchief round her throat which seems soaked in blood. The face and hands were besmeared with blood, as if she had struggled. She appeared to have been on her back and fought with her hands to free herself. The hands were turned to her throat. The legs were wide

apart and there were marks of blood upon them. The entrails were protruding and were lying across her left side.[16]

Inspector Joseph Chandler heard that another woman had been murdered at 6.10am. He went to the scene and saw the body, noting that the woman's skirt had been drawn up as far as her knees. A portion of her intestines was lying above her right shoulder and there were pieces of skin on both shoulders. After summoning Dr George Bagshaw Phillips, the surgeon attached to police division H, which covered the district, an ambulance and more men, he ensured no one went near the body and covered it with sacking. Once the others had arrived and the body was moved, he then examined the ground. There was a piece of coarse muslin, a small-tooth comb, and a pocket hair comb in a case, which were found by her feet. Close to her head he saw an envelope with two pills inside. On the back was a seal marked with 'The Sussex Regiment' and it was stamped 'London 3 Aug. 1888'. Elsewhere in the yard was a leather apron, saturated with water, not far from a water tap, and a box of nails, which were found to belong to a resident of the house. There were bloodstains on the fence and the floor where the body had been found. Some cheap rings had been removed from the woman's fingers.[17]

Dr Phillips arrived at Hanbury Street at 6.30am and examined the body properly at Whitechapel workhouse. He noted that the body was generally cold but there was some warmth remaining and it was just beginning to stiffen. He also observed that 'the throat was dissevered deeply'. It had been cut from left to right, and this had been done twice. To his annoyance, as in the case of Mary, the body had been stripped of its clothes before he got there. There were bruises on it. The body had also been mutilated after death. Shockingly, the woman's bladder and uterus had been removed from her body. He thought that the weapon used was 'a very sharp knife, probably with a thin, narrow blade, and at six to eight inches in length, probably longer'. It could not have been either a bayonet or a surgical instrument. It could have been a slaughterer's knife, ground down, but it was too long for a cobbler or leather worker's tool.[18]

There were also indications that the killer had some anatomical knowledge, as had been noted at the previous inquest. Dr Phillips said 'My own impression is that anatomical knowledge was only less displayed or indicated in consequence of haste. The person evidently was hindered from making a more complete dissection in consequence of the haste'. As to the removal of the organs, he said 'I think the mode in which they were extracted did show some anatomical knowledge'. He thought death had occurred by 4.30am and possibly earlier, that there had not been a struggle prior to death, and that the woman had been partially strangled first; the bruising on the chin suggested this.[19] The doctor's comments led some to believe that he was suggesting that the murderer was a doctor, but clearly he was not. Known doctor murderers tend to be poisoners.

The body was identified later in the morning by Amelia Palmer. It was that of Annie Chapman, née Smith, aged 47 on death and thus the oldest Ripper victim. She had been married to John James Chapman, a coachman, who had died in 1886, but the two had lived apart for several years though she had received a weekly allowance from him. They had had three children who lived with their father. In recent years Annie had lived in a variety of common lodging houses and was well known at one of the thirteen in Dorset Street. Her life of late had been miserable and she had suffered physical abuse (she had been in a quarrel and fight with another woman a few days prior to her death) and lacked even enough money for a cup of tea. Like Mary she drank to excess.[20]

Annie had been drinking in the Britannia pub on Friday 7 September. She was seen on Dorset Street at 5pm, when she told Amelia she was feeling unwell. Amelia last saw her at the same spot ten minutes later and Annie said 'It is of no use going away. I shall have to go somewhere to get some money to pay my lodgings'. Annie was in the common lodging house at 35 Dorset Street run by Timothy Donovan in the early hours of Saturday morning, having arrived at midnight, drunk. She had often stayed there in recent weeks. Donovan recalled that between 1.30am and 1.45am Annie had said to him, 'I have not sufficient money for my bed. Don't let it'. She needed another eight pence for her night's lodging. She then said, 'Never mind Tim, I shall soon be back. Don't let the bed'. With that she left, at about 1.50am. She walked towards Paternoster Row and onto Brushfield Street, as seen by John Evans, a night watchman. He said she was going in the direction of Spitalfields Church and that she was slightly inebriated.[21]

The inquest was begun at the same place and by the same coroner on 10 September and continued for the next three days. Dr Phillips did not want to detail or discuss the exact nature of the mutilations in court, but was pressed by the coroner to do so. He said that the mutilation would have taken at least a quarter of an hour and probably longer. He also remarked that 'the operation was performed to enable the perpetrator to obtain possession of these parts of the body'.[22]

A key witness was Mrs Elizabeth Long, who was walking along Hanbury Street with her husband in the early hours of 8 September on their way to Spitalfields Market. It was about 5am. She said:

> I saw a man and a woman standing on the pavement talking. The man's back was turned towards Brick Lane and the woman's was towards the market. They were standing only a few yards nearer Brick Lane from 29 Hanbury Street. I saw the woman's face. Have seen the deceased in the mortuary, and am sure the woman I saw in Hanbury Street was the deceased. I did not see the man's face, but I noticed he was dark. He was wearing a brown low crowned hat. I think he had

on a dark coat, but I am not certain. By the look of him he seemed to me to be a man of over 40 years of age. He seemed to me to be a little taller than the deceased.

Further questioning elicited that he looked like a foreigner (presumably meaning Jewish) and was 'shabby genteel' rather than being a dock labourer or a workman. They were talking pretty loudly and she heard him say 'Will you?' and she replied 'Yes'. They did not seem to be drunk and she had often seen people talking like that so did not pay much attention, as she carried on her journey.[23]

Amelia Richardson was a widow who lived at 29 Hanbury Street. She had gone to bed early but had a fitful sleep, waking at 3am and only dozing thereafter. She had heard nothing suspicious. Another resident, Harriett Hardiman, had heard nothing either. John Richardson, Amelia's son, recalled coming to the house at about 4.50am as he was concerned about potential burglary. He admitted that the back yard was often used by prostitutes and their clients and he had had to turn them out. However, he had not seen nor heard anything of significance.[24]

Baxter concluded the inquest by thanking those assembled and commenting on the social deprivation to be found among the lodging houses of Spitalfields: 'there is much in the nineteenth-century civilisation of which we have small reason to be proud'. He said that Annie's movements between 1.45am, when she left the lodging house, and 5.30am on Saturday 8 September, when seen by Mrs Long, were unknown. The brief exchange of words overheard by Mrs Long was clearly that of a client and a prostitute. He then discussed the discrepancies in the estimates of the time of Annie's death, but claimed that these were not unusual. She was not in the yard at 4.50am but was found dead there at 6am. He thought that the doctor's assessment of death occurring at 4.30am was wrong.[25]

Baxter believed that the killer had put his hand around Annie's throat and so rendered her speechless, before cutting her throat and mutilating the body. He noted that there was talk that the murderer must be mad, but the dissection of the body showed that he was clear headed enough to do what he did, perhaps with the intention of selling the uterus that he had removed. This might net him £20. He added 'His anatomical skill carries him out of the character of a common criminal, for his knowledge could only have been obtained by assisting at post mortems, of frequenting the post mortem room'. He therefore thought that this limited the pool of suspects and that allied with Mrs Long's description, and the fact that the killer had bloody hands and was away from home early on Saturday morning, should make it possible to apprehend him. The jury brought in the murder verdict and added that Whitechapel needed a proper mortuary rather than the workhouse shed.[26]

This murder suggested that the killer had been fearful of being disturbed after he had killed Mary; there had been cuts to her abdomen, perhaps preliminary to dissection, but nothing more. In the case of Annie he had been undisturbed for longer. With two murders by the same hand within a week, and after the other two killings earlier in the summer, the people of Whitechapel were understandably worried while the police made every effort to apprehend the killer. In this they were unsuccessful.

On 27 September the Central News Agency received the following letter, dated two days earlier:

> Dear Boss,
> I keep on hearing the police have caught me, but they won't fix me just yet. I have laughed when they look so clever and talk about being on the right track. That joke about leather apron gave me real fits. I am down on whores and shant quit ripping them till I do get buckled. Grand work the last job was. I gave the lady no time to squeal. How can they catch me now. I love my work and want to start again. You will soon hear of me with my funny little games. I saved some of the proper red stuff in a gingerbeer bottle over the last job to write with but it went thick like glue and I can't use it. Red ink is fit enough I hope ha ha The next job I do I will clip the lady's ears off and send to the police officers just for jolly wouldn't you Keep this letter back till I do a bit more work then give it out straight My knife's so nice and sharp. I want to get to work right away if I get a chance good luck
> Yours truly
> Jack the Ripper
> Don't mind me giving the trade name.[27]

The letter may well have been a hoax, but it is important in that it gave the unknown murderer a label by which he would be known forever after. Chief Inspector John Littlechild, writing about the letter in 1913, wrote 'it was generally believed at the Yard that Tom Bulling at the Central News was the originator'. Littlechild thought that it was 'a smart piece of journalistic work' and that Bulling's boss, Charles Moore, was the brains behind the phrase.[28]

Unfortunately the murderer's appetite was unsated. Just over three weeks after Annie's death he struck again, but this time he claimed not one victim, but two. He clearly had enjoyed his first two murders and, having got away with them, wanted to repeat the experience. Given the number of lone women on the streets at night it was unfortunately all too easy for him to find victims.

At 12.40am on Sunday 30 September, Morris Eagle was returning to the International Men's Working Club at 40 Berner Street, having attended a meeting there the previous night and then having taken his girlfriend home. He found that the front door was locked, so he went through the gateway into the yard, known as Dutfield's Yard. He did not recall seeing anything untoward there and went into the club where he met a friend and they sang songs for twenty minutes. Then a man called Gidleman came upstairs and told them, 'there is a woman dead in the yard'. They all went down and Morris recalled the sight: 'I saw a woman lying on the ground in a pool of blood near the gates. Her feet were towards the gates, about six or seven feet from them. She was lying by the side of and facing the club wall'.[29]

However, the first man to see the corpse, not that he knew it, was Louis Diemshutz, the club's steward, who was driving his pony and cart into the club's yard. It was about one o'clock. The pony shied at some object on the ground but its master could not distinguish what it was. So he jumped down and struck a match. He could see from the dress that it was the body of a woman, whether drunk or dead he could not tell. He immediately went into the club for help from his comrades there and then went out to the street to find a policeman. He found one in Grove Street, Constable Henry Lamb, and said 'Come on, there has been another murder' and together they went back to take a closer look at the woman. It was then that they could see that her throat had been cut.[30]

While waiting for a doctor to arrive, the police took the details of the thirty men in the club and searched them. The buttons on the top of the bodice of the victim were open, blood was flowing from her and the body was still warm. PC Lamb thought she was dead, but could see no sign of any struggle. The clothes were undisturbed. He kept the crowd back as he waited for help to arrive. The victim had a spray of flowers attached to her coat.[31]

Mr Frederick William Blackwell was the first surgeon on the scene at 1.16am. Although the woman's hands were cold, most of the body was warm. Her right hand was bloody but the left held a small packet of cachous (breath sweetener lozenges). He noted the deadly wound: 'In the neck there was a long incision which exactly corresponded with the lower border of the scarf. The border was slightly frayed, as if by a sharp knife. The incision in the neck commenced from the left side, 2 inches below the angle of the jaw and almost in direct line with it, severing the vessels on that side, cutting the windpipe completely in two and terminating on the opposite side'.[32]

Blackwell thought that death had occurred between 12.46 and 12.56am. There was a minimum of blood and she would not have been able to have made a noise prior to death. He thought 'the murderer probably got hold of the silk scarf, which was tight and knotted, and pulled the deceased backwards, cutting her throat in that way'. He also considered that the killer put his hand over her nose and mouth before doing this.[33]

On her person was found a padlock key, a small piece of a pencil, a comb, a broken comb, a spoon, several buttons, a dress hook, a piece of muslin and several scraps of paper.[34]

Elizabeth Tanner was the deputy of a common lodging house at 32 Flower and Dean Street, and she identified the deceased. She had lodged there on and off since 1882 and was known there as 'Long Liz'. She had slept there on the Thursday and Friday evenings before she died. She had been born in Sweden and alleged that her husband and children had been drowned while aboard *The Princess Alice* (this latter story was completely invented). She was rather secretive about her past.[35]

Her full name was Elizabeth Stride, née Gustafsdotter, wife of John Thomas Stride, a carpenter. She had been born on 27 November 1843 at Torlandsa near Gothenburg in Sweden. She came to England in 1866 and married Stride in 1869; they lived in Poplar in 1871 where Elizabeth was described as being a servant. She had been a member of the Swedish church since 1866. Elizabeth was very poor.[36]

Elizabeth Tanner had last seen Liz alive on Saturday 29 September, when the two women had been together at the Queen's Head pub in Commercial Street. The two then returned to the lodging house. The two women went to different parts of the building and then never saw each other again. Catherine Lane, a charwoman, who also lived in the lodging house, remembered seeing her there between 6 and 7pm that evening. She was wearing a long coat and a black bonnet, which she had not had on previously. Before leaving she asked Catherine to keep a large green piece of velvet for her until she returned. She also asked another occupant, Charles Preston, a barber, for a clothes brush, but he did not have one. They were in the kitchen at that time. On leaving she did not say where she was going or why, but she was very short of money and only had sixpence, earned from cleaning the lodging house earlier that day.[37]

Liz Stride was then seen at a quarter to midnight by William Marshall, a labourer. She was standing on the pavement opposite 58 Berner Street. With her was a man and they were talking together. Unfortunately there was no light nearby and Marshall could not see the man's face distinctly. However, he was able to note that he wore a black cutaway coat and dark trousers. He seemed to be middle aged and wearing a cap. The latter was round, with a small peak, of the type that a sailor might wear. He was about five feet six, rather stout and decently dressed, a businessman, not a labourer. He looked like a clerk, rather than a dock labourer, a sailor or a butcher.[38]

Furthermore, Marshall did not think the man had whiskers and was rather more sure that he was not wearing gloves nor carrying a stick or umbrella. The pair stood there for some time and the man kissed the woman. He also spoke a few words, saying 'You would say anything but your prayers', at which the woman laughed. The tone of voice seemed that of a clerk, or an educated man. The pair then walked away towards Ellen Street and not towards the club. Both seemed sober. It was about midnight.[39]

PC William Smith saw a couple in Berner Street just after half past twelve. The two were talking. The man had a parcel wrapped in newspaper with him and was about five feet seven tall. He wore a dark felt deerstalker hat and was wearing dark clothes and a cutaway coat. He was clean shaven, aged about twenty-eight and of a respectable appearance. Both were sober but he did not hear any conversation.[40]

Another witness had seen the couple at about a quarter to one. James Brown, a dock labourer, had just been out for his supper and saw two people near the Board school. The man had a long dark coat, was about five feet seven, and of average build. He could not detect any speech or whether the man wore a cap.[41]

There was a final and perhaps most important sighting. Israel Schwartz saw a man and a woman at the gateway to the club, very near where Elizabeth's body was found. He said that 'the man tried to pull the woman into the street, but he turned her round and threw her down on the footway and the woman screamed three times, but not very loudly'. The man was aged about thirty, and wore a dark jacket and trousers with a peaked cap. He had a moustache and was five feet five inches tall, with brown hair and broad shoulders. This might well have been the killer. Schwartz walked away but was pursued by another man who was nearby, but Schwartz did not know if these two men were acquainted.[42]

Two days after the murder, Thomas Coram found a knife outside 253 Whitechapel Road, which was used as a laundry. It was a foot long and an inch broad, with a handkerchief tied round the handle. The blade was discoloured. He brought this to the attention of PC Joseph Drage, who picked it up and thought it was covered in blood. He thought it had been placed there recently and passed it to Dr Phillips.[43]

Another possible piece of evidence was supplied by Mr Packer, who ran a fruiterer's on Berner Street. He told the police that at 11pm on the night of the murder two people came into his shop. He thought that one was Elizabeth Stride, as she had a flower on her clothing. They bought half a pound of grapes, then left in the direction of the club. Her companion was a young man, aged 25–30, with a long black coat, buttoned up, and a soft felt hat. He was broad shouldered and spoke with a quick, rough voice. However, Packer's evidence was discounted because he gave numerous and varied accounts of the same story.[44]

Michael Kidney was a waterside labourer of 38 Dorset Street, Spitalfields and had been living with Elizabeth since 1885; they had apparently had an argument on Tuesday 25 September, though he claimed not, causing her to leave him for the lodging house.[45]

Unlike the previous inquests, this one was held in the Vestry Hall of St George's in the East, beginning on Monday 1 October. As before, Baxter presided. Initially the identity of the victim was unknown, but the name of Elizabeth Stride was being bandied about. Baxter did not want to discuss her identity on the first day of the inquest, so after the jury had viewed the body and statements had been taken from the club members, the inquest was adjourned until the next day.[46] Mrs Malcolm initially identified the deceased as her sister Mrs Elizabeth Watts and this caused some confusion.[47]

On 3 October, a very disgruntled Kidney was giving evidence and he said that the police were inept as they had not caught the killer. He had been to the Leman Road police station, where he had claimed 'I could give information that would enable the detectives to discover the man at any time'. If he was given a detective to command he would be able to find him, he said, but could offer nothing more concrete despite the coroner trying to pry his knowledge out of him, saying 'I have had over a hundred letters making suggestions'. Kidney had no knowledge that Elizabeth had any enemies, which was the case with the previous victims.[48]

Dr Phillips was asked on the fifth day of the inquest to make additional remarks about the murder and in particular the weapon used. He said that the knife found on the High Street could have been the murder weapon, but he thought it probably was not. The knife used, he said, was shorter than that used in the previous murders and was not sharp pointed. He thought the murder was done in seconds and could not account for the victim's right hand being bloody. He thought that the killer would not have been bloodied as the blood went away from him as he cut her from behind. He also said the cutting had been less than that which had occurred on Annie's neck.[49]

The inquest was concluded on 23 October. Baxter discussed the question of the identity of the deceased and her final movements. He then queried whether the man seen with her at just before midnight was the same man who was seen with her in the next hour. The descriptions did not exactly tally, but this was not conclusive. He could not suggest any motive for the murder. Could it have been a copycat killer? 'There had been the same skill exhibited in the way in which the victim had been entrapped, the injuries inflicted, as to cause instant death and prevent blood from soiling the operator and the same daring defiance of immediate detection, which…had hitherto been only too successful'. The jury returned the inevitable verdict of murder by person or persons unknown and Baxter thanked the jury and police for all their efforts.[50]

The early hours of Sunday 30 September were to yield another horror. Catherine Eddowes was born in 1842 in Wolverhampton but was living in Bermondsey with her family by 1843. She was one of seven children and her father was a tin plate worker. She lived with a man called Thomas Conway, a hawker, from at least 1861–1871, living in Hackney and St George's in the East and then Chelsea by 1881. They had two sons and a daughter together; once they were adults the children did not want their mother to find them because she was always wanting money from them. From 1881 Catherine with a man called John Kelly, a labourer, having split from Conway because of her drinking. They lived in a common lodging house at 55 Flower and Dean Street, known as Cooney's (there were at least thirty lodging houses on this street). She had also suffered great poverty, as had some of the previous victims. In her case she had been in numerous workhouses: at Southwark in 1873–1874, at Greenwich Workhouse in 1876–1877 and later at Holborn in 1880 and 1888.[51]

Kelly last saw Catherine alive on Saturday 29 September at 2pm in Houndsditch. She said that she was going to Bermondsey to see her daughter, Annie. She told Kelly that she would be back by 4pm. She did not go there. The couple had been hop-picking in Kent earlier in the week but made little money and were penniless by Saturday; Kelly had even had to pawn his boots for a few pence. The two seemed to be on good terms with one another.[52]

City Constable Lewis Robinson, at half past eight that evening, was on High Street Aldgate and saw a crowd gathering near number 29. He saw a drunk woman lying on the pavement. This was Catherine. No one knew where she lived and she was unable to walk by herself. The constable called a colleague and they took her to the Bishopsgate Street police station. She was asked her name but refused to answer, so was put in a cell. She remained there until 1am on 30 September. Then PS James Byfield asked her for her name and address, which she gave as Mary Ann Kelly of 6 Fashion Street, Spitalfields, which given the next victim, was ironic in retrospect, but given that her lover's surname was Kelly it is not too surprising. She was now sober and said that she had been hop-picking recently. She was then released.[53]

The officer who set her at liberty was PC George Hutt, acting under Byfield's orders. He took her to the exit and asked her to close the door when she left. She said to him, 'All right. Good night, old cock'. She walked in the direction of Houndsditch. It was 400 yards from the police station to Mitre Square.[54]

Joseph Lawende had been with friends in the Imperial Club, Duke's Place, leaving at 1.30am. About five minutes later, he saw a man and a woman at Church Passage, Duke Street, which led into Mitre Square. The woman had her hand on the man's breast and he was taller than her. The man wore a cloth peaked cap. He looked rather rough and shabby. Joseph Levy was with Lawende and he remembered seeing the two, as well as thinking 'they were up to no good'. They did not hear the people speak. Levy thought the man was about five foot three and later identified the woman as Catherine Eddowes.[55]

PC Edward Watkins of the City Police was on a nightly beat on Sunday morning of 30 September. It was a quiet night and he passed through Mitre

Square at 1.30am. Mitre Square falls just within the boundaries of the City of London and so was policed by the City Police rather than the Metropolitan Police, who had investigated the earlier murders. His lantern was affixed to his belt and as usual he looked into the passages and corners of the square. He recalled 'I next came into Mitre Square at 1.44, when I discovered the body lying on the right as I entered the square. The woman was on her back, with her feet towards the square. Her clothes were thrown up. I saw her throat had been cut and the stomach ripped open. She was lying in a pool of blood'. Touching nothing, he fetched George Morris, a night watchman at a nearby warehouse, saying, 'For God's sake, mate, come to my assistance' and then called for help and another constable soon arrived, followed by the doctors and senior officers.[56]

Inspector Collard and Dr Frederick Gordon Brown, the surgeon attached to the City Police, arrived just after 2am. Near to the body were the woman's few meagre possessions: several buttons, a thimble and a tin containing two pawnbroker's tickets. There was no money. Her head and neck were in a pool of blood but there was no blood in front of her. Given the liquid state of the blood, the murder must have taken place very recently. Judging from the lack of marks on the ground and the state of the victim and her clothes, there was no evidence that any struggle had taken place.[57] Dr Brown noted:

> The clothes were thrown up. The bonnet was at the back of the head. There was great disfigurement of the face. The throat was cut across. Below the cut was a neckerchief. The upper part of the dress had been torn open. The body had been mutilated and was quite warm – no rigor mortis. The crime must have been committed within half an hour... There were no stains of the blood on the pavement.[58]

The other medical man on the scene was Dr Sequeria. He noted that the body was found in the darkest part of the square, but even so there was sufficient light from the street lighting to enable the killer to do what he did. He thought death occurred at about 1.45am. He differed from his colleague in one viewpoint, however, as he did not think that the killer had much anatomical skill nor was he seeking any particular organ.[59]

Meanwhile police constables were sent out in all directions from Mitre Square. Men found in the streets were questioned and searched. There was house-to-house questioning in the immediate vicinity of the murder. Nothing tangible was found. Empty houses were searched. No one had heard any suspicious footsteps.[60]

During the search of the nearby streets, PC Alfred Long, at 2.55am, found a portion of a white apron taken from the deceased in a passage off Goulston Street, which is a few minutes' walk to the north-east from Mitre Square. There were bloodstains on it, so presumably the killer had been there. The apron piece had not been there half an hour earlier when he had passed by previously. He also found, chalked on the wall nearby, the following message, 'The Juwes are the men that will not be blamed for nothing'. Instructions were given by the City Police for the message to be photographed, but the Metropolitan Police, fearing an anti-semitic riot, had it washed off. Sir Charles Warren, the Commissioner of the Metropolitan Police, came down in person to see that this was done at five in the morning. He later had to justify his actions to the Home Secretary. The message may or may not have been written by the murderer. Enquiries were made at nearby houses but no one had seen or heard anyone in the vicinity of the passage.[61]

Meanwhile, Catherine's body was taken by ambulance to the City Mortuary after it had been seen in situ by Dr Brown. Once there, in the presence of Inspector Collard and the doctor, the clothes were removed. Dr Brown then examined the body. He thought that death would have been immediate from the throat wound. Unlike the other three victims, the face had been mutilated. There were cuts on the nose, cheeks, eyelids, jaw, lips and mouth. Elsewhere, the left kidney had been cut out and so had most of the uterus. These had not been found. These injuries were caused when she was lying on the ground.[62]

The cuts led the doctor to make a number of conclusions about the murderer. He said 'The way that the kidney was cut out showed that it was done by somebody who knew what he was about'. He added 'He must have had a good deal of knowledge as to the position of the abdominal organs, and the way to remove them'. This is what had already been noted at previous inquests. As to the weapon, it 'must have been a sharp pointed knife... at least six inches long'. Because the kidney was covered by a membrane it would easily be overlooked when a body was cut open.[63]

Someone used to cutting open animals might have the skills necessary, but the organs could not be used for any professional purpose. It would have taken the killer at least five minutes to remove the organs as an absolute minimum. Brown also thought that the killer would not necessarily have been bloodstained because he would have knelt by the body when dissecting it. He said that the only purpose of the facial mutilation was to disfigure the face. The victim would not have been able to cry out so it could all have been done very quietly indeed.[64]

Mr S.F. Langham was the coroner for the City of London and the inquest was held in the Coroners' Court in Golden Lane. It began on 4 October. The victim's sister, who had identified the body, gave a tearful account of her sister's life of poverty and misery. It was ascertained that the distance between Berner Street and Mitre Square was but three-quarters of a mile, or about 12 minutes' walk, so the killer could have easily got there after having killed just before 1am. Although there had been talk of offering rewards to catch the killer, the Home Office had not approved this. However, the City of London put a price of £500 on the murderer's head. The hearing was resumed on 11 October.[65]

At the second hearing, Annie Phillips, daughter of the deceased, gave an account of her mother's tragic life and family estrangements because of her behaviour. There was discussion about the decision to erase the Goulston Street graffiti, and discrepancies about what exactly was written there. Daniel Halse, a City detective, stated that it had read 'The Juwes are not the men that will be blamed for nothing'. He thought it had been recently written and that it had been written in a good schoolboy's style of round handwriting. However, PC Long brought his notebook along to confirm in writing what he had said verbally. Unlike Baxter, the coroner did not feel it was necessary to summarise all the witness statements, but he did say that 'the crime was a most fiendish one could not for a moment be doubted, for the miscreant, not content in taking a poor defenceless woman's life, endeavoured so to mutilate the body as to render it unrecognisable'. He hoped the police would pursue their enquiries and that the reward would help bring the killer to justice. The jury then brought in the inevitable verdict.[66]

On the day after the murders, George Lusk, chairman of the Whitechapel Vigilance Committee, a mild-mannered businessman, received a peculiar package through the post. He thought it was a bizarre practical joke, for it contained part of a human kidney, once preserved in alcohol, and a note which read:

'From hell
Mr Lusk
Sor
I send you half the kidne I took from one woman presarved it for you tother piece I fried and ate it was very nise. I may send you the bloody knif that took it out if you only wate a while longer
Signed Catch me when
you can
Mishter Lusk'.[67]

This was duly reported to the police and examined. The fact that Catherine Eddowes had had her kidney removed on the previous night seemed to suggest that it might have been from the killer himself, taunting Lusk. There is much doubt about whether it came from the murderer, however. The police also received many crank letters and postcards, some purportedly coming from the killer. Infamously in 1978–79 the West Yorkshire Police received letters and a cassette from a man claiming to be the Yorkshire Ripper, which were also hoaxes. Unsolved crimes often generate such anonymous communications.

After this 'double event' there was no further murder for a month. Some felt that the killer had ceased his evil work. In this they were to be disappointed. The final outrage was the worst of all.

Mary Jane Kelly, also known as Marie Jeanette Kelly, lived with Joseph Barnett, a fish porter who also worked in the markets, in a room with the address 13 Miller's Court, just off Dorset Street, reached by a short passage. They had lived there since the beginning of the year, but they separated on 30 October on account, said Barnett, of the fact that Marie had allowed Maria Harvey, a prostitute, to stay with the couple in the room despite Barnett's objections. However, he visited her on both Tuesday 6 November and Thursday 8 November. They parted on kindly terms and the latter was a brief visit. As he was unemployed he had no money to give her, for which he was sorry. He had left her between 7.30 and 7.45pm. Marie Harvey was also present then, and recalled him saying to her, 'Mary Jane, I will not see you again this evening'.[68]

Unlike the previous victims, little is known for sure about Marie, the youngest by far of the Ripper's victims, and most of it is what she had told Barnett. She claimed she had been born in Limerick and then moved with her family when quite young to live in south Wales. Her father was called John, a gaffer in a Carmarthen ironworks. She had a sister and six brothers. She had been married to a collier when very young but he had died in a mining accident and she then lived in Cardiff. She arrived in London in 1884 and worked in a West End brothel, or so he said that she had told him. She then briefly lived in Paris before returning to England, this time to London's East End. She had lived with a succession of different men, in Ratcliffe, Stepney and Poplar.[69]

Barnett had met Marie in Commercial Street. They had had a drink together and arranged to co-habit, first in George Street. She was interested in the murders and Barnett would read her the relevant stories from the newspapers. Julia Vanturney, a neighbour, recalled that Barnett would not allow her to go out at night and that she was fond of another man, also called Joe, a costermonger.[70]

Mary Ann Cox was another neighbour, living at 5 Miller's Court. She had seen Marie at a quarter to midnight on 8 November. She was very drunk, which was not uncommon. She was in Dorset Street and went into Miller's Court. She was not alone and Mary Cox recalled that with her was 'a short stout man, shabbily dressed. He had on a longish coat, very shabby, and carried a pot of ale in his hand'. He had a dark coat and a hard billycock hat. He had a blotchy face and a full carotty moustache. She could not recall his hair, however, but he was clean shaven and was aged about 36. He was not carrying anything but the beer pot in his hand. The two women said goodnight to each other. Marie added 'I am going to have a song... A violet I plucked from my mother's grave when a boy'. Julie Vanturney recalled that Marie often sang Irish ballads.[71]

Mary returned to her room and left fifteen minutes later. When she returned, at 1am, she could still hear Marie singing. She went out again, returning at 3am. By this time, the light in Marie's room was out and all was quiet.[72]

Elizabeth Prater, another neighbour, recalled returning home at about 1am, but did not go to her room, which was above that of the deceased, until about 1.20. She went to sleep ten minutes later and did not awake until about 3.30–3.45, when her kitten, Diddles, woke her. She then recalled hearing the cry 'Oh murder' from the court. It was not heard again, but such a cry was not unusual, so she took no notice of it. Sarah Lewis heard the same cry, but at almost 4am. She did nothing either. Julia Vanturney did not remember such a cry in the night.[73]

Sarah Lewis was visiting a friend at Miller's Court just after 2am. She saw a stout-looking man, with a black hat and not very tall, looking up at the rooms there and he seemed to be waiting for someone. She also saw a man and a woman together; the latter worse for drink. She had also seen a man with a woman that morning on Commercial Street, near the Britannia pub. He was short, pale faced, with a black moustache and was about forty years old. Two days earlier he had tried to inveigle Sarah to follow her into an entry. He was carrying a black bag.[74]

However, Caroline Maxwell, wife of a lodging-house deputy, had a rather different recollection of Marie's last movements than the previous witnesses. She recalled that between 8am and 8.30am on Saturday 9 November she had seen Marie at the entrance of the court. It was unusual to see her at such an early hour and the two women conversed briefly. Marie told Caroline that she felt unwell and Caroline sympathised with her. She was then seen outside the Britannia pub, talking to a man, at some time before 9am. He was stout, wearing dark clothes and a plaid coat.[75] This account conflicts with the testimonies of Elizabeth Prater and Sarah Lewis, which suggest the murder occurred several hours earlier.

There was another witness statement, this time by a man. George Hutchinson told police that he had met Marie at the end of Commercial Street at 2am. She asked him for money but he had none. Shortly after she passed by, she returned with a man. She made a proposition to him and he agreed with it. They went into Miller's Court, pausing at the entrance where she said 'come along you shall be comfortable'. Hutchinson stayed nearby for three-quarters of an hour, but neither reappeared. He recalled that the man was carrying a parcel with a strap. Unlike most of those men seen with the victims, this man was very respectable in appearance, with an astrakhan coat and a gold chain. He was about 35 years old, with a pale complexion, dark eyes, and a slight moustache. He was stated as having 'a Jewish appearance'.[76]

After day broke later that Saturday, Thomas Bowyer was ordered by his boss, John McCarthy, to go to 13 Miller's Court to collect the rent that was owed to McCarthy as he was the landlord of the property. It was 10.45am. The rent was in serious arrears to the tune of 29s (it was 4s 6d per week) and he went to the place and knocked on the door. There was no reply. Numerous knocks went unanswered. So he went around the corner and looked through the little window of the property. It was broken and so he put his hand through it and lifted the curtain. He recalled 'I saw two pieces of flesh lying on the table'. The table was in front of the bed.[77]

Bowyer then took another look at the little room and recalled, 'I saw a body on this bed and blood on the floor'. He left and went to see Mr McCarthy in his chandler's shop at 27 Dorset Street and told him what he had seen. McCarthy recalled that Bowyer said 'Guvnor, I knocked on the door and could not make anyone answer. I looked through the window and saw a lot of blood'. The two men returned to the scene so McCarthy could verify what his employee had said. They then went to the Commercial Street police station and spoke to Inspector Beck.[78]

Dr Phillips was called out by the police and arrived at about 11.15am. The door was locked and, looking through the broken panes of glass, he could see that he could not render any medical assistance. Nothing could be done immediately, though police stopped anyone leaving the court, and they were told that bloodhounds were on their way. Detective Inspector Frederick Abberline of the CID, who was in charge of the Ripper investigation on the ground, was also then present. So they waited. At 1.30pm, hearing that the order for the dogs had been countermanded, McCarthy broke the door open under Superintendent Arnold's supervision. He noted, 'The mutilated remains of a woman were lying, two-thirds over, towards the edge of the bedstead, nearest the door'. The deceased had an undergarment on and had been moved after death. There was much blood under the bedstead and the doctor surmised that her throat had been cut when she was lying on the right side of the bedstead.[79]

Abberline recalled that there had been a large fire in the grate that night, so hot that the spout of the kettle had melted. Sifting through the ashes, he found remnants of clothing, mainly those of a woman, but also part of the brim of a hat. He thought that these items had been burnt so as to provide a light in the room for the killer to undertake his mutilations. Other than that there was only a candle atop a broken wine glass. He found a clay pipe, belonging to Barnett, who told him that the key to the door had been missing for a long time, so the door was put on the latch and that could be easily lifted from the outside by putting one's hand through the broken window.[80]

The inquest took place at Shoreditch Town Hall on 12 November. It was overseen by Dr MacDonald, MP, coroner for the North East division. Barnett identified the body. After hearing his evidence and that of the neighbours and those who arrived on the scene the next day, he asked the jury whether they wanted to adjourn the inquest in order to hear additional evidence, or whether they thought they had heard enough to decide how the woman had died and to leave the evidence for the magistrates' court. They decided on the former and so returned the only verdict possible, that this was murder by an unknown assailant.[81]

Dr Thomas Bond undertook the post mortem, which does not make for pleasant reading. He had seen the body on the bedstead and noted that:

> The whole of the surface of the abdomen and thighs was removed and the abdominal cavity emptied of its viscera. The breasts were cut off, the arms mutilated by several jagged wounds and the face hacked beyond recognition of the features. The tissues of the neck were severed all round down to the bone.
>
> The viscera were found in various parts, viz: the uterus and kidneys with one breast under the head, the other breast by the right foot, the liver between the feet, the intestines by the right side and the spleen by the left side of the body. The flaps removed from the abdomen and the thighs were on a table.

He also noted that the bed clothing in the corner was saturated with blood and on the floor was a pool of blood about two feet square. There were splashes of blood on the wall in line with the neck.

The details as uncovered in the mortuary were even worse. The face was badly cut, with nose, ears, eyebrows and cheeks all partially removed. The lips had been cut and there were additional marks thereon. The throat had been cut down to the bone. The air passage had been cut and both breasts had been cut off. Skin had been stripped from both thighs and the abdomen. The left calf had been deeply gashed and both arms and forearms had received jagged wounds. The lower part of the right lung had been torn away. The heart was missing. The stomach gave evidence of Marie's last meal: fish and potatoes.[82]

This behaviour on the killer's part was the culmination of his earlier attacks. He had been able to completely destroy Marie. He had done far less in his earlier attacks, but now he had the time to do even worse, which had not been possible in earlier instances. Working inside he was undisturbed.

Subsequently there were other killings locally. Rose Mylett, found strangled in nearby Poplar on 20 December 1888, and whose killer was never found, has sometimes been added to the killer's tally, as has the dismembered torso which was found in September 1889 in Pinchin Street, Whitechapel. Neither seem probable, though, due to discrepancies in the *modus operandi*.

There were no more murders which even remotely resembled the Ripper's handiwork until the early hours of 17 July 1889. A policeman found the body of a middle-aged woman in Castle Alley. Her throat had been cut. Dr Phillips examined her and noted that there were other stabbings carried out on her abdomen. She was identified as Alice MacKenzie, who had left her lodgings in Gun Street and was last seen alive at 11.40pm in Brick Lane. She was in a hurry. The murder took place between 12.30am when a policeman patrolled Castle Alley and 12.45am when he returned. There was debate over whether she had been killed by the Ripper; Dr Phillips thought the knife used was smaller than in the other murders, and the mutilations were different and the killer was left-handed rather than right-handed.[83]

The last murder sometimes attributed to the Ripper took place in the early hours of 13 February 1891. PC Thompson was passing through Swallow Gardens. He saw the body of a woman lying on the street. Her throat had been cut and she was dying. Because life was not extinct he did not investigate the running footsteps which might have been those of the killer. Frances Coles, a 31-year-old prostitute, was the victim. A middle-aged sailor, Thomas Sadler, was known to have been with Frances on the previous day and he was arrested, but was later discharged due to lack of evidence. There were no mutilations on the body and although the murder was never solved she was probably not a Ripper victim.[84]

No one was ever charged with the murders. This is despite a major manhunt on the part of the police. House-to-house searches occurred, men were questioned, extra manpower was deployed in the streets and handbills and posters were distributed. It was all to no avail. The police, and the Commissioner in particular, were seriously criticised in the press for their incompetence. The press lapped up the case, reported it widely, and it has been said that Jack the Ripper was in part a media creation. The press certainly helped to build up his reputation. There were also vigilance patrols by local civilians on the streets.

However, it was a difficult case to solve. In part this was because of the primitive technology and methods available to the police. No crime photographs were taken at the scenes of the first four murders and the preliminaries to the post mortems were rudimentary. There was no DNA, of course, and the introduction of fingerprinting was several years away. There were no real clues left by the Ripper. No one saw the murders happening and the witness statements about men seen with the victims beforehand varied. There was no obvious or inter-personal motive for the murders. The police had no experience of dealing with serial killers; indeed this was a very new phenomenon and the police had no knowledge of this type of crime and criminal. Unless a killer confessed, or was caught in the act or apprehended immediately afterwards, there was little real chance of him being brought to justice. The Ripper had no accomplice, so he could not be betrayed. The police needed good luck and this was lacking.

Had the killer continued, he might have eventually made mistakes that led to his being identified.

Hundreds of suspects have been identified over the years, usually relying on the weakest of evidence that would never stand up in court. Sir Melville MacNaghten, appointed Assistant Chief Constable after the murders, wrote a memorandum on 23 February 1894 to refute the possibility raised in the press that a young man called Thomas Cutbush was the Ripper, stating that there were only five murder victims of the Ripper. He also wrote:

> No one ever saw the Whitechapel murderer; many homicidal maniacs were suspected but no shadow of proof could be thrown on anyone. I may mention the cases of three men, any one of whom might be more likely than Cutbush to have committed this series of murders.
>
> (1) A Mr M.J. Druitt, said to be a doctor & of good family – said to have disappeared at the time of the Miller's Court murder and whose body (which was said to have been upwards of a month in the water) was found in the Thames on 31 December – or about 7 weeks after that murder. He was sexually insane and from private information I have little doubt but that his own family believed him to have been the murderer.
>
> (2) Kosminski – a Polish Jew – and resident in Whitechapel. This man became insane owing to many years indulgence in solitary vices. He had a great hatred of women, especially of the prostitute class, & had strong homicidal tendencies: he was removed to a lunatic asylum about March 1889. There were many circumstances connected with this man which made him a strong suspect.
>
> (3) Michael Ostrog, a Russian doctor and a convict, who was subsequently detained in a lunatic asylum as a homicidal maniac. This man's antecedents were of the worst possible type, and his whereabouts at the time of the murders could never be ascertained.[85]

MacNaghten wrote in his memoirs, published twenty years later, of the killer, whom he did not name, that 'his brain gave way altogether and he committed suicide, otherwise the murders would not have ceased', adding 'the individual who held London in terror resided with his own people; that he absented himself from home at certain times, that he committed suicide on or after 10 November'. Sir Robert Anderson, Head of Scotland Yard, in his memoirs, concurred with MacNaghten as regards the second suspect, writing that the killer was 'a low class Polish Jew' (unnamed in his memoirs) who was later incarcerated, but the only witness refused to testify in court. Chief Inspector Donald Swanson, appointed by Anderson to oversee the Ripper investigation, agreed, as is known by his notes in his copy of Anderson's memoirs, writing 'Kosminski was the suspect'. Between them they probably knew more than anyone else about the killer other than the man himself. On 19 October, as a side note in his report about the Elizabeth Stride murder, Swanson wrote, because Schwartz had heard the word 'Lipski' (a Jew found guilty of murder in Whitechapel in 1887), from the man who assaulted Elizabeth, 'The use of the word Lipski increases my belief that the murderer was a Jew'. However, there is good cause to doubt that any of these men were the killer.[86] Much of what MacNaghten wrote about these men is factually incorrect.

Aaron Kosminski was a young Polish hairdresser who lived in Whitechapel in 1888. He was sent to Colney Hatch asylum in 1890 and died in 1919 in Leavesden Asylum. He was known to have threatened his sister with a knife. However, other reports show that he was a pathetic creature, not washing and eating food from the gutters and incapable of the terrible, but also cool and controlled, actions of the Ripper. There is also the suggestion that David Cohen, who was also sent to an asylum and died there, was the 'Polish Jew'. In recent times, Kosminski has emerged as a leading suspect, though on tenuous grounds.

Montague Druitt was a doctor's son who attended Winchester College and then New College, Oxford. He was a barrister and also a schoolmaster at a private school in Blackheath, south-east London, from 1881–88. He was also a capable cricketer. However, his mother was sent to an asylum and on 31 December 1888 his body was found in the Thames. He had drowned and had left a note stating that he feared he was going to go insane, like his mother. There is no positive reason to believe he was violent or a criminal.

Michael Ostrog is again very unlikely to be the killer. He had a long record as a thief and a conman, both in Britain and elsewhere. As with Druitt there is no record that he was at all violent, apart from once pulling a revolver on a police superintendent when being arrested in 1873.

There was another contemporary suspect, as revealed by Inspector Littlechild in a letter to George Sims in 1913:

> amongst the suspects, and to my mind a very likely one, was a Dr T (which sounds much like D). He was an American quack called Tumblety and at one time was a frequent visitor to London and on these occasions constantly brought under the notice of the police, there being a large dossier on him at Scotland Yard. Although a Sycopathia Sexualist subject he was not known as a sadist (which the killer unquestionably was) but his feelings towards women were bitter in the extreme, a fact on record. Tumblety was arrested at the time of the murders in connection with unnatural offences, and charged at Marlborough Street, remanded on bail, jumped his bail and got

away to Boulogne and was never heard of afterwards. It was believed he committed suicide, but certain it is that from this time the Ripper murders came to an end.[87]

Again, according to many historians the American Dr Francis Tumblety does not fit the bill as the Whitechapel murderer (homosexual murderers tend to kill men, as in the case of Denis Nilsen) and if he had been a serious suspect it seems curious that he was released on bail. He was also rather too old to be the killer, aged 55 at the time of the murders.

It seems to this author that the murderer suffered violent rages, and was probably a local man who knew the streets and alleyways very well indeed. He was violent but could also appear trustworthy and respectable to approach women who would not suspect him, and could walk the neighbourhood at night without arousing suspicion. His motive seems to have been an extreme hatred of women, perhaps stemming from fear, and perhaps focussed on prostitutes in particular. He wanted to destroy the objects of his hatred, not just by killing them but by destroying them utterly, which he achieved in the case of his final victim. He also took parts of some of his victims away so he could relive the pleasure that his fiendish work had given him; a common trait among serial killers. He had probably committed earlier crimes before he turned to murder, perhaps attacks on women that had gone unreported and that were never linked to the later killings, which was also a characteristic of the Yorkshire Ripper case in the 1970s. He was probably an insignificant little man, indistinguishable from his peers, and perhaps mentally tortured by the fact he could never reveal what he would deem his cleverness. Perhaps self-satisfaction was enough.

It is perhaps noteworthy that the gap between the first two murders was short, but those between the second and the third and fourth, and the fourth and fifth, were longer. This may be because in the second, fourth and fifth murders the killer was able to do what he wanted to his victims and was thus temporarily or permanently sated, whereas he had been interrupted in his first and third murders so felt he needed to kill again quickly in order to satisfy his desires.

The FBI profile, compiled in 1988, seems sensible enough. The killer would have been a lust killer, would be white, male and in his mid-to-late twenties. He would have had a domineering mother and a weak or absent father so had no good role model. He would have grown up socially and mentally detached from others. He could have grown up committing acts of lesser cruelty and violence, perhaps to animals. His job might have been that of a butcher or a man who worked in a mortuary or hospital. He would have had regular working hours. He would have average or less than average intelligence. He was unmarried and socially awkward. He lived or worked in Whitechapel and killed not far from his home. He probably drank prior to the murders. He would not have committed suicide but stopped because he felt that he was close to being suspected after having been interviewed (though serial killers usually carry on until stopped). This suggests a degree of self-preservation, which many serial killers lack. He may have revisited the murder scenes and gone to the victims' graves.

The identity of the killer will probably never be known, but this is not the whole of the story. We also need to consider the women who unfortunately were his victims and the children they left behind. There are also important social questions that arose from these killings; the murders shone a harsh spotlight on the deprivation of the district. To focus on the killer's identity to the exclusion of all else is to miss much of the importance of this grim episode.

The East End has changed vastly since 1888, though it is still a centre of social deprivation and prostitution is all too visible. Many of the streets and houses known then no longer exist and so in some ways there is a very different feel to the district. Yet it is unlikely that these killings will ever be forgotten, both because of their brutality and the fact that they were unsolved.

The Whitechapel murders would cast long shadows over how future serial killers were referred to. We shall see in later chapters that references and comparisons were made to Jack the Ripper during later serial murders. The notoriety of the Ripper murders also led to them being immortalised in wax at Madame Tussaud's, and later in the London Dungeon, as tourist attractions for entertainment and titillation, which is a far cry from their grim reality.

Chapter 2

The Deptford Poisonings, 1885–89

During the same year as Jack the Ripper was committing his appalling crimes, there was another serial killer at work, whose crimes are now almost forgotten, despite the fact that the killer was identified and was more prolific. There are no known photographs of the killer or their victims. This is the only known example of a London female serial killer; or perhaps two. This is a more substantial version of these murders than the one which appeared in the author's *Foul Deeds and Suspicious Deaths in Lewisham and Deptford*. It is unfortunate that there are no surviving police files for these murders, indicative of the almost non-existent police investigation into them (for reasons which will become apparent), so most of this chapter is taken from press reports, which covered it in detail. The case appeared in many British newspapers, national and local, but most of all it featured in the weekly newspaper which covered north-west Kent, *The Kentish Mercury*. Most of the information in this chapter is taken from the extremely detailed statements in the reports therein for the inquest and magistrates' court hearings.

Female serial murderers are rare. When women kill, they tend to commit domestic killings, preying on those who are nearest, but clearly not dearest, to them, rather than leaving the home to find victims as most male serial killers do. Money tends to be their common motivating factor, whereas for men there are usually others such as sadism, sex and power. In the nineteenth century there was Amelia Dyer, who was a baby farmer, taking unwanted babies for money and promising to care for them. She actually killed them and was eventually arrested, tried and hanged in 1896. The number of her victims is unknown. Another was Mary Ann Cotton, the first female serial poisoner, who poisoned many of her family, including most of her children and three of her husbands, for the insurance she had paid premiums for. Again the final tally of her victims is not known. She was hanged at Durham Prison in 1873.

Poison was relatively easy to acquire in the nineteenth century. Arsenic was often the poison of choice because it was cheap, easily accessible and had little taste so could be easily introduced into food and drink without the victim noticing, and deaths from arsenic could usually be passed off as food poisoning and other causes. Deaths among the poor, especially the young and the old, were common, and so an arsenic poisoning would usually go unnoticed by doctors and would only be uncovered if suspicions were aroused by someone associated with a victim, whether relation, friend or official. It led to agonising and slow deaths.

Deptford was a small, but very crowded urban parish which partly adjoins the south-west bank of the Thames, but was part of north-west Kent until 1889 when it officially became part of the county of London. From 1513–1869 there had been a royal dockyard there, but with the end of wooden naval ships it had closed, leading to large-scale unemployment for the skilled and semi-skilled workers who lived there. Deptford retained its industrial character, with its mills and works, but increasingly jobs were for the unskilled and it became more and more impoverished. Major employers were the City of London's Foreign Cattle Market and Stone's Foundry.

The 1894 Medical Officer of Health's Report for Greenwich and Deptford noted that of a combined population of 165,413, there were 3,691 deaths and of these almost half were of the very old or the very young. 881 were infants under one year old and 854 of aged 60 or over. There were 145 inquests into these deaths (less than 5%).[1]

The principal character in this story is Mrs Amelia Winters. She was born Amelia Goodman in Deptford on 30 January 1827, to a working-class couple, Isaac and Mary Goodman, the third of at least three children. In 1841 they lived in a house on Thames Street. She married Joseph Winters, of Huntingford, Kent, a labourer, on 29 January 1854 at St Nicholas' church, Deptford. They had several children: William, born in 1856; Elizabeth, born in 1859; Isaac, born in 1861; Emma, born in 1865 and Anne, born in 1864. The family lived at 1 Charles Street in 1861, then at 3 Regent Street, Deptford in 1873, when Isaac, Emma and Anne had all been baptised on the same day. In 1881 they also let rooms to seven workmen. They then lived at 149 Church Street, Deptford, but moved to 153 later that decade, which was a three-storey house.[2]

In 1881 Elizabeth Winters, their eldest daughter, married Thomas Frost, who had been a lodger with the Winters family earlier that year. He was a carpenter like his father. Mrs Amelia Winters kept a general store for some years. She was apparently too free in giving credit to poor customers and so had to close the business. When they were at 3 Regent Street the neighbours protested that the house was noisy due to the quarrelsome nature of its occupants and because it was alleged to be used for gambling and as a brothel on Sundays. They wanted the landlord to move the family.[3]

Yet the Winters family themselves, if not their visitors, seemed decent and hardworking, not prone to gossip or drink. They were, though, bad-tempered and often used foul language. When speaking to those whose good opinion she desired, Mrs Winters could make herself agreeable and it was said that she:

though an uneducated woman had a considerable degree of cleverness. She was a woman of a remarkable type of character, resolute, commanding and possessing great influence over those she came into contact. Imperious and intolerant of the least opposition to her will, she was the autocrat of the house.[4]

Mrs Winters liked pigeons, fowl and rabbits, which the children kept as pets, and was fond of children. She would give tickets for children's treats to poor neighbours. She would give gifts to sick neighbours and was very hospitable. She was a loving mother, was proud of her children and took sole care of one of her grandchildren for many years.[5]

Insurance was big business in the nineteenth century and many poor people paid small sums to cover their own or their relatives' funeral costs. Agents called at the payer's house every week to collect the premiums and would, if payments were kept up, pay out on death.

From 1885 to 1888, the Liverpool Victoria Legal Friendly Society accepted payments from Mrs Winters in respect of twenty-two people aged between nine and seventy-three, including family members and those who lived with them. Five of these were increased to double the original sum, and two of these persons died shortly afterwards. In total Mrs Winters paid the company 7s 6d per week and the policies totalled £240. The company paid out £45 12s, with no distrust or suspicion. She also took out thirteen policies from 28 April 1884 to 14 January 1889 with the Prudential Assurance Company. These included policies for William Sutton and the Boltons, for which payments were increased. Two policies were also taken out for Mrs Elizabeth Jane Frost; one of these by her daughter-in-law, Mrs Elizabeth Frost.[6]

The first known death in this series of murders took place in 1885. Benjamin Winters, the 54-year-old wooden-legged younger brother of Joseph Winters, a widower and a labourer, spent spells of time in the Greenwich Union Workhouse, Woolwich Road, from 1880–1884. He had been insured by Mrs Winters for 18 guineas. He was readmitted but left the Vanburgh Hill Infirmary on 21 May 1884. In 1885 he left the workhouse for a short holiday and went to Mrs Winters' house. He was soon taken ill, with sickness, diarrhoea and stomach pains, all the classic symptoms of arsenic poisoning. Dr Joseph Brough Macnaughton, who had just taken up practice in Deptford, attended him, but he died shortly afterwards of a fit and Mrs Winters collected the insurance money on her brother-in-law's life.[7]

On 18 July 1886 there was another death, when a child whose life Mrs Winters had insured in the previous year died. This could have been William Winters, aged five and a grandson of Mrs Winters. He was removed from the infirmary to Mrs Winters' house in the summer of 1886. A woman calling herself the boy's mother collected the £5.[8] Then there was Anna Bolton (née Goodman), a widow of William Bolton, a cutler, and now aged 63, who was insured in March 1886 for £3 1s. She died at Friendly Street on 10 November 1886 and payment was made out to a woman who claimed to be (and indeed was) her sister, 'A.W. Winters'. Anna was James Samuel Bolton's mother and Sidney Bolton's grandmother and Mrs Winters' older sister. Dr Macnaughton and Dr Roberts attended her in her last days. Mrs Winters received £1 10s insurance money.[9]

Better documented are the three last victims, whose deaths were investigated in 1889. On 26 September 1885, a policy on the life of Elizabeth Jane Frost for £9 9s was made by Amelia Winters, who told Mr Jones, agent for the Liverpool Victoria Insurance Company, that she was her next-of-kin. Stephen Barry collected the premiums from June 1886.[10]

Mrs Elizabeth Jane Frost was a 54-year-old widow and lived in a room at 57 New King Street, Deptford, which she had rented from Mrs Ellen Collins since November 1887. She had been born in Robertsbridge, Sussex, in about 1834 and had married Thomas Frost, a carpenter. By about 1861 they were living in Walworth, Surrey, but had moved to Deptford by about 1862; in 1871 they were living at 47 Henry Street with their children. In the next decade Thomas died and the family were then divided.[11]

Elizabeth Jane Frost's children were Thomas (1863–?), Emma (1864–1906), Alfred (1877–?) and Ann (1860–1942), all of whom except Alfred were married by 1886. Thomas, who had crucially married Elizabeth Winters, now Frost, in 1881, visited his mother several times a week, as did his sister Emma Dalamain. Mrs Elizabeth Jane Frost would also visit her daughter Emma Dalamain at her home at 8 Czar Street. Normally, Mrs Elizabeth Jane Frost was in good health. On 2 February 1888 she had been at 153 Church Street doing some needlework and had dinner there at 2pm. On 3 February 1888, Mrs Dalamain was told by Elizabeth Frost, her sister-in-law, that her mother was unwell. Mrs Dalamain visited her at once and found her sick in bed. She said that she felt very bad and had stomach pains. Her face was swollen and she was very thirsty, suffering from sickness and diarrhoea, unable to keep any food down.[12]

Mrs Dalamain asked her mother why she had not visited her on the previous day. Mrs Frost said that she had been doing some washing at Mrs Winters' house. She had had some brandy after dinner once she had got home. It was obvious that the woman had been sick and so her daughter spent much of the next few days with her. Mrs Winters and Thomas Frost brought beef tea, whisky, oranges and brandy to the sick woman. They came each day. Mrs Dalamain often gave the food and drink to her mother.[13]

Unfortunately Mrs Elizabeth Jane Frost complained that the brandy hurt her and that she could not really drink it. The beef tea made her sick. She vomited after taking it. Mrs Dalamain made her mother a meal of mutton broth and fish. This was on Sunday 5 February and she kept it down. Sometimes Mrs Winters and Mrs Elizabeth Frost would stay the night and her daughter Emma also did so. Mrs Winters summoned Dr Macnaughton on Friday 3 February. Mrs Winters thought the woman had bronchitis, but Mrs Dalamain thought this was not so.[14] Walter Clyde Frost, a son of Mrs Elizabeth Jane Frost, suggested to Mrs Winters that he should stay a night with his mother and the woman replied, 'No' and that he could do no good.[15]

Dr William Freke Hingston of 215 Evelyn Street, Deptford, the district medical officer for north Deptford, was called by Mrs Dalamain on Monday 6 February and he arrived the next day. He could see that the patient's condition was very serious. She was puffy about the face and he was pessimistic. He thought her kidneys were out of order and prescribed a saline mixture with bromide. He recommended that she be transferred to the infirmary. Dr Macnaughton was present and when he heard this suggestion he was angry, 'How dare you fetch the parish doctor?' He said that the woman was his patient, not anyone else's, and lambasted Mrs Dalamain for being a very bad young woman and an undutiful daughter. Mrs Winters also castigated Mrs Dalamain as having no business to interfere. 'How dare you take her away?' They eventually left.[16]

Mrs Dalamain remained with her mother until 8pm when she left to nurse her sister, Mrs Anne Woodgate, at Rotherhithe. She remained with her sister all the next day. That evening, her little brother went to enquire how her mother was. Mrs Dalamain had not applied to the parish for an order for removal of her mother to the infirmary as she did not now believe it necessary. She had tasted the drink her mother had been given and she thought it tasted unpleasant and that something was burnt. Mrs Elizabeth Jane Frost died on 8 February 1888, just after noon.[17]

Dr Macnaughton issued the death certificate. He stated that she had died of stomatitis inflammation of the mouth and secondary cause bronchitis; although he believed that alcoholism was the true cause, he never put that down on any death certificate. On 9 February Percy Crampton, on behalf of the Liverpool Victoria Legal and Friendly Society insurance office, paid the claim of £8 5s in gold and silver to Mrs Winters.[18] Mrs Elizabeth Jane Frost was duly buried at the nearby Brockley Cemetery and her death caused no public comment. On 9 November 1888 Mrs Dalamain learnt that there had been an additional insurance policy made out for her mother's life; namely that which Mrs Winters had paid. Mrs Dalamain had also paid one for her mother's life to meet burial costs.[19] She did not act on this knowledge.

William Sutton was insured on 23 July 1887 for £8 14s. Stephen Barry was a collector for the Liverpool Victoria Legal and Friendly Society. Barry saw Sutton but did not speak to him. He did not know if Sutton was aware of this insurance. It was possible to insure lives without the subject's knowledge. The society would only not insure someone if it was against that person's will, but

Barry saw nothing dishonest in the transaction and it was commonplace in the insurance world. Sutton's son at Deal had also paid an insurance policy for his father.[20]

William Sutton had been born in 1814 in Canterbury and had been a mariner, a costermonger and a labourer. By at least 1841 he lived in Deptford; at Creek Street in 1851. In 1861 he, his wife Edith and their daughter lived in Griffin Street, Deptford. In 1878 he lived at 4 Hamilton Street, Deptford. Crucially his daughter Mary Ann Sutton had married William Winters, a labourer and Amelia Winters' eldest son, in 1878. Since about 1885, Sutton had been an inmate of the Greenwich Union Workhouse. Although infirm and partially sighted, he had fairly good health for a man of his age and had received no medical attention since May 1888. His wife died in 1887. He left the place at 10am on the morning of Tuesday 4 December 1888. He had not been discharged, but had been allowed out and may have been collected by someone. On 5 or 6 December, William Henry Jordan, the Workhouse Master, received a letter about Sutton. It stated that he was ill and would not return. The writer of it was resident at 153 Church Street, Deptford, but the letter was subsequently lost and Jordan could not remember the author. He therefore discharged Sutton from the workhouse inmates' register and soon received his workhouse clothes back.[21]

Sutton often went to Mrs Amelia Winters' house and that was where he went on this occasion. He was her brother-in-law. His daughter, Mrs Mary Ann Winters, had insured his life with the Prudential in order that he could be properly buried. Her father was not very well when he arrived at the house and in the afternoon his condition became worse. He was made a bed on the sofa and there was talk of returning him to the workhouse. In the meantime, Dr Macnaughton was called. Sutton complained of feeling sick, of diarrhoea, being short of breath and of heart pains. He seemed to be in a great deal of pain. Macnaughton asked about the man's diet and was told that he had been given mutton broth for dinner, and the doctor thought that this sudden change in diet might have upset his stomach and he had often seen such happen when people left the workhouse and its simple, plain diet. He advised that he not be moved for a few days and gave him some medicine, which made the patient vomit. This was made up of cerium and opium. Mrs Winters suggested that if he got better he could return to the workhouse.[22]

The old man was then brought to his daughter's house at 61 Berthon Street. Anthony Pengelly, a sailmaker of 16 Berthon Street and a Scripture Union reader, visited the sick old man on the evening of 6 December between 6 and 9pm. He was ill and lying on the sofa in the parlour and Pengelly could tell that he was unwell. 'You appear very ill, my brother', Pengelly remarked, and held his hand, 'Have you been ill long?' Sutton replied, 'only since I came out of the House. I was well when I left the Workhouse, but after I had something to eat and drink, I was sick and whenever I got a drink I was sick and got a burning here', pointing to his throat. His face was contorted and he knew he had not long to live.[23]

The doctor called on the next two days and thought that Sutton was getting better. He then prescribed soda, gentian and drachm of chlorodyne. Mrs Frost and Mrs Winters attended Sutton in the next few days. Mrs Edson, who also lived at 61 Berthon Street in Deptford, recalled the old man eating bread, butter and jam, which made him sick. He also suffered from a fit when Mrs Winters and Mrs Frost were there. However, he died on 8 December and was buried without any further fuss in Brockley Cemetery, just as Mrs Frost had been ten months previously. Dr Macnaughton considered that Mrs Winters had been very kind to the deceased. He readily wrote out a death certificate, registering it as due to senile decay. He was not surprised by the old man's death. The death of a poor old man in Deptford was commonplace. He was paid 5s for his visits.[24]

Sutton's life had been insured by Mrs Amelia Winters and she went to the Liverpool Victoria Legal and Friendly Society insurance office to collect the money. As he had done so ten months earlier, Crampton paid out, later recalling making the payment of £8 14s on 11 December to an elderly woman who said she was the deceased's only sister (not true). There had been two policies on the old man's life and these did not need a written application; one had been very recently increased.[25]

James Samuel Bolton was born in Deptford in 1850 and in 1888 was living at 5 Creek Street, Deptford, being employed at Messrs Hill's chemical works as a labourer. He had been separated from his wife, Sarah Ann Rebecca, a year his junior, probably in about 1883. They had four children and the youngest was Sidney Bolton, born on 17 September 1878. Mrs Amelia Winters was James Bolton's aunt as his mother (who had died in 1886) had been her sister. His youngest daughter was Mary Ann Minnie, born in 1872. Both children had apparently been deserted by their father earlier that year and spent over three months in the workhouse until he collected them from there in July. They began to attend Lucas Street School in September 1884. There were two other children, both of whom were older and seem to have lived with their mother in nearby New Cross. In the summer of 1887, Mrs Winter began to care for Sidney and Mary and their father contributed 10s per week for their upkeep. He then lived next door at 155 Church Street, with Mrs Frost. Mrs Winters told him she would insure them for a halfpenny a week at the doctor's club and a penny a week at the Prudential Assurance. This was said in front of her husband.[26]

Mrs Winters had already insured the lives of the two children from January 1887 for £5 each and paid a penny a week for each. This was increased in October to £20 12s each, which was the limit for children of that age. This was from the Liverpool Victoria Insurance Company.[27]

The Deptford agent for the Prudential Insurance Company was, from September 1888, a Mr Coleman of 25 Edward Street. He called at 153 Church Road weekly to collect the premiums. He usually collected it from Mrs Winters but occasionally from Mrs Frost. There was a penny for each of the two life policies on Sidney Bolton.[28]

From the beginning of November 1888 Mary became ill with pain in her stomach and vomiting and continued in this state for the next nine weeks. It came on very suddenly and she was often sick. Mrs Amelia Winters nursed her. Dr Macnaughton attended her each day and prescribed a bismuth mixture and recommended a diet of milk, lime water and soda water. Mrs Frost fetched medicine from his surgery and sometimes administered it. The doctor took a sample of the girl's vomit, which was yellow and black, when she was sick in his presence, but he did not take it away with him. Mrs Greenway, another of Mrs Winters' married daughters, and Mrs Matthews also assisted in the nursing. Her father suggested that she be removed to the infirmary but she said she did not want to go because Mrs Winters had told her that it was a nasty place. Dr Macnaughton would not sanction this either. Mrs Winters said that she thought recovery was unlikely. Mrs Bolton of Walpole Road, New Cross, the girl's mother, said that the sicknesses came on after meals. Just before Christmas Mary noticed her tea tasting strange. Her father became adamant that she be sent to hospital and Mrs Winters demurred, arguing that to do so would lead to her death. Bolton would give it another day. When he returned the next day he saw that she was less ill, with the doctor making house calls only every other day. Mary told her father that she had had bread and milk that morning and had not been sick. She began to improve and was no longer sick, so her father decided she did not need hospital after all.[29]

After Christmas 1888, Sidney became ill; he had not been ill when his sister had been. Mrs Winters took him to Dr Macnaughton's surgery, telling him that the boy was suffering from diarrhoea. He made the same prescriptions and recommendations as he had for the sister. From 1 January the doctor regularly attended him at Mrs Winters' house. The boy complained of sickness, vomiting and stomach pains. He was sometimes sick before eating and sometimes afterwards. He asked his sister to taste his tea and she agreed that it was unpleasant. He suffered from intense thirst and at the end of January began to suffer from convulsions. The doctor stated 'I cannot do anything more for him'. Hitherto, the boy had been in the best of health.[30] He vomited after meals. Mrs Winters and Mrs Frost took care of him in the day times when he was confined to his bed.[31]

Bolton was very busy in January 1889 and for two weeks saw nothing of his son. He was occupied in moving from one house to another and did not think his son's condition was serious. When he did see his son, he looked thin and ill and complained of stomach pains, but was not in pain otherwise. He told his father that Dr Macnaughton had seen him. Bolton saw his son again three days later, but never saw the doctor. His son told him he was not suffering much. Three days later Mrs Winters summoned Bolton and the boy was much worse. He had had two fits and from then on Bolton visited his son each day, once staying with him all night. He was very thirsty and drank water all night. Mrs Winters said he had had nothing for a week but water. Bolton's wife also visited her son, but did not speak to the father. She stayed six nights with him and he was not sick on any of these occasions. The boy's elder brother also visited.[32]

His father visited three or four times a day. However, on 11 February 1889, Sidney Bolton died. His mother was present at his death. The doctor completed a death certificate, putting the causes down as gastrodynia, diarrhoea and convulsions. Bolton then visited Mrs Winters and discussed funeral arrangements. He later recalled that he would spend 50s on it and she said that this would be very mean and if he could not pay she would. He then inquired about the insurance payments. She told him she had missed payments and the premium had run out.[33]

Later that day, Mrs Winters visited Coleman and told him about Sidney's death. He arranged to visit her at her home that evening. He met her, Mrs Frost and Mrs Emma Greenaway (another of Mrs Winters' daughters) and he produced a claim form. He then asked Mrs Winters a few questions about the deceased's family. Mrs Winters lied and told him that the boy's father was dead, and so he asked about the boy's mother. Mrs Winters lied again and said 'this is the mother', pointing to Mrs Frost, who obligingly said 'I am the mother'. Coleman said 'I want your name on this paper'. He asked her to write her name but she said that she was unable to do so. He asked her for her name – Sarah Bolton was given – and he wrote it on the form himself.[34]

Mrs Greenaway was then asked by Coleman to sign her name as a witness, which she did. She had not previously taken part in the conversation and had stood at the back of the room. Mrs Winters then gave him the two insurance policies and the receipt book for payments made, together with the death certificate. Coleman took all these away and forwarded them to his employers' head office that very evening.[35]

By 13 February, Coleman had received a reply from his head office and a cheque for £10. He then went to 153 Church Street and met Mrs Winters and Mrs Frost. He drew their attention to the letter accompanying the cheque. He needed the late boy's father's signature. Mrs Winters lied again and told him 'You can't, for he is dead'. Her daughter said he had died six months ago and her mother corrected her to say it was nearer seven. Coleman told them 'It does not matter to me how long he has been dead as long as he is dead'. He then pointed to the cheque and told Mrs Frost 'I want your signature there'. As she was illiterate he wrote her name and address on the receipt. 'Before you make a cross, I want a witness for the mark'. Mrs Winters left the room and sent a little girl to find someone. A man, introduced as Thomas Frost, arrived and signed the receipt after the cross had been made. He then left, as did Coleman, who posted the receipt to his employer.[36]

The funeral was at Brockley Cemetery on 16 February. On the same day, Bolton had a meeting with Mr Baker, Superintendent of the Prudential, and Mrs Winters, following the receipt of a communication from him. Mr Coleman and one Mrs Cremer were also present, but not Mrs Frost. Mrs Winters and Baker conversed with the upshot that Baker gave Bolton £7 and Mrs Winter £3.[37] The payout would have been £20 had Sidney lived for another two days. As with Mrs Frost and Sutton, Sidney was buried without any public attention to the matter.

At the beginning of March, however, Bolton's suspicions were aroused. He heard that Mrs Winters had received £20 from the Liverpool Victoria Insurance Company for his son's death in the previous month. He said nothing to Mrs Winters about this, but informed the police instead; possibly Inspector Phillips, who later represented the police at the inquest hearings. He believed that there had only been the Prudential insurance policy on his son's life.[38] This led to a warrant from the Home Office to exhume the body, organs of which were sent to Guy's Hospital, and thus set about an inquest.[39]

On 1 April Dr Thomas Bond of Westminster Hospital, who had performed the post mortem on the last of Jack the Ripper's victims, Mary Jane Kelly, and Dr Charles Alfred Hebbert, demonstrator of anatomy at the same hospital, had Sidney's coffin opened in the presence of his father. There was much decomposition on the surface of the body. It was thin but not emaciated. Dr Bond opened up the skull. Despite the slight congestion on the brain, it was not diseased. The intestines, heart, liver and kidney were removed. They concluded that death was due to inflammation and irritation of the mucus membrane of the intestine, but they could not initially tell whether this was due to disease or an irritant poison.[40]

Dr Thomas Stevenson was an eminent toxicologist, lecturer in forensic medicine and chemistry at Guy's Hospital. He was often called in by the Home Office in poisoning cases as an analyst and attended the high-profile Pimlico case in 1886 (and others later chronicled in this book). It was he who analysed the organs. He found traces of arsenic in the intestine and so concluded that death had been caused by its administration. In his opinion it had been given in small quantities and at frequent intervals, probably in food. Convulsive fits were unusual for children but they were symptoms of those poisoned by arsenic.[41]

On 18 April the inquest on Sidney Bolton commenced at the Brakespear Arms, Brockley Road, Deptford, with Mr Wood, the deputy coroner of west

Kent, in charge. The body was viewed by the jury at the cemetery that day. The purpose of the first day was to identify the body, then to adjourn. The boy's father had already confirmed that the body was that of his son (about two weeks prior to the inquest). Amelia Winters was too ill to attend. On 25 April Bolton gave his evidence to the jury. It was adjourned.[42]

On 9 May, evidence was given by Sidney's parents about his final illness, as well as by Dr Macnaughton. Representatives of the Liverpool Victoria attested to the insurance policies taken out by Mrs Winters and their lack of suspicion. Medical evidence was brought forward to show that the lad had met his death by arsenic poisoning. The inquest was adjourned for another three weeks.[43]

Suspicions were being aroused about earlier deaths. On 14 May, in the early morning, acting under a Home Office warrant, Sutton's body was exhumed. The body was in an advanced state of decomposition. The contents of the stomach were handed over to Dr Stevenson for analysis. There was much excitement locally and Mrs Winters remained very unwell.[44]

The inquest was resumed at the Brockley Arms on 30 May. Mrs Amelia Winters was again unable to attend due to ill health and a note from Dr Francis Taylor was produced by Inspector Phillips. Dr Macnaughton said that she had a temperature of 110 Fahrenheit, had had an attack of diarrhoea, was very weak and unable to leave her bed.[45]

The inquest on Sidney Bolton resumed at the Brakespear Arms on 1 June 1889. This time the enquiry was also incorporating that of William Sutton. The jury had to go to the cemetery to view his body. Evidence of his departure from the workhouse, subsequent illness and death was then given by a number of witnesses. Such was the local feeling against the Frosts and Winters that when Mrs Frost and her husband returned from the inquest they were attacked by a large crowd of between 300 and 400 women, throwing stones and flour at them and preventing them from going home. They were forced to hide under the arches of the railway bridge and stayed there for hours.[46]

Regarding Sutton, the doctors found that the stomach and intestines showed all the signs that an irritant poison had been used. There were traces of arsenic in both stomach and liver, especially in the latter, where it was clear that a fatal dose had been administered. It would have been taken some hours before death as most had disappeared from the alimentary canal.[47]

There was another exhumation, this time of Mrs Frost, on 15 June. Present were doctors Macnaughton, Bond and Hebbert of Westminster Hospital. The organs were removed for analysis.[48] There was evidence of large quantities of arsenic in the intestines and this was the cause of her death. They noted that the symptoms of bronchitis and arsenic poisoning were similar. The body was remarkably free from decomposition and there was no sign that death was due to either bronchitis or alcoholism; so much for Dr Macnaughton's earlier assessment.[49]

The inquest was concluded on Tuesday 9 July. Representatives of the insurance companies and lawyers for both Treasury and defence were present. Again, the jury had to go to the cemetery to view an exhumed body. This time it was that of Mrs Elizabeth Jane Frost and there were many witness statements about her illness and demise. Medical evidence was given to the effect that Mrs Frost and William Sutton had died from arsenic poisoning and insurance agents testified that Amelia Winters had paid insurance premiums and collected the payouts after the deaths. The jury had to decide whether these deaths were due to misadventure or murder. They concluded that deaths had come about by wilful murder by Amelia Winters and Elizabeth Frost. The latter, who was in court with her baby Thomas, was immediately arrested. She was taken to the police station, charged with murder and remanded in custody. Her mother was too ill to attend and it was stated that she was dying.[50]

Meanwhile, William Winters of 61 Berthon Street visited his mother at nine in the morning of 12 July. She was in bed and he recalled the scene, him leaning over her and asking:

'Mother, if you have done anything, pray, tell me'.
'My boy, I have ruined the family'.
'Never mind, mother, whatever you have done, tell me. Do you know anything about old Mrs Frost and giving her anything?'
'Yes'.
'Who gave it to her?'
'I gave it to her.'
'Does Lizzie [Mrs Elizabeth Frost] know anything about it?'
'No, she knows nothing about it; nobody knew anything but myself.'
'Where did you get the arsenic from?'
'I did not know what arsenic is.'
'What was it you gave her?'
'It is what you use for the head, for vermin – precipitate powder.'
'Does Mrs Frost know anything about the deaths of the old man and the boy?'
'They are all as innocent as the babe unborn.'
'Did you give them something?'
'Yes.'
'Ask all belonging to me to forgive me. Don't say about this till I am dead.'[51]

Mrs Greenaway of 53 Reginald Road also visited her mother and had almost exactly the same conversation as above, but she asked 'Oh, mother, how could you have done such a thing?' and there was no reply. Another daughter, Annie Matthews, called that evening and a similar conversation ensued. They went out to find Dr Henry George Cundy, the rector of St Paul's, Deptford, so he could hear the confession too, but he could not be found.[52]

The principal player in this drama had only a little longer to live. Mrs Winters died in the early morning of Sunday 14 July at her home in Church Street. A coffin of polished oak with black furniture with 'Amelia Winters, died 14th July 1889. Aged 59 years' inscribed on it was delivered to 153 Church Street.[53] Naturally she had insured her own life as well as those of others. She had insured her life with the Prudential for £10 and with the Liverpool Victoria Company for £8.[54]

Dr Hingston provided the death certificate. There was a question as to whether an inquest should be held to examine whether her death could be due to suicide or murder, as her death was certainly convenient for the rest of her family. However, the doctor thought it was marasmus or a general wasting away of the body, and she certainly had been unwell for twenty weeks and had been unable to attend the inquest hearings. The registrar initially declined to accept the death certificate, as he had every right to do if he disagreed with the doctor. The coroner was appealed to and he decided not to hold an inquest and so the death certificate was accepted.[55]

Amelia Winters was buried on Monday 22 July by Messrs Chappell and Sons. There was such local hostility against her, following her confession to murder, that the house where the body remained prior to the funeral was watched night and day so that any attempt at removal would be met by a demonstration by the crowd. Some used the phrase 'Jack the Ripper' in relation to her. However, in the early hours of that morning a hearse brought the body to the undertakers. It was believed that burial would take place in Ilford, as the Brockley cemetery was closed on Mondays. However, it did take place at Brockley cemetery, with only the widower, his sons and the officials present.[56]

Mr Smith, officiating at the service, said that he had known the deceased for thirty-three years. His words reflected on Mrs Winters' recent activities; he exhorted those present to beware of the sin of covetousness and to be sure to earn their money honestly. He said the Lord's Prayer but when it came to the sentence in the burial service 'We commit her body to the ground in hope of the resurrection to eternal life' he omitted the words 'sure and certain'. The (unmarked) grave was under two lime trees, between the cemetery wall and a footpath, near the graves of Sidney, Sutton and Mrs Frost and eighteen yards away from that of Jane Maria Clousen, murdered on Kidbrooke Lane in 1871.[57]

There was no such escape from earthly justice for Winters' eldest daughter, however. On the same day as her mother's funeral, Mrs Frost was brought before the Greenwich Magistrates' Court on the charge of the three murders. A huge crowd was present. Mr Kennedy was the magistrate, Mr Angus Lewis for the Treasury and Mr J.C. Seard for the defendant. Lewis argued that Mrs Winters' confession should not be taken as being true as she may have made it to absolve her daughter of any wrongdoing. These statements were then read out in court. Evidence was then called as to the forgery allegedly committed by Mrs Frost; principally by Bolton and Coleman.[58]

The hearing was concluded on the next day. Sarah Bolton was examined and then Coleman was re-examined as to the insurance payments. Other insurance agents also provided evidence. Mrs Frost made no reply and reserved her defence. She was then sentenced to attend the Assize court at the Old Bailey where her trial would commence.[59]

The Winters family had additional troubles of their own. William Winters had been assaulted by one Margaret Grace, who shouted 'There go the murderers' before throwing a stone and mud at him. When the father, his two sons and a daughter left the court, a large and hostile crowd awaited them, angered by the sentence of a 14s fine or two weeks in gaol given to Margaret Grace. The police had to restrain the latter and the Winterses returned home by a circuitous route, but on entering Church Street they found another crowd. Police were needed to ensure their safety and meanwhile the crowd paid the fine of their attacker. Eventually all calmed down.[60]

Mrs Frost was put on trial for forgery at the Old Bailey on 29 July. Charles Matthew and Mr A. Gill were the prosecuting counsel and Mr Warburton was for the defence. The principal witnesses were Bolton, his estranged wife and Coleman, who gave much the same evidence as has already been noted about Sidney's life being insured by Mrs Winters and Mrs Frost signing the document as if she were Sarah Bolton, the boy's mother, to verify it being truthful. She was found guilty.[61]

On 21 October Frost appeared at the Old Bailey to be tried for murder on the three coroners' inquisitions; of Sutton, Bolton and Mrs Frost, to which she answered not guilty. Mr Gill, on behalf of the public prosecutor, suggested that there was insufficient evidence to support the coroner's warrant against her for the said offence. He recalled that Mrs Winters had exonerated her daughter on her deathbed. The jury then found her not guilty, but she was sent down for the forgery charge.[62]

Frost was sentenced to seven years in prison for forgery. An editorial in the local newspaper viewed this as very severe, which was believed to be because of the suspicion entertained by the court that she may have been involved in the murders as well. However, the editorial argued that this was unfair as Frost had been acquitted of that charge, and that she had been under her mother's thumb. The column regretted that the whole truth of the murders could never be ascertained. Frost now faced seven years to meditate on her offence.[63]

The deputy coroner made an assessment of the woman in the dock:

> there is yet little doubt that she was aware of the deeds that had been done in that unhappy house, if not indeed an active and conscious participant in them. But as we saw her in the dock of the Old Bailey... her finely chiselled features and almost classic face expressing desolation and despair as we never saw them depicted before on the human countenance, we could not restrain the pity that went out to one we thought was most probably the dupe and tool of the older and stronger sinner. There was no trace upon that face, white and motionless as sculptured marble, of hardened sin. If she has sinned, as no doubt she has, and that grievously, her sin has found her out, and she is bearing its bitter punishment.[64]

Frost was sent to Woking Female Prison, at Knaphill, Woking, Surrey, and is noted there on the 1891 census. It had opened in 1859 as the first purpose-built prison for women, but it closed in 1895. Whether Mrs Frost had left by then, with remission for good behaviour, or whether like other inmates she was transferred to Aylesbury Prison in 1895 for a short spell, is unknown.

A newspaper article made the following assessment of Mrs Amelia Winters:

> enough is known to satisfy the most sceptical that this woman, who has confessed the perpetration of three murders, was a systematic poisoner, the number of whose victims it is not possible to tell, but who pursued her hideous trade with a cold remorselessness, which in recent times we have no parallel.[65]

There was never any investigation into how the poisoning actually occurred. We only have details of the three last cases. The first step was to insure potential victims; all people whom Mrs Winters had easy access to, including family members and lodgers. Next was to provide them with food and drink when they were at 153 Church Street. What could be more natural than to provide a meal for a visiting relative? Mrs Elizabeth Jane Frost was doing work at the house on 3 February 1888 and was given lunch; Sutton was provided with a hearty meal on visiting from the workhouse on 4 December of that year. And both the Bolton children were fed once they began to stay there in 1887.

Mrs Frost and Sutton were given large doses of arsenic and then probably given smaller doses in the next few days as Mrs Winters and her daughter visited both of them with further food and drink. Both died in a matter of a few days. The Bolton children were a different case because their parents often visited, and so dealing with them would need more care, because if they died within a short space of time there would be greater suspicion from the parents. Mary was poisoned first, being given small doses in her food and drink. When her father demanded she go to hospital, Mrs Winters was resistant to the idea. Naturally if she did go there, the doctor might note that she was being poisoned as the symptoms were all there. Even if he did not, without being poisoned her symptoms would cease and she would recover, which would suggest that there was something wrong at 153 and thus might spark suspicions.

Mrs Winters could not allow that, so she ceased the poisoning and Mary recovered. She then turned her attention to the younger, and perhaps weaker, brother. She was fortunate that his father had been unable to visit for a crucial fortnight and that when his mother stayed the night, no poisoning occurred – perhaps Mrs Bolton fed the child herself and so he was momentarily safe. Eventually, though, the poisoning increased and within the span of a few weeks, the boy was dead.

It is possible that the arsenic used was procured from Bolton's own home, 6 Church Street, where he was then working as a bird stuffer. He kept four of five pounds of arsenic in a tin canister in an unlocked drawer in his workshop. Mrs Winters came there to clean the place, though he was out when she did this. He thought that Mrs Frost accompanied her and said that he never gave her any arsenic.[40]

Clearly Mrs Winters had no qualms about killing her relatives (including her own sister) for money. In an age when there were no universal old-age pensions or any other form of what would later be called social security, the workhouse beckoned for many elderly people unless they had a supportive family nearby who were able to help them, or had savings. Many poor old people feared and hated the regimentation and basic diet that the workhouse offered. So it is possible that Mrs Winters was acting in order to avoid such a fate.

Was her motivation entirely based on money? She may have enjoyed the power of life or death over others, which as an elderly woman she could not have gained otherwise. Other poisoners, such as doctors John Bodkin Adams and Harold Shipman, certainly enjoyed the power that poisoning gave them, as well as the fairly minor monetary gains. She may also have resented her relatives and harboured grudges against them that we do not know about.

It is possible that there were other victims, but this cannot be known for certain. Neighbours evinced surprise that so many of Winters' grandchildren died shortly after birth from 'convulsions'. Mrs Winters was spoken of as being 'a clever person'. Possibly a dozen babies died in such a way. William Winters had married Mary Ann Sutton in 1878; Elizabeth Winters had married Thomas Frost in 1881 and Emma Winters had married Herbert Greenway in 1885, so plenty of grandchildren could have been born. The Frosts only had a baby boy alive in 1889, the Winterses had two daughters living in 1891 (aged eleven and eight) and the Greenways had no children alive by 1891, so certainly some of the babies probably died, though whether all by Mrs Winters' hand is uncertain. Then there was an unnamed lodger, friendless but in excellent health. He was sick one morning and sick in the night. He left the house and was sick again, and a day or two after returning, died.[67]

This sort of circumstantial evidence is common in poisoning cases where not all of the victims can be identified. All we can be sure of is that at least six people died prematurely at Amelia Winters' hands from 1885–1889, but there were quite possibly more, and she possibly practised on the babies. This was perhaps taking the Darwinian principle of 'survival of the fittest' to its logical extreme, without any moral scruple whatsoever. There was never any suggestion that she had any faith in any tenet of Christianity.

It could also be argued that George Dear, aged 34 on death and a labourer employed at Mumford's Mill, Deptford, who had been a lodger at 153 Church Street from at least 1881–89, was another victim, for he committed suicide at his new lodgings in 66 King Street, Blackheath, on 20 July 1889. He was found hanging from the ceiling of an outhouse. Although he had had bronchitis recently, he had given evidence at the inquest hearings and was known to have been very upset about the poisonings. He later learnt that Mrs Winters had insured his life without his knowledge. He may have thought that he had also been poisoned by her and so sought a speedier death.[67]

Mrs Winters was not the only one to blame in this squalid episode of criminal history. There were also her unwitting accomplices. The coroner, Mr E.N. Wood, stated:

> To my mind, the facilities given by some insurance companies to effect wholescale life insurances are direct incentives to wicked persons to destroy such lives for the sake of the insurance money. From the evidences it is certain that insurances can be and are effected upon the lives of persons who have no knowledge of any such proceedings, that insurances are effected by persons who have no insurable interest in the lives insured, and there is nothing to prevent an adult life being insured at the same time in several offices unknown to each other, so that the amount insured in this way on one life may amount to a considerable sum.

Dr Macnaughton also came in for heavy censure for failing to recognise the symptoms of arsenic poisoning in three patients that he attended who died within the same year.[68]

Mrs Winters was fortunate to die when she did and is perhaps unique among serial killers who were detected in this period. Undoubtedly she would have been tried for murder had she lived and it is difficult to see how she could have avoided the fate of Mary Cotton, who had been hanged for similar offences in 1873. She had a clear motive and the opportunity to commit murder. These were crimes committed on vulnerable and trusting people – the old and the young– who were also the killer's relatives. The sums she gained from these deaths may seem very limited, but to Mrs Winters they were not so inconsiderable and represented the ability to buy little luxuries. In many ways she is comparable to the better known Mary Cotton. Both were working-class women who preyed on their own families for relatively small sums of money.

As to the fates of the characters in this story, it is unclear how much guilty knowledge Mrs Frost possessed, but she was given the benefit of the doubt as regards the murders, although there can be no doubt about the forgery. She was living with her sister-in-law Mary Ann Winters in 1911, in West Ham, assisting in the family business, but she returned to Deptford eventually and died there in 1945 at a ripe old age, without any further comment. The Winterses adopted her baby son Thomas in 1889. Her husband died in 1936 and it is not known if they were ever reconciled. Joseph Winters benefitted from his wife's will to the extent of £58, a not unsubstantial sum, being partly at least the proceeds of crime. When he died on 12 April 1898 he left a slightly smaller sum to his eldest son, Isaac, now a boiler maker. Mary Bolton married John Albert Edward William Taylor, a labourer, in 1893 in Southwark. Her father died in 1918, at 121 Friendly Street, Deptford.

It is uncertain if Mrs Winters acted alone. Most poisoners do. Certainly Mrs Frost acted as an accomplice in signing herself as Sarah Bolton and was involved in the insurance payments. She also took food and drink to her mother's victims and nursed Sidney Bolton. Did she abet her mother in the poisonings? Or did she have, at least, guilty knowledge? She was certainly in a position to have done both as she visited her mother-in-law with Mrs Winters, and both came bearing food and drink. Likewise she could have done so as regards Sidney. But there is nothing more to go on apart from the fact that she had opportunity and the prime mover was her mother, though she may well have lied on her deathbed to shield her daughter. Her guilt must remain not proven.

Chapter 3

The Lambeth Poisonings, 1891–92

No sooner had south London been cleared of one poisoner, with the death of Mrs Winters and the imprisonment of one of her daughters in 1889, than another emerged. This time it was rather closer to the centre of the city, though still south of the Thames. As before, the first victims were not initially recognised as such and it was only when more women were murdered that justice was to eventually prevail. These murders are not well known; there are very few books about them and there have been no film or TV dramas to date.

Ellen Donworth, born in Kensington and the second daughter of Michael, an Irish labourer, and Minnie, his wife, was aged 18, and in the early evening of 13 October 1891 told Ernest Lennett, the man she lived with at 8 Duke Street, Westminster, that she was going out to see her mother who lived in a house on the Wandsworth Road, but she did not do so. Instead, she went to Morpeth Place. Here she was seen with several men, going into a house with them, one at a time. She also had a quick drink with Constance Lindfield, another prostitute, at the nearby Lord Hill pub.[1]

At 7.45pm she was found by a man called James Styles of 47 East Street, Lambeth, at Morpeth Court on Waterloo Road near the pub, in a state of collapse. She fell on her face and he picked her up. She was conscious, but in great pain, and told him that a man in the street had given her two drops of 'white stuff' to drink. She was taken first to her home. John Johnson, assistant to Dr Lowe, medical officer of health for the district, was summoned. He could tell she was suffering from tetanic convulsions and seemed to be dying and so ordered her to be taken to St Thomas' Hospital, where she arrived at 9.20pm. Martha Northfield, her landlady said that Ellen had said 'a gentleman with a tall hat and a dark beard had given her something white to drink', corroborating what Styles had said. Unfortunately, Ellen died that night in hospital. The post mortem revealed that there was a quarter of a grain of strychnine and a trace of morphia in her stomach.[2]

Dr Thomas Killick was the house physician and he performed the post mortem. He said that it was novel to find two poisons together. He said that the morphia would intensify and mask the effects of the strychnine. Although only a quarter of a grain of the latter had been found, the poison which caused death had been absorbed into the system.[3]

There was an inquest on 21 October, resumed on 23 October. An open verdict was returned. The death was deemed 'mysterious' and 'suspicious', but that was it. It is conceivable that it might have been suicide or murder. The grounds for the first assumption were that the young woman had just given birth, but her baby soon died. The man she was cohabiting with had been unemployed for six months and so was sending her out onto the streets as a prostitute. She was very depressed because of all this. Despite the verdict, a man named William Seater was charged with her murder, Constance Lindfield having allegedly seen him with Ellen on the night of the murder. There was insufficient evidence to try him on the capital charge and on 23 November he was released.[4]

Inspector George Harvey of L Division had been present at the inquest. He later related that the man Styles, a jewellery salesman, was a suspect. He was questioned by the police, but not charged. He was a tall man, with drooping shoulders and a straggly beard. He was middle-aged, with a peculiar look in his eye and a worn out appearance. He was not identified by any of the witnesses as being the man seen with Ellen. In south London the case caused 'a fearful sensation' and was known as the 'Lambeth mystery'. There the matter rested.[5]

The coroner received a letter written on 19 October to the effect that if he paid the writer £300,000, he could reveal the name of the murderer. A.O. Brien, detective, was the name on the letter.[6]

Unknown to the public, a letter was sent concerning this death to Alfred Smith, but was opened by Mr Alfred D. Acland of W.H. Smith's. He received it on 6 November and it read as follows:

London 5th November, 1891

Sir, On Tuesday night 13th October (last month) a girl named Ellen Donworth but sometimes called Ellen Linell, who lived at 8 Duke Street, Westminster Bridge Road, was poisoned with strychnine. After her death, among her effects were found two letters incriminating you, which if they ever became public property would surely convict you of the crime. I enclose a copy of one of the letters which the girl received on the morning of 13th October (the day on which she died). Just read it, and judge for yourself what hope you have of escape if the law officers ever get hold of these letters. Think of the shame and disgrace it will bring on your family if you are arrested and put in prison for this crime. My object in writing to you is to ask you if you will retain me as your counsellor and legal adviser. If you employ me at once to act for you in this matter I will save you from all exposure and shame in this matter; but if you wait until arrested before retaining me, than I cannot act for you as no lawyer can save you after the authorities get hold of these two letters. If you wish to retain me, just write a few lines on paper, say: 'Mr Fred Smith wishes to meet Mr Jayne, the barrister, at once'. Paste this in one of your shop windows at 186 The Strand, next Tuesday morning, and when I see it I will drop in and have a private interview. I can save you if you retain me in time but not otherwise. Yours truly, H. Bayne.

This was obviously an attempt at blackmail, but it failed to have the desired effect. Acland passed the letter to his solicitor.[7]

A few days later, a Clerkenwell magistrate received a letter to say that there was enough evidence to hang Mr Smith and if the police did not act he 'would make it hot for them'.[8] Again, no action was taken.

Unremarked by the press at this time was another death. Matilda Clover, alias Phillips, aged 27, and whose father was Henry Clover, a coarser, lodged in two rooms on the second storey at 27 Lambeth Road in October 1891, where she had been for some months. Two years earlier she had given birth to a baby boy who lived with her. She could let herself out of the house but had to ring the doorbell to be readmitted. She was prone to drink and on 13 October had had 11s worth of brandy. Robert Taylor of London Road, Southwark, knew her. He said 'She was a domestic servant and had been living a loose life'. She was 'peculiarly marked with small pox'.[9]

In particular, Matilda had been keeping company with a man she called Fred. Taylor recalled that one evening he had met her in a pub and she told him about him. On being asked what she did for a living she said 'I could form my own opinion'. In September she introduced Taylor to 'Fred', who apparently gave her plenty of money. Fred was a man in his thirties and was the father of her child.[10]

On 20 October, a letter arrived for Matilda, asking her to meet the writer outside the Canterbury Music Hall at 7.30pm that evening. She did so and went out. Later that evening, Lucy Rose, the servant, let Matilda into the house. She was with a tall, broad man, aged about 40, wearing a silk top hat. He was also seen by Elizabeth Masters and Elizabeth May. They noticed he had a moustache but no beard. Matilda left the place to buy two pint bottles of beer, returned and spent another hour there with him before he left and she went to bed. She was a prostitute and this was known to Mrs Emma Vowles, the landlady.[11]

At about three the next morning, Matilda began to scream in pain, which woke up Lucy, who slept in the room under hers. She got up and together with the landlady and another woman they entered Matilda's room.[12]

They found Matilda in great agony, complaining that she had been given poison. She was lying across the foot of her bed with her head fixed between bedstead and wall. There were moments of relief and then the fits came on again and she was twitching and her eyes rolled terribly. She was vomiting. They went out to find Dr Robert Graham of Upper Kennington Lane, but without success. Once Matilda's fits passed, she spoke quite rationally and asked to see her child.[13]

On the morning of 21 October, at 7am, Francis Coppin of Westminster Road, assistant to Dr McCarthy, was called to the house. He saw Lucy, and then was shown Matilda. She was in convulsions, and tremors, with a quick pulse and covered in sweat. He thought she was suffering from epileptic fits and convulsions due to excessive drinking, which in his fourteen years' experience of the district was far from uncommon. He learnt that she had been given a pill and sent out the landlady's grandson for medicine. He remained in the house for only 12 minutes. He gave her a mixture which turned black. After leaving, Coppin was sought again but could not be found.[14]

Matilda died at nine in the morning on 21 October 1891. Dr Graham eventually arrived (he had been with a woman giving birth) and discussed what had happened with the landlady. He had seen Matilda for previous illnesses, first of all on 13 October and then on a daily basis. He believed that she was suffering from alcoholism, so prescribed bromide of potassium and sedative medicines. He had last seen her alive on 19 October. He wrote a death certificate to state that Matilda had died from delirium tremens. She was buried at Tooting Cemetery on 27 October by the parish overseer.[15]

On the night of her death, Emma had sent for Matilda's aunt. The aunt said, 'I think it is very strange for a young girl to go off like this. From her drawn up condition I should think she died in great agony'. However, Emma suggested to the aunt why her niece had died, telling her, 'The girl had a bottle of brandy the other day'. She also told the grieving relative what the doctor had said, 'If she had given up the drink I think I could have pulled her through'. So they concluded that death was due to excessive drinking and that was that. Elizabeth May and Elizabeth Masters heard of Matilda's death and that it was due to natural causes. No one notified the police about the death. Curiously, on the morning of the previous day, Lucy had noticed a letter in Matilda's room, but it had gone by the next morning.[16]

It should be noted that in 1891 there were nineteen deaths in Lambeth due to alcoholism and only three known murders.[17]

Meanwhile, the killer was still on the prowl for more victims. Louisa Harris, who lived at 44 Townshend Road, St John's Wood, with Charles Harvey, a painter turned bus driver, and was known as Loo Harvey, had good reason to remember an evening on 21 October 1891. Firstly her boyfriend had lost his job a few days earlier, perhaps leading her to pursue a new way of making money. Secondly, she was at the Alhambra music hall that night and met a man there who arranged to see her outside after the show. They met in Regent Street and spent a night together in a hotel in Berwick Street. The man told her he was a doctor at St Thomas' Hospital and that he was from America and was planning to return. Would she accompany him there? He was cross-eyed, bald, but had a moustache. He wore a dark suit and a top hat. He had an old-fashioned gold watch and spectacles. He asked for Louisa's address, but she gave him a false one, number 55, as she did not want a visit from him at home.[18]

The next day he told her that she had a few spots on her forehead, but he could cure her of these with some pills he could obtain. They parted but arranged to meet that night on the Embankment near to Charing Cross station at 7.30pm as a prelude to going to a show at the Oxford Music Hall. She agreed and told him she was a servant. Louisa told Harvey about what had happened and he went with her to the rendezvous, though keeping out of sight. Harvey waited in Northumberland Avenue and Louisa kept her appointment with the man, saying 'Good evening, I am late' and asking him if he had brought the pills, which he had made at Westminster Bridge Road. He said he had.[19]

The man asked her if she would like a drink of wine first and she asked if she could have the pills beforehand. He refused and they went to the Northumberland pub and had their wine. She was even bought flowers from a woman selling them there. The two left and it was then explained that they could not go to the music hall as he had an appointment at St Thomas' Hospital at nine, but if she could she meet him outside at 11pm they would spend the night at a hotel as before. He then gave her the pills and suggested she eat some figs after swallowing them.[20]

Louisa was given two pills and told to swallow, not bite them and she then put her hand to her mouth as if to swallow them as instructed. However, she managed by sleight of hand to put the pills in her left hand and then put her right hand to her mouth. He asked to see her right hand, which was empty, then her left (she had by then thrown the pills away). Satisfied, he gave her five shillings and suggested she take a cab to the music hall and meet him as arranged at 11pm.[21]

Louisa waited outside the hospital until 11.30pm, but the man did not appear, so she went home. A month later she saw him at the corner of Piccadilly and Regent Street. He did not recognise her but arranged to have a drink with her that evening. They met at a pub in Archer Street and had the drink. She reminded him of their earlier assignations, but he denied all knowledge of them and departed swiftly, evidently displeased.[22] Fortunately Louisa was an astute and cautious young woman.

Dr William Henry Broadbent of Seymour Street received a letter with a London postmark on 30 November. In it he was told that if he paid £2,500, then the writer would suppress all knowledge that he had about the doctor concerning Matilda's death. This was at a time when no one suspected that there was anything untoward about Matilda's death.[23]

The letter read as follows:

London 26th November 1891

Sir, Miss Clover, who lived a short time ago at 27 Lambeth Road, S.E., died at the above address on 20th October (last month) by being poisoned by strychnine. After her death a search of her effects was made, and evidence was found that showed that you not only gave her the medicine which caused her death, but that you had been hired for the purpose of poisoning her. The evidence is in the hands of one of our detectives, who will give the evidence either to you or the police authorities for the sum of £2,500 (two thousand five hundred pounds) sterling. You can have the evidence for £2,500 and in that way save yourself from ruin. If the matter is disposed of to the police it will of course be made public by being placed in the papers, and ruin you forever. You know well enough that an accusation of that sort will ruin you for ever. Now sir, if you want the evidence for £2,500, just put a personal in The Daily Chronicle, saying that you will pay Malone £2,500 for his services, and I will send a party over to settle this matter. If you do not want the evidence, of course, it will be turned over to the police at once and published and your ruin will surely follow. Think well before you decide on this matter. It is just this – £2,500 on the one hand, and ruin, shame and disgrace on the other. Answer by personal on the first page of The Daily Chronicle any time next week. I am not humbugging you. I have evidence strong enough to ruin you forever.

M. Malone.[24]

Dr Broadbent took the letter to the police. It reached Inspector John Tunbridge of Scotland Yard. With the doctor's sanction they had an advert placed in the newspaper on 3 December and kept a watch on his house for two days to intercept any callers in response to it. None came, so the inquiry was called off. It was assumed that the letter was by a madman and letters of that type were not uncommon. No enquiry was made at 27 Lambeth Road, nor were the police in L Division, which covered that district, informed.[25] However, only Matilda's murderer knew that she had been poisoned by strychnine and thus the writer of the letter was clearly the murderer.

Although there were no more murders for several months, the case was recalled in the following year when there were further poisonings, which it was surmised 'may possibly be three links in a single chain'. Reference was made to Jack the Ripper, in that the three victims 'belonged to the class of unfortunates that recalls the series of crimes which in the public mind is with the name of Jack the Ripper'. The recent killer was not forgotten and there are further references to him in this chapter.[26]

Alice Marsh, aged 21, and Emma Elizabeth Shrivell, aged 18, had lodged on 15 March at Mrs Emily Newman's house at 27 Stamford Street, paying her 5s per week for the use of one room. She was the wife of a brewer's labourer. She thought they were respectable servant girls. They were not allowed to entertain men there and so they left. She recalled after their departure that a man did call to see them, but she would not allow him into the house further than the mat. He was tall, with a fair moustache, young and looked like a gentleman. She saw the girls once after they had left and they told her that they were doing very well. They told her that their current landlady allowed them to do what she had not.[27]

The two had moved to two rooms on the second floor of 118 Stamford Street, Blackfriars. Their landlady was Charlotte Vogt, to whom they paid 15s a week rent from 22 March. Alice was from Hampshire and worked as a servant in Brighton where she had a good character. In 1891 she had been working as a housemaid at 5 Thurlow Park Road, Lambeth, in the household of German military outfitter Adolphus Cori. She left the job six weeks previously as she was not receiving her wages due and was looking for work in a biscuit factory. Emma was from Brighton, being born there in 1874, and was baptised at St Peter's church on 18 September 1875. Her mother was dead and her stepfather was Henry Washer, a fish hawker, and she was the second of at least four children, resident at 38 Castleton Road, Brighton, in 1881. The two young women lived at 170 York Road in London in 1890.[28]

They returned to Brighton in September 1890; allegedly Emma had been seeing a member of Parliament who gave her the return train fare and advised her to find a job as a servant. Apparently Emma lived with one Frank Pimm, who had known her since 1887, at 38 Carlton Road, and she also received money from one Pedro Glenzo, an Italian who also went by the name of Joe Simpson of Walham Green. The young women had returned to London as recently as March 1892. Emma's aunt recalled that the two young women had travelled up to London together, but she did not know why; one reason was to work in a biscuit factory. Emma had had no money when setting off on her journey and had had to pawn some of her possessions to afford the train fare. She had written to her aunt three times when in London but had not told her anything about her life there. The two had lived in London together two years ago for two months at Mrs Mary Eden Matthews' house.[29]

Charlotte recalled that they were very quiet and that they were attempting to find work in the theatre. They went out every night but had few visitors. As to the girls' real occupation, two witnesses made suggestive comments. A man later said 'The house in question is let out to girls of this description. There are many others in the neighbourhood'. Mrs Matthews said 'she did not know exactly how they got their living but she could give a good guess'.[30] On Monday

11 April, between 6 and 7pm, Emma asked Charlotte's servant to go for powder. She had been eating fish and was unwell because of it.[31]

At about a quarter to two on the morning of the next day, PC George Cumley was on his beat along Stamford Street. He saw a man being let out of number 118 by a young woman. The man was aged between 45 and 50, and wore a dark coat and a top hat. He was five feet nine or ten, moustached and wore glasses. He walked smartly away on leaving his companion.[32]

At half past two on the same morning, Charlotte's husband heard cries. Charlotte went up and found Alice in the passage screaming and Emma, who was calling for Alice, in her room, both in agony. Vogt then went for the police.[33]

Vogt saw an empty salmon tin on the table and two empty plates nearby. Emma, who was lying on the floor and leaning on the sofa, asked her repeatedly, 'Do you think we have been poisoned?' and asked how Alice was. They told her that a gentleman had given them a pill each. 'How foolish it was to take it from a stranger' the landlady said and they said 'He is not a stranger, he is a doctor'. They could not remember exactly when they had taken the lethal pills.[34]

Mrs Vogt heard Alice again, so went down to see her. She was lying on the floor, twitching as if the pain was going off and then passing, only to return again. She tried speaking to the girl when she was conscious.[35]

PC William Eversfield arrived at 2.30am. He found Alice lying in the passage in her night dress. In the room nearby was Emma, lying on the floor in her dress. He gave them mustard and water and then put them in a cab to St Thomas' Hospital. They did not vomit en route. Alice died on the way and Emma soon after arrival, but not before she had made a statement.[36]

However, the officer had spoken to Emma on the journey. She told him that they had had tea with a man on the previous day and afterwards he had given them three long pills. They had then invited him to their rooms that evening. They had then had the tinned salmon and became so ill they were unable to stand. Emma had met the man before and he was known to her as Fred and also as Clifton, the same names mentioned in the case of Matilda.[37]

When Inspector Lowe went to the house and looked in one of the girls' rooms, he found a letter on the sideboard. It was from a man accepting their invitation to tea. There was no envelope to be found, but it had been addressed from a hotel in Chatham. A number of pawnbroker's tickets were found for shops in Brighton. No poisons were located, however.[38]

The letter read:

> Prince of Wales Hotel April 10
> Just a few lines to say, that all being well, I shall be in London tomorrow (Monday) and shall hope to have the pleasure of seeing you at 118 Stamford Street between six and seven in the evening. Pleased

to accept your kind invitation to take tea with you. We can then go to some place of entertainment for the rest of the evening. Kind regards to your friend. Please remember me to her. With best wishes to yourself, believe me to remain yours faithfully, George Clifton.[39]

Dr Cuthbert Wyman was house physician at St Thomas' Hospital. He received the two women; Alice was already dead and Emma was in fits of convulsions for another two hours prior to her death. He carried out post mortems and diagnosed strychnine poisoning in each case. There were no signs of any disease and the stomach contents were sealed for analysis.[40] In all, there were six grains of strychnine in Alice and two grains in Emma.[41]

Sir Thomas Stevenson, who had been involved in the Deptford poisonings in 1889, undertook to examine the stomach contents on 16 April. He received three sealed jars. The first was marked with Alice's name and contained her stomach and organs. The second contained Emma's vomit and the third her organs. In the first he found 6.75 grains of strychnine. A fatal dose was less than one grain. The stomach contained portions of salmon, bacon, cheese and apples. In jar two were fish, currants and 1.46 grains of strychnine. In the third were 1.8 grains of strychnine. He also received the remains of the salmon and the tin, but there were no traces of poison there.[42]

The question of the identity of the murderer was posed at the inquest. This lay in the fact that no chemist would ever supply such a large quantity of strychnine to a customer. Therefore, the killer must be a man connected directly or indirectly with the medical profession. It was then that the previous mysterious death of the year before was recalled, having been dismissed somewhat summarily. The description of Ellen's killer was that he was a man 'tall, dark and cross eyed', and in the latter murders he was 'tall, with a fair moustache, 29 or 30 years of age and of an exceedingly gentlemanly appearance'. In both cases, he had been at pains to conceal his real name. It was suggested that he might be an American or a Frenchman because his method of murder seemed more appropriate to a man from either of these countries than an Englishman.[43]

On 13 April, Mr G.P. Wyatt, coroner for east Surrey, opened the inquest. Emma Stevens of Brighton identified Emma's body as being that of her niece. Rebecca Walker identified Alice as her daughter by her first husband. Evidence was given by the landlady, police officers and the relatives of the deceased. It was then adjourned to await further medical evidence.[44]

On 25 April a letter was received by Dr Joseph Harper of Bear Street, Barnstaple, in Devon. It said that unless £15,000 was paid, the writer would prove that Harper's son (Walter, a medical student lodging at 103 Lambeth Palace Road) was the poisoner. It also contained three circulars pertaining to Ellen Donworth's death. There was also a newspaper cutting about a mysterious poisoning in south London. The doctor knew no one called W.H. Murray, who had allegedly written the letter. He showed it to his solicitor, then his son, and finally handed it to Inspector Tunbridge on 1 June.[45]

Alfred Ward, a sergeant in L Division, was asked to make enquiries into the deaths of Emma and Alice. During his investigations he talked to many women in the district. One was Lucy Rose, servant at the house where Matilda lodged. She told him about the death of Matilda Clover. He wrote up a report of this and passed it to Inspector Harvey.[46]

In the meantime, two letters were sent to the coroner, though he never mentioned these during the inquest proceedings. The first read as follows:

> London 2 May 1892
> Coroner Wyatt, St Thomas Hospital, London
> Dear Sir – will you please give the enclosed letter to the foreman of the Coroner's Jury in the inquest on Alice Marsh and Emma Shrivell, and oblige yours respectfully, William Henry Murray.

The letter in question was rather longer and read:

> Dear sir – I beg to inform you that one of the operators has positive proof that William [sic] Harper, medical student at St Thomas' Hospital, son of Dr Harper of Barnstaple, is responsible for the death of Alice Marsh and Emma Shrivel having poisoned these girls with strychnine. This proof you can have by paying my bill for services to George Clarke of 20 Cockspur Street, Charing Cross, to whom I will give proof on paying my bill. Yours respectfully, W.H. Murray.

Murray also wrote a very similarly worded letter to the police.[47]

When Dr Harper showed the letter mentioned above to his son, Walter Joseph Harper, who was at St Thomas' Hospital, the young man was surprised. He had heard of only one of the four young women mentioned therein. Nor did he know anyone called Murray. He and his father could not determine if this was an attempt at blackmail or a practical joke.[48]

The inquest was resumed on 5 May. Dr Stevenson gave his evidence, as did the two landladies and the police. Summing up, Wyatt urged the jury to find that this was a case of murder by poison, but there was no evidence to suggest who the killer was. The jury took only a few minutes to concur with him, but they added the following statement:

> We are of your opinion, sir, as to the suggestion as to the verdict being the proper one for us to find. We desire to say that the police has exercised not near enough energy in the matter – to trace out the matter;

but we are of opinion that Constable Eversfield did his duty well, and promptly in rendering the assistance to the deceased.

Wyatt said that the police had been endeavouring to trace the killer and so that portion of the jury's statement was unfair, so they withdrew it.[49]

Suspicions began to be aroused that Matilda Clover had been poisoned. Application was made to the Home Secretary with the result that on the evening of 5 May her corpse was exhumed and Mr Steers, the assistant keeper, was present to testify that it was the same corpse which had been buried in the previous year.[50]

On 6 May Dr Stevenson and Mr Dunn, senior examiner at Guy's Hospital, went to the cemetery and examined the deceased. She was in a good state of preservation and following a dissection he could find no signs of disease. He extracted several organs and examined them for any presence of alkaloid poisons, of which strychnine is one. He found traces of it in the stomach, liver, brain and the fluid on the chest. He tested this poison on a frog and it died, showing the characteristic signs of strychnine poisoning. Altogether he found a sixteenth of a grain of strychnine and while a twelfth of a grain is the maximum medical dose permitted, this was accounted for by the fact that the victim had vomited frequently and her stomach was empty on death. He concluded, 'I have no doubt that taking into account the vomiting and the length of time, it did point to a much larger dose – a little more than half a grain has killed – but one grain is usually about a fatal dose'.[51]

It is now necessary to introduce a major character into this narrative. Dr Thomas Neill Cream had been born in Glasgow on 17 May 1850. He went with his parents, Scottish-born William and Irish-born Mary (née Elder) to America later in the decade, and by 1861 lived in Quebec. His father was recorded as a clerk in 1861 and Cream first went into business with him. He soon developed an interest in medicines and went to the Guild College, Montreal, where he took a degree. He then travelled to London and attended lectures at St Thomas' Hospital, but did not take a degree. He then went to Edinburgh where he was successful in this. Returning to Canada in 1879 he practised medicine in Ontario for some years. He arrived back in London on 5 October 1891 and briefly stayed at Anderton's Hotel in Fleet Street, before taking lodgings at 103 Lambeth Palace Road on 7 October, where he stayed until January 1892. While there he visited John George Kirby's chemist's at 22 Parliament Street. He explained he was a medical student and needed to buy nux vomica, which contains strychnine, and capsules. He did so and signed the poisons register.[52]

From 7 April Cream was again staying at 103 Lambeth Palace Road, after a brief trip across the Atlantic (from 7 January to 2 April 1892), and was interested in reading about the mysterious deaths in the newspaper they took there. He discussed the case with the landlady's daughter, Emily Sleaper, and even asked her to visit 27 Lambeth Road about a strange death that had occurred there, but she refused. He said it was a cold-blooded murder. He also asked questions about a fellow lodger, Harper, and told Emily that Harper was the poisoner. Emily refused to believe him, but he insisted that the police had proof.[53]

Cream was fascinated with the murders. In May he was taking refreshment with Mrs Margaret Armstead, a photographer's wife whom Cream had dealings with. They discussed the murders, Cream exclaiming, 'What a dreadful murder it was in Stamford Street'. She replied, 'Yes, it is terrible. They ought to be hanged whoever did this'. Cream added that he had seen the two girls in the streets previously and had seen them soliciting clients on the bridge.[54]

He made similar remarks to John Haynes, an engineer, in April. Cream told him about Dr Harper, who, he alleged, was being trailed by the police. He alleged that Harper had made a girl in Brighton pregnant and then had procured an abortion for her. This news became known to prostitutes in London who threatened to blackmail him, so he obtained strychnine and poisoned four prostitutes with this and also one Louisa Harris. Haynes asked why, if he knew all this, he did not contact the police? Cream replied that there was blackmail money to be obtained by keeping quiet.[55]

Cream was also engaged to a young lady from Berkhamsted called Laura Sabbatini. They had met in November 1891. On 3 May 1892 he asked her to write the letters to the coroner and jury in the inquest of Emma and Alice. She did so, but asked him if he had the evidence he referred to and he told her that a detective whose name he would not mention had it. Then she asked who 'Murray', who was allegedly writing the letters, was, and Cream told her that he would tell her that sometime.[56]

On 17 May the killer sought another victim. On both this day and the next he met Violet Beverley, a London-born prostitute of 3 North Street, Kensington Road, aged 20, who had a two-year-old daughter and a husband who was abroad. He offered her what he called 'an American drink' but she declined it. He also showed her a number of pills, but again she did not take any. 'The man' called himself Dr Neal.[57]

On 19 May DS Patrick MacIntyre was approached by Cream, who complained that he was being followed. The detective did not know of the investigation, so made enquiries. Cream told him that a woman had told him that the police were suspicious of him for being involved in the two recent poisonings. He later said that a detective called Murray had stopped him in the street and accused him of being Dr Harper, the poisoner.[58]

The investigation was certainly progressing. Alfred Ward had seen the reports of the two constables from the night of 12 April and on 12 May his attention was drawn to a man seen on Westminster Bridge Road whose description tallied with the suspect. The man watched women as they passed and seemed particularly interested in prostitutes. From then on a watch was kept by the police on this man.[59]

On 26 May Tunbridge was instructed to investigate all four deaths. He went to 103 Lambeth Palace Road to meet Dr Cream because of his allegations of persecution by the police. He talked to him about his business and he showed him his medicine case. Therein was a bottle of strychnine pills and the detective asked him about them and on being told what they were and that they had been sugar coated, Tunbridge stated, 'the bottle contains quite a large quantity of strychnine and it would be highly dangerous that they should fall into the hands of the public in any quantity'. Cream said he would not sell any. At that time Tunbridge did not know how Matilda had died.[60]

Suspicions, though, were aroused and the police had all the blackmail letters. Walter de Grey Birch was a handwriting expert employed at the British Museum in their Manuscript Department. He compared the blackmail letters with samples of Cream's handwriting and found that they were the work of the same man.[61] Tunbridge arrested Cream on 3 June at Lambeth Palace Road. Cream protested his innocence, 'you have got the wrong man, fire away'. He showed him the writing on the letter to Dr Harper and took him to Bow Street station, where he was formally charged. Cream's room was then searched. Apart from the silk top hats, there were papers with Matilda's, Emma and Alice's addresses, initials and dates on them.

On 11 June there was an identity parade, following statements made by Elizabeth May and Elizabeth Masters. Twenty men, most with moustaches and top hats, though none with a squint, were assembled with Cream. Elizabeth Masters failed to recognise him and left the room, then Elizabeth May came in and she picked him out. She left and then the men were told to remove their hats. Elizabeth Masters went in a second time and this time she did pick him out. Evidence was produced about Cream's involvement in Matilda's death. On 9 October 1891 it was ascertained he had arranged to meet Elizabeth Masters. He did not meet her, but she saw him in Lambeth Palace Road with Matilda after the latter turned and smiled at him. He then followed Matilda back to her lodgings. Masters waited for him but as he did not reappear, she went home.[62]

On 22 June the inquest on Matilda Clover was opened at Tooting and Dr Braxton Hicks was the coroner. There were several adjournments. Cream, when asked questions at one hearing on 13 July, was very unhelpful. He insisted that his solicitor had advised him not to testify in court, 'I refuse to be sworn whatever the consequences'. He even refused to confirm his name or give his profession. It was at this hearing that the jury had to decide on the cause of Matilda Clover's death and they declared:

> We are unanimously agreed that Matilda Clover died from strychnine poisoning and that it was administered by Thomas Neill with intent to destroy life and we therefore find him guilty of wilful murder. The jury especially also desire to draw special attention to the loose way in which medical certificates are given... great credit should be given to the police for the manner in which the evidence has been prepared.

Cream looked pained and anxious.[63]

Some light amusement was found in a letter addressed at this time to the coroner, which was read out in court and even Cream laughed:

> Dear Sir, The man you have in your power, Dr Neill, is as innocent as you are. Knowing him by sight, I disguised myself like him and made the acquaintanceship of the girls that have been poisoned. I gave them the pills to cure them of their earthly miseries, and they died. Miss L. Harris has got more sense than I thought she had, but I shall have her yet. Mr P. Harvey might also follow Loo Harris out of this world of care and woe. Lady Russell is quite right about the letter and so am I. Lord Russell had a hand in the poisoning of Clover. Nelly Donworth must have stayed out all night or she would not have been complaining of pain and cold when Annie Clements saw her. If I were you I would release Dr T. Neill or you might get into trouble. His innocence will be declared sooner or later. And when he is free he might sue you for damages. Yours respectfully, JULIAN DE POLLEN, alias Jack the Ripper. Beware all, I warn warn but once.

After the inquest was over, there were the magistrates' court hearings, as the lesser courts to which the defendant's case is heard. These were at Bow Street before Sir John Phillips, with lawyers representing both Crown and defendant. The second session was on 27 August when McCulloch's evidence was heard.[64]

Inspector Jervis travelled to Canada for any information about Cream that could be acquired there and had a lead from the Montreal police who had received a letter about a man who had known Cream and had relevant information. Further information about Cream came from John Wilson McCulloch, a Canadian travelling salesman, who became acquainted with him in the first week of March 1892 while both were staying in the same hotel. They talked of drugs and medicines and Cream showed him a bottle of pills, declaring 'This is poison' and told the shocked McCulloch 'I give these to women to get them out of the family way'. He then said that he walked the streets of London, such as Waterloo Road, at nights between 10pm and 3am, meeting prostitutes and using their services, and wearing a disguise. He also said that he was an abortionist. On one occasion he suggested to McCulloch that he could murder a man for his money, stating 'I could give that man a pill and put him to sleep, and his money would have been mine'. His friend was doubtful, 'I ought to have done it' added Cream.[65]

Lucy Rose reappeared at the court and it was shown that she had been unable to pick Cream out from a number of other men and so her recognition of him in 1891 was suspect. Waters was the solicitor for Cream and he complained of the unconstitutional way in which seven charges had been rolled into one. He did not call any evidence, and advised his client to plead not guilty. Cream was then formally committed to trial at the Old Bailey and he returned to Holloway Prison.[66]

The trial took place on the afternoon of Monday 17 October, before Justice Hawkins. Leading for the Crown were Sir Charles Russell, QC and Bernard Coleridge, QC, MP. Defending were Messrs Geoghegan and Warburton.[67] Cream was charged with all four murders, the attempted murder of Louisa Harris and attempting to extort money from others. To all these charges he pleaded not guilty. Russell focussed on the murder of Matilda Clover and went through the other cases of murder and blackmail. The defence tried to cast doubt on the identity parade, arguing that Cream had six days' hair growth on his face and so obviously was the man in question, and stated that one witness had not initially recognised him.[68]

The trial continued on the next day.[69] It continued for five days in total. Defence counsel argued that the man 'Fred' might be the murderer; he doubted Lucy's identification, questioned Dr Stevenson's evidence over Dr Graham's, as well as the identifications of the prostitutes and policemen of Dr Cream. Finally he made a plea for mercy and a statement on the awfulness of the death penalty. It was a desperate speech. After all the speeches, examinations and cross examinations, the jury took just ten minutes to come to their unanimous decision. Cream was guilty and thus Hawkins sentenced him to death. He was sent to Newgate Prison, next door to where he had been tried, and there was in regular conversation with the prison chaplain.[70]

There was comment in the press about the murders. One thought that the 'pitiless atrocity is almost unparalleled in the black annals of human crime'. Greed and the pleasure of inflicting suffering were seen as his motives and his victims were taken from a defenceless class of women; his blackmail victims were not in that category and it was there that he failed.[71]

After the verdict, Cream's solicitors tried to gather evidence to show that their client was insane and so should not hang. They produced affidavits from a number of people in Canada who knew him and they stated that following his release from Joliett prison, Illinois, on 29 July 1891, he was insane. His brother and sister-in-law, with whom he stayed after his sentence, were convinced that he was not sane. A London vicar thought he was irrational and odd. His London optician thought he took drugs. A man in Canada who had campaigned for Cream's release in 1891 met him afterwards and thought he was mad. However all this was not deemed sufficient evidence to prove Cream was insane and so there would be no reprieve. Cream took this news quietly and without comment.[72]

The date for the execution was 15 November. On the day before, Cream was moody, restless, silent and paced up and down his cell incessantly. He woke at six but could not eat breakfast. When he was about to put his collar on, he was advised 'I wouldn't put that on this morning if I were you'. The chaplain arrived at seven and just before nine, Colonel Hillman, the governor, and other officials came into the cell. Mr Metcalfe, the deputy sheriff, asked if there was anything else he wanted to say 'because now is the time'. Cream said that there was not, except to thank all the prison staff for their care of him in his last days. James Billington was the hangman. After Cream had been executed, there was an inquest on his body and the black flag was raised over the prison.[73]

After Cream's death further revelations were made about his time in Canada and America. His murders in London were by no means his first forays into serious crime. His wife died in mysterious circumstances in 1877, as did at least two other women. In 1879, after qualifying as a doctor in Edinburgh, he was in medical practice in Ontario. The body of a young woman was found on the premises and, understandably, demand for his medical services fell, so he set up shop in Chicago. There Julia Faulkner died, as a result of an abortion carried out by Cream in 1880. He was arrested and charged with murder but was acquitted. In the following year he was having an affair with the wife of Daniel Stott; Cream gave his lover a bottle of poisoned medicine with which to kill her husband. It was deemed a natural death, but Cream insisted that there should be an investigation. In October 1881 he was convicted of the murder and sentenced to life imprisonment, but this was commuted and concluded in 1891, leaving Cream a free man.[74]

Cream never made a confession or a statement explaining how he committed his murders or why. Bearing in mind Louisa's experience, we can see that he made the acquaintance of prostitutes by meeting them in the streets of Lambeth, close, but not too close, to where he was lodging in Lambeth Palace Road. He would then spend some time with them, paying them for their services in their rooms. Sometimes he would write to them to suggest a meeting, as in the cases of Matilda and Emma and Alice (he was able to remove the first letter but not the second). Shortly after meeting he would suggest that they had an ailment, which he as a bona fide doctor could cure by use of his pills. Some of the women he met would agree to take the pills, but not all of them, and whether Louisa and Violet were the only ones who declined is impossible to know, as they were the only ones to come forward. His victims were all very vulnerable and possibly gullible enough to be taken in by his veneer of respectability and professionalism as a medical man.

Whether Cream was a sadist or not is uncertain. He was not present when his victims died or even when they began to experience their death agonies. It would often take hours of pain before they died. Possibly he enjoyed the knowledge that he was the instrument of agonising death from afar. Perhaps he enjoyed the power of life and death that the poisons gave him, like doctors Shipman and John Bodkin Adams in the twentieth century.

However, perhaps the major motive was financial. He had little money and no income. He did not take the possessions of his victims as they all had next to nothing. Rather he aimed to use the murders as tools in his blackmail conspiracies. The letters sent to prominent men to gain money were presumably a means to enrich himself. Yet if this was his plan, he had a spectacular lack of success. His bluff failed on all three occasions.

The first two murders went by almost unnoticed. Matilda's death was put down to alcoholism, which was not unreasonable, and Ellen's death, though poison was detected, was not treated as murder and though there was a police investigation it seemed to begin and end with Slater, who brought the victim to public attention. Had Cream stopped there, in the knowledge that his attempts at blackmail had failed, it is probable that he would never have been detected. But like most serial killers, early success bred over-confidence and in the case of Emma and Alice there was no doubt that their deaths were murder and a more thorough investigation began. As part of this, the first two murders were found to be what they really were, and thus witnesses emerged who could provide evidence of Cream's activities in the case of Matilda's though not Ellen's death.

Cream also had that desire, as some serial killers do, to insert himself into the murder investigation. Unable to boast to anyone of his cleverness in these murders, he did the next best thing and boasted of inside knowledge about the murders and the identity of the killer. He even talked to detectives about it.

Cream is not as well known now as he once was, as his crimes have been overshadowed by more terrible ones. It seems that his chief claim to infamy now is that he is one of hundreds of men accused of being Jack the Ripper. This is based only on the alleged words of Billington, the hangman, who claimed that Cream's last words before he made his fatal drop on the gallows were 'I'm Jack the–'. Yet the reports of the execution, such as the one noted above, make no reference to this, nor did the *Notable British Trials* book on the case and nor did a recent scholarly treatment of the murders. Even if he did say it, it would seem impossible for he was, in 1888, incarcerated in the Joliett prison in Illinois, as he had been since 1881. Supporters of his candidature as the Ripper allege he might not have been in prison; perhaps another man was there in his stead, perhaps he escaped. Even so, the methods of murder and the motive in 1888 and 1891–92 are radically different. The 1888 murders were committed by a knife-wielding murderer who wanted to dissect dead women and take away their organs. He was a sexual sadist. Cream used poison and not a knife; he was not interested in taking body parts, but rather was interested in monetary gain which the Ripper was not. Nor did Cream even vaguely resemble any of the men seen with the Ripper's victims. He does, however, fit the stereotypical and wholly erroneous image often associated with the Ripper – he was a doctor and wore a top hat. However, as we shall soon see, he was not the only poisoner who was to be retrospectively accused of the earlier murders in Whitechapel. After his death a wax statue dressed in his own clothes was exhibited at Madame Tussaud's Waxworks in London.[75]

It is ironic that in the year of Cream's first two London murders, a short story was published in which the hero states, 'When a doctor goes wrong he is the first of criminals. He has the nerve and he has the knowledge... It's a wicked world and when a clever man turns to crime it is the worst of all'.[76]

Chapter 4
The Southwark Poisonings, 1897–1902

We have already read the stories of two serial poisoners in south London. We now come to a third. To lose one 'wife' might seem to be a misfortune, but to lose three seems like carelessness, to misquote Oscar Wilde's *The Importance of being Ernest*. George Chapman, born Seweryn Klosowski in Kolo, Poland, on 14 December 1865, seems to have been remarkably unfortunate with the women he called, for propriety's sake, his wives. Yet he is best known today, not for his verifiable murders, but, because (as with Dr Cream), he has become one of the many men suspected of an entirely different set of well-known murders.

Klosowski, born in 1865, was the son of Antoni Klosowski, a carpenter of Nagorna, a suburb of Kolo, and his wife Emilia. Like most Poles, they were Catholic. From 1873–78, after the family moved from his birthplace, Klosowski attended Krasienen school and his conduct was good. From 1880–85 he was apprenticed to Moshko Rappaport, a barber surgeon in Zwolen, where he was diligent in his studies and work. He was then employed at Praga hospital in Warsaw from 1885–86 as a surgeon's assistant. It is important to note that he was not a surgeon or a doctor and his medical skills were those similar to a paramedic now. He left Poland in either 1887 or 1888 and arrived in England, though it is not known exactly when or why. In 1888 he was working in Whitechapel, which had a large population of immigrants from Poland. He took a job in a hairdresser's shop at 70 West India Dock Road, run by Abraham Radin, and was employed there for five months. He said he was a doctor's assistant in Warsaw.[1]

In 1889 Klosowski was employed at a barber's shop in Cable Street. Life was not all work and no play. Klosowski was a regular at the Polish club in St John's Square, Clerkenwell. It was here that he became friendly with Stanislaw Baderski, a tailor. Klosowski went out with one of Baderski's sisters, Lucy Baderska, then aged 16 and born in Posen, Polish Germany, for a few weeks before getting married on 29 October 1889, at St Boniface's Church, Union Street, Whitechapel. The couple had a son, Wladyslaw, born on 6 September 1890 at the White Hart pub, who died on 3 March 1891. The newlyweds first lived in Cable Street and then, by 1890, in Whitechapel High Street, Commercial Road and Greenfield Street. They went to America in 1891 and Lucy returned alone in February 1892, pregnant again (Cecilia was born on 12 May 1892 and lived until 1960). Klosowski returned in May and the couple lived together at 2 Tewkesbury Buildings, Whitechapel, where he was listed as being a hairdresser.[2]

Klosowski and Lucy split up, but it is not known why or exactly when. They were never divorced, as this was expensive and few couples bothered. He was employed as a hairdresser's assistant at John Haddon's hairdressers shop at 7 West Green Road, Whitechapel, towards the end of 1893. Annie Chapman (the same name as the Ripper's second victim, ironically enough), born in 1875, met him there and they became friendly. He suggested she move in with him as his housekeeper so they could live together. At about this time he anglicised his name to George Chapman, and will be referred to as such from now on. Annie lived with Chapman from November 1893 to November or December 1894 and they had a child together, William, who died in 1896, but Chapman left her and failed to provide any money for the child's upkeep.[3] It is interesting to note that none of the three women whom Chapman later cohabited with bore children.

In the following year Chapman was keeping a hairdresser's shop at Tottenham High Street from January to March. Later that year he ran one opposite the Bruce Grove railway station. He then became a hairdresser's assistant at a shop at 7 Church Lane, Leytonstone, run by William Wengel.[4]

It was there that he met Mary Spink. She was born Mary Isabella Renton in Pudsey, West Yorkshire, in 1858, so she was a few years older than Chapman. Her mother, Sarah Ann, and her grandmother, Mary Smith, were employed as pork butchers in Leeds in 1871, her father, William, having died in 1869, and she was then living with them. She was still living in Leeds in 1881, but moved to London. However, on 16 December 1883 she married Shadrach Spink at St Paul's Church, Stepney. He was employed by the Great Eastern Railway as a porter at Leytonstone station. They had two sons, Shadrach, born in 1884, and William, born in 1888, but the couple separated in 1888 before William was born, Spink taking Shadrach with him. Mary had £530 from her grandfather's will to tide her over. In 1891 she was living with her younger son at a house in Mornington Road, Leytonstone, and was able to support the two of them out of this private income. By 1895 she lived with her brother Joseph, a corn chandler at 1 Mornington Road. Mary Spink then moved to lodge in John Ward's house in Forest Road, Leytonstone.[5]

Chapman was lodging at John Ward's house, too, when he began to make Mary's acquaintance. This developed into romance and this was not something that Ward's wife, Caroline, liked. Chapman said that they were soon to marry, so it did not matter. Ward saw them kissing and cuddling on the stairs. Shortly afterwards, on 27 October 1895, the two went out early one Sunday morning and on their return Chapman announced 'Mr and Mrs Ward, allow me to introduce you to my wife Mrs Chapman'. He told Ward that they had been married in a Catholic church in the City and when Mrs Harris asked to see the certificate, he told her that 'our laws are different to your laws' as he was a Polish Jew, or so he said. They were not married; it would have been illegal as both were already married to living spouses. Ward later recalled Chapman complaining that he could not gain control of his 'wife's' money as he wanted to acquire business premises. They left to go to Hastings in March 1896.[6]

The couple and her son William lived in rooms in a house at 10 Hill Street, Hastings, from March 1896. At this time Chapman ran a barber's shop at Albion Mansions, George Street in the town, using Mary's remaining money from her trust fund to establish the business, and his wife and son went there to eat. In 1896 the remainder of Mary's funds were paid into Chapman's bank account at Hastings. Relations between the couple, though, were poor. They were known to quarrel. Chapman sometimes struck his wife about the face and neck. She also suffered from violent sicknesses and stomach pains. The vomit was green. Medical help was never sought. Later the family moved to lodgings in 1 Coburg Place in February 1897. Chapman wrote his name in Russian to a fellow lodger. She recalled Mary being intemperate but in good health. Mrs Martin, housekeeper at Albion Mansions, recalled that Mary 'vomited a good deal in May' and afterwards 'appeared very poorly'. Chapman had a revolver and borrowed the four-volume *Family Physician* from a Mrs Greenaway and never returned it.[7] His interest in medical matters was clearly revived.

It was when they were in Hastings that Chapman bought poison from a William Davidson, a chemist on the High Street, on 3 April 1897. He bought an ounce of tartar emetic, a white powder and more importantly a deadly poison – 146 grains of antimony; two of which can be fatal; ten to twelve grains would certainly be so. The chemist discussed medicines with Chapman and believed that he had some knowledge of them. Davidson said that Chapman was 'an intellectual man to talk to on medical subjects'. Alice Penfold, a servant, recalled Chapman accosting her in the street and introducing himself as a manager of a pianoforte shop and a single man. They walked out together on two occasions. One day he said he thought she was ill and she complained of having a cold and so he told her he had studied medicine and gave her some of the white powder, which would cure her. However, she destroyed it. Why he wanted to harm her is unknown. He later wrote to her in London, asking her to visit, but she did not do so.[8]

The Chapmans returned to London in September 1897, Mary complaining before departure of being unwell and Chapman had a radical change of career, for reasons which are never explained. He turned his back on the career of the hairdressing forever and began a wholly new one. On 28 September, Chapman opened a new bank account at the London City and Midland Bank, depositing nearly £300. He took the licence of the Prince of Wales beerhouse, 20 Bartholomew Square, Finsbury, in September 1897. Mrs Martha Doubleday recalled Mary as 'a nice woman, rather stout, with a fresh complexion' but she soon lost weight. She became thin and ill and the concerned husband asked Mrs Doubleday if she would sit up with his wife at night time, which she did. She also advised Chapman to call Dr John Rogers of Old Street, which he did, but only after his wife's friend had sat up with her on two or three occasions and Mrs Susan Paget had threatened to call the parish doctor.[9]

Chapman occupied a couch on the second floor and his wife had the bed, both in the same room. She complained of pains in the head and sickness. She vomited a lot every night. Chapman gave her brandy that he obtained from the bar downstairs. That was her only nourishment; there was no food and no fire was lit in the patient's room. After taking brandy she was always sick.[10]

Mrs Susan Paget and her husband worked at the pub and recalled that Chapman was not convinced that the illness was dangerous. Mary said that her husband put a red substance in water for her to drink, but on being confronted with this, he told her to ignore what his wife said because of her being delirious.[11]

Mrs Elizabeth Waymark saw the terrible state that Mary was in from 11 December. She noticed that Chapman often felt her pulse. Mrs Waymark would say 'She is very bad' and he would reply 'Yes, I know what to do'. Mary would say 'Do, do, kiss me'. He then took her hand.[12]

On about 11 December, Chapman sent a note to the doctor, who arrived in the daytime, when Mrs Doubleday was not there. The latter did see medicine bottles when she next called, and it was Chapman who always administered the contents. The vomiting continued and there was frequent diarrhoea. Chapman and the doctor would discuss the case in the bar, away from his wife and her friend.[13]

Another woman came to nurse Mary; Mrs Jane Mumford. She was a neighbour and from 18–25 December 1897 helped with the night-time nursing. She recalled Chapman not allowing her to give Mary anything; he alone gave her drinks of what she presumed was medicine in a wine glass. Once Chapman said 'she seems queer' and 'she drinks a good deal of brandy'. She also noted that he read a lot of medical books, and he told her he had once been a doctor at sea. He claimed that what he gave her would cure her of her dipsomania and that he would tell all once she was better.[14]

The idea that Mary was an alcoholic came from suggestions Chapman made to Mrs Paget. On one occasion she was in the bar and Mary was there. Chapman said to his wife, 'Get out of it, you cannot get drunk here', but Susan never saw her drinking. On another occasion, she asked him if Mary was ill and he replied 'Get about your business. She will be back again into the bar to get drunk again'. Chapman explained that she suffered 'delirious tremens after drink'. On questioning him about the red liquid in the drinks he gave her, he said 'I told you before that she is delirious; you must take no notice of it'. She retorted 'Delirious or not, I quickly moved in and I can quickly move out'. Her husband also had words with Chapman and told him 'Mr Chapman, if you have no respect for your wife and want to kill her, I have respect for mine, and you won't kill her'. Mrs Waymark did not think Chapman seemed kind or attentive to his wife either.[15]

On Christmas morning, Mary was unconscious and was very much worse. Mrs Doubleday went downstairs to bring Chapman up to the sick room, but on arrival he merely shook his head and retuned downstairs. Mrs Waymark also told him how serious it was, at least three times. Later, Mrs Doubleday went down to tell him that his wife was dying. He did not come up immediately and when he did, she was already dead. He looked at the body and said 'Polly, Polly, speak'.[16]

On the evening of Christmas day, Chapman called for Henry Pierce, an undertaker. He wanted a coffin for his 'wife' that very night, which he was told was not possible. He would have to wait until the next day at noon. Pierce went upstairs to view the body. He thought it was very yellow and that struck him as unusual. Nevertheless he supplied what was wanted and the burial went ahead on 30 December at St Patrick's Roman Catholic Cemetery, Leytonstone. Every expense was spared by her husband and Mary was buried in a common grave, unmarked by any headstone.[17]

After the death, Chapman's main concern was to send Willie Spink to Dr Barnardo's Homes for Orphaned Children, but he could not show that he was an orphan, so was unsuccessful.[18] Dr Rogers attributed Mary's death to phthisis. Although Chapman was in tears over her death, he did not inform her relatives of it and her brother Joseph was unaware of her death until a month later, despite living in Leyton.[19]

Having failed to offload Willie at Barnardo's, Chapman palmed him off to Shoreditch Workhouse, explaining that his mother was dead and his father had deserted him. He never saw his adopted son again. He returned to the pub and advertised for a barmaid. Along came Bessie Taylor by about 20 March 1898. As with Mary she was a few years Chapman's senior, but unlike her she had never married and had no children. She had been born on 15 June 1861 at Budworth in Cheshire and was baptised on 14 July. She was the fourth of seven children born to Thomas, a farmer, and Betsy. She was still living with them in 1881 in Heatley when her father was listed as being a commission agent and she had then no listed occupation.[20]

Bessie's life underwent a radical change in the 1880s, though her whereabouts in 1891 are unknown. However, according to a friend and fellow employee, Elizabeth Painter, she had been a housemaid at Streatham in 1896, then a manageress of a restaurant in Peckham and at that time lived with fellow servant Elizabeth. It was also said that she had worked as a manageress in restaurants in London and thereabouts for ten years. Bessie left Peckham in 1898 and was soon working at the Prince of Wales pub.[21]

Bessie and Chapman allegedly underwent a form of marriage at Easter 1898, though as with his previous 'marriage' this was a fiction. According to her brother James, a salesman living in Hornsey, his sister was 'a remarkably saving woman', though probably she did not have much money. Initially the 'marriage' seemed happy and the 'newlyweds' would visit him on Sundays and they would go off for a day's cycling together.[22] Taylor also recalled that, 'they seemed to be on good terms – he treated her kindly and properly – she seemed to be fond of him and they seemed to be happy', yet he admitted to only having seen them together on six occasions.[23]

The couple left the pub later that year and resided in Bishop's Stortford in Hertfordshire, in August 1898 running the Grapes pub there. Chapman told a county court bailiff there that he had been a steward on various American liners and could obtain will forms, telling him that his wife wanted to make a will. Elizabeth Painter visited just after Christmas and learnt that Bessie had been to the local hospital due to having lumps on her face. She was a little better on her return. Chapman was angry about her absence and telling the customers she would be in hospital and constantly scolded her and threatened to shoot her.[24]

The stay in the Hertfordshire town did not last long, and they returned to London, taking the licence of the Monument pub in Union Street, Southwark, on 23 March 1900, where Bessie would work as a barmaid. Mrs Martha Stevens, a nurse, recalled that Bessie at first 'seemed pretty well in health'. However, relations between the two were sour; Chapman threatened her with his gun and from at least December 1900, she suffered abdominal pains, sickness and diarrhoea. She was fatigued and languid. Her brother William recalled that she complained of being 'on fire'. He said that when he had seen her in Bishop's Stortford she had been strong and healthy; now 'she appeared to be very ill and shrunken; she had gone like a little old woman'. She was sick and had violent internal pains and it was so serious that her mother came down from Cheshire to see her.[25]

Elizabeth Painter was a frequent visitor. She noticed what William did not: that Chapman ill-used his 'wife', 'He was not kind to her... he was always carrying on at her'. She was sick after eating and had head and stomach pains. Chapman appeared attentive, taking Bessie's pulse and examining his medicine bottles. When Elizabeth asked about these, he said that it was a complication of diseases. He would often tell Elizabeth, when she paid her visits, that her friend was dead, when this was not so.[26]

Mrs Stevens recalled that Bessie increasingly complained of being exhausted and suffering from stomach pains. She suggested to Chapman that Dr James Stoker of 22 New Kent Road look at her. The two went to his surgery in December 1900 and he gave her some medicine. He thought she was suffering from constipation and so treated her accordingly. She seemed to improve, and

Mrs Stevens nursed her in the days before Christmas. She noticed that her patient had vomiting, diarrhoea, great pain and complained of a burning throat and perspiration. Her vomit was green, thick and slimy, as had been the case with Mary, though no one save Chapman would have been aware of that.[27]

Chapman gave Bessie milk, water, brandy and water and champagne to drink. At first Mrs Stevens was only with her in the daytime. Bessie's mother, Stevens and Chapman brought her food and the latter would hold her hand in a friendly way. He seemed very attentive and supportive of all possible remedies for his 'wife'. Bessie was occasionally better and one day just after Christmas she went downstairs and played the piano. Dr Stoker heard this and he said to Mrs Stevens, 'Capital'. She also took short walks.[28]

Dr Stoker was called on 1 January 1901. This was the first time he had made a home visit. He then came daily throughout Bessie's illness. He noted the vomiting, stomach pains and diarrhoea of the bedridden patient. The vomit was green and the stomach was very tender. He prescribed medicines for her. She would get better and then would have a relapse. He wondered if the problem might be 'womb trouble'.[29]

As he was not satisfied with the cause of the illness, Dr Stoker consulted colleagues. Dr Sutherland, an expert in female illnesses, was one he talked to. Dr Thorpe of Southwark Bridge Road diagnosed hysteria and another internal malignant trouble. Dr Patrick Cotter thought it was a cancerous disease of the stomach or intestines. A portion of her vomit was sent to the Clinical Research Association, for any sign of cancer. There was none. Chapman seemed happy to pay all the fees required and accepted what the doctors told him. Bessie's condition worsened and on 12 February the doctor thought that the situation was very bad indeed, but he could not recollect whether he thought she was dying at that stage.[30]

Mrs Stevens was with Bessie on 13 February. At 1.30pm she thought she was dying so called Chapman, who came immediately, just as she was dying. 'I think she has gone' he said. He began to cry. Dr Stoker signed the death certificate and gave the cause as 'intestinal obstruction, vomiting and exhaustion'.[31] On 14 February 1901, Elizabeth called at the Monument pub and asked if Bessie was better and Chapman replied, 'She is much the same', when in fact she was dead.[32]

On the day of her death, William Tull, manager to a local undertaker, called at the pub after Chapman had called at the shop earlier. He brought a coffin with him. He was shown Bessie's body upstairs and he coffined her. He later had the body conveyed to St Pancras station.[33]

A mourning card for Bessie read:

In loving memory of Bessie Chapman, wife of George Chapman and daughter of Thomas P. and Betsy Taylor, who died February 13th 1901 aged 36 years and was interred at Lymm, February 15th.

Her brother paid for her to be laid to rest in the family vault as Chapman claimed he had no money. There was also the following verse:

Farewell my friend fond and dear
   Weep not for me one single tear
   For all that was and could be done
   You plainly see my time was come.[34]

Chapman met Bessie's relatives at St Pancras Station on 15 February and they all travelled up to Lymm churchyard in Cheshire. Her brother recalled that, 'he seemed to have been very sorry to have lost her when she died – he behaved in every way that I should expect a man to who had just lost his wife'.[35]

Chapman remained at the Monument for the next few months, living with a potboy, Henry Hope, aged 18 from Cheshire. He was not to remain single for long, however.

Maud 'Chapman' was the youngest of Chapman's 'wives' by far. She was born on 17 February 1883 in Croydon as Maud Eliza Marsh to Robert and Eliza. Her father was variously described as being a groom and a carman and was also a labourer. She was baptised at St John's Church, Croydon, on 27 May 1883 and the family were living at 48 Stanley Road, Croydon, in 1891.[36]

Maud had worked as a barmaid in the Duke of York, a Croydon pub, in 1901 and in two private houses in Croydon in the same year, but by August was out of work and advertised in *The Morning Advertiser* newspaper for a position. She had an answer and went with her mother to the Monument and met Chapman. They talked with him and the older woman noticed a ring on his finger. Chapman explained that he was a widower. Maud accepted a live-in job, at the rate of 7s per week after it was learnt that a family were also living there. Within a week Chapman had given her a gold watch and a ring which led her father to say 'It seems funny he had given her that so soon'. This was in August. However, Marsh visited his daughter and thought that all seemed well. The next month, Maud and Chapman visited her parents in Croydon to tell them that they wished to marry and sought permission. Maud's father was then in hospital and so the couple saw him there and visited her family at other times, once showing her mother the will he had made in her favour, dated 13 December 1901.[37]

Apparently Chapman had asked Maud, 'How would you like to become Mrs Chapman?' When Maud told her father this, he advised caution. She said she would and soon afterwards Chapman visited her father with her. The next time she saw him she was wearing a ring.[38]

Chapman and Eliza allegedly married on 13 October 1901; another fabrication. Her mother visited later that day and saw confetti on the floor of the Monument pub. Nellie Marsh, a younger daughter, said 'Maud married this morning'. This was news to Mrs Marsh. Chapman suggested she have dinner with them and she accepted. She then saw a wedding ring on her daughter's hand and other rings that Chapman had given her. She learnt that the marriage had taken place in a Catholic church on Bishopsgate Street, though her daughter was not a Catholic. When the question of the marriage certificate arose, Maud told her 'George has got it and put it with his other papers'.[39]

There was another momentous event to take place in Chapman's life that year. The Monument pub, the licence of which he had held since the previous year and was about to expire, was damaged by fire on 25 October. There was a suspicion that Chapman had caused the fire to claim insurance money on the overvalued premises, but he gained nothing financially from the incident and managed to evade being charged with arson.[40]

The Chapmans took the licence of the Crown pub at 213 Borough High Street on 11 November 1901. In June of the following year Chapman took legal action against Alfred Clark and Matilda Gilmor for conspiracy to defraud him of £700. Maud supported her 'husband' in the ensuing court hearings. Clark was found guilty and sentenced to three years, imprisonment.[41]

Louisa Sarah Morris, one of Maud's sisters, later claimed that she was worried about her from April 1902. She had been to her sister's bedroom and had seen a bottle and a syringe and on asking her about these, Maud said that these were what Chapman 'used on her' and later, that he gave her 'stuff to take'. She told Chapman that it was strange that the doctors could not discover what ailed her. He replied, 'I could give her a pinch like that and 50 doctors could not find out what the matter was with her'. She then asked 'What do you mean?' and then he said 'Never mind'. When she was alone with Maud she asked her whether Chapman was violent towards her, 'Yes. He held my hair and banged my head'. It was not all one-sided. 'Did you pay him back?' 'Yes, I kicked him'. On another occasion, when the three were taking tea together, Maud said 'What do you think? George here says I won't live to be 28'. Louisa asked 'How does he know?' and Chapman replied 'More you won't'.[42]

Maud was in Guy's Hospital in July 1902. Louisa recalled visiting her there at the end of the month, when she was in the Queen's ward. Maud told her that she was 'very bad' and the doctors could not tell what the matter was. Maud asked Louisa to ask if Chapman could see her. Had he done so already? Louisa asked. 'Not for a day' replied Bessie. Louisa went to the Crown and asked the question, but Chapman said that he was too busy to visit. Louisa said that she could manage the pub while he went to the hospital, so he agreed. He cycled there and returned in the evening and on being asked by Louisa about her sister's health he merely said 'very bad'.[43]

Another sister, Alice Marsh (ironically sharing the same name as one of Dr Cream's victims), also visited Maud that summer. She saw Chapman first and asked how her sister was. 'She's in bed, dying hard' he replied. Alice then saw her sister in bed with a cup of tea and suggested that she should be in hospital or call a doctor. Maud said of the tea she was holding, 'George has made this, but I can't take it or it would make me sick'. She added that Chapman would not want her to go to hospital again. When tasked with medical assistance, Chapman told Alice 'If she wants to go anywhere, she can have a doctor; there's one around the corner'. The sisters took him at his word; he gave them half a crown, Maud took an hour to dress and they left the pub to go to a doctor's house, but he was not in so they went to Guy's Hospital instead. Maud told her 'We must not let George see us going'.[44]

At the hospital, Maud undressed, lay on a couch and was examined by several doctors. She found this to be a painful experience. They gave her a draught to drink and a prescription. They then went back to the Crown where Chapman was angry about where they had been. Next morning, Chapman gave Maud a drink and stood by to watch her drinking it. Maud later said to Alice that if he had not been there she would not have drunk it.[45]

While in hospital, Maud wrote Chapman a letter:

My Dear Husband,
  Just a line to let you know I am no better. I had no sleep last night; was in pain all night long and have not been much better today. I came on queer in the night, and of course, that made matters worse. I will try, dear George, to get better so as to come home and help you. I am sorry to hear your back is so bad but I will rub it well, when I come home... My own darling husband I think this is all. So with love I remain your ever loving wife, Maud.[46]

Dr James Targett, an obstetric surgeon at Guy's, recalled Maud being there from 28 July to 20 August. He later recalled being unable to diagnose her complaint. At one time he thought it was an inflammation of the covering of the bowels.[47]

There was a strange conversation between Chapman and Florence Rayner, a young woman who had once served behind the Crown's bar. He kissed her and asked her to accompany him to America. She objected, saying, 'No, you've got a wife downstairs and don't want me'. Chapman commented, 'Oh, I could give her that (putting his thumb and finger together) and there would be no more

Mrs Chapman'. He pestered her at other times, 'Be my sweetheart, will you?' and she refused saying, 'No, I won't'. When she left and found work in a pub, the Forresters in Peckham, he followed her there and she asked after his wife's health. He then said 'If you had not been such a fool, you might have been at the Crown now'. That was the last time he would voluntarily see her and when she asked him for a reference he refused.[48]

Maud fell ill again in October. As in the case of Bessie Taylor, Dr Stoker was called by Chapman to visit her. Chapman said that she was suffering from diarrhoea and vomiting, so the doctor prescribed for her and then made a visit. He saw her but did not make an examination until the next day. Seeing that she could not keep food down, he then concluded that inflammation of the stomach was the problem. Six days later he advised going to hospital but she was against that. In that case, the doctor told Chapman she must have a nurse and on 17 October Jessie Toon was employed. The doctor then recommended bismuth powder.[49]

Maud's father noticed his daughter was ill on his visit on 16 October. Chapman was very attentive to her but every drink he brought her made her sick. Her mother stayed with her from 19 October. Alice visited her on 20 October. She asked Chapman at the bar how she was and he told her she was very ill. She went to her sister's bedroom. Chapman often visited and felt her pulse. He also gave her a mixture in silver paper but after having that Maud was sick. She was sick several times that day. On leaving on that day she said goodbye and Maud replied, 'Goodbye, you won't be seeing me again'.[50]

Jessie recalled that Chapman prepared injections for Maud and gave her medicines. He would not allow her to give her any of these. She heard the doctor talking to Maud's mother about the need for a post mortem if Maud died and this angered Chapman. He said that his mother-in-law was always trying to make trouble.[51]

Mrs Marsh visited her daughter at the Crown. She asked Chapman how her daughter was and he said that she was no better but did not say what was ailing her. Maud was bedridden, complaining of stomach pains, of excessive thirst and vomited frequently. Chapman seemed most solicitous and supplied her with drinks, such as brandy and water and just iced water. However, after these drinks she vomited green liquid. Mrs Marsh stayed with her daughter overnight, but vomiting and drinking continued.[52]

On Tuesday 21 October Mrs Marsh talked to Dr Stoker in Chapman's presence, asking him if there was anything he could do and he was despairing. Dr Francis Grapel was the Marsh family's doctor from Croydon, and he was summoned at Maud's father's suggestion and, after examining Maud along with Dr Stoker, told her mother their conclusions. Mrs Marsh then said to Chapman 'Dr Grapel thinks Maud has been poisoned'. Chapman said he could not see how this could be and suggested that it might be the rabbit she had eaten. To which she said 'Dr Grapel says you don't find arsenic in rabbits'. 'I cannot think what it was then' replied Chapman.[53]

Marsh was suspicious, so contacted Dr Grapel, who told him 'Your daughter is very ill but I do not see why she should not get better if the sickness can be stopped. My opinion is that she has been poisoned with arsenic. How she got it I could not tell'.[54]

Jessie was given careful instructions by Chapman as to what to do and say. If asked by the doctor what was given to Maud she was to tell him that it was only beef tea, milk and eggs. Chapman was also aware of what his mother-in-law was saying about him and to pre-empt such, instructed Jessie to say:

> It's that wicked old cat. She has been raking up all this. If Maud dies, she wants to have her cut about and show me up. Now, Jessie, be careful what you say to her and take particular notice of what she says to you, and ask her in the course of conversation – not to think we are inquisitive or want to know – whether she thinks there is anything wrong or any foul play.[55]

There was no improvement on that day. Vomiting, diarrhoea and thirst continued. She only had brandy and water to drink. Mrs Marsh stayed with her daughter all night. On the next morning, Maud woke at 3 or 4am and her mother, sleeping in an armchair nearby, woke and was asked for a drink, so Mrs Marsh gave her soda and a very little brandy. She vomited. Mrs Marsh also had some of this drink and she felt very ill, too, just as her daughter had. During her brief absences, Chapman went to the room. At 9am Maud had another fit and her hands and lips had turned to a dark shade.[56]

Mrs Marsh called Chapman to come up after this new development. He went over to his 'wife' and she said 'I am going, George'. 'Where?' asked Chapman. 'Goodbye, George'. These were her last words. Chapman looked very upset and there were tears in his eyes. Maud died at 12.50pm on 22 October.[57]

Jessie Toon noticed that Maud's lips were nearly black, and that her mouth, hands, face and parts of her arms were discoloured. On the following day she suggested to Chapman that the bedclothes should be sent to a laundress. Chapman said 'I have destroyed them'.[58] On the same day Alice went to the mortuary with Chapman to see the body. They went back to the pub to have tea. Chapman asked 'Ah, there's a chance for you now as a barmaid. Will you come?' She replied 'No, a barmaid's place wouldn't suit me'.[59]

Dr Stoker arrived shortly afterwards. Chapman asked him for a death certificate but the doctor said that he could not issue one. Mrs Marsh asked why not and he told her that he was not satisfied with the cause of death. Chapman asked 'Why not?' The doctor said that he could not think why she had died so suddenly. Chapman said that it was exhaustion, because of diarrhoea and sickness. Dr Stoker stated that he would like to carry out a post mortem, asking what caused the sickness and diarrhoea. Chapman had no reply to this.[60]

A telegram was sent to Dr Grapel, who had returned to Croydon. The doctor expressed his surprise and said, 'I saw no symptoms which should have brought about death so soon'.[61] He told Dr Stoker, 'Look out for traces of arsenical poisoning'.[62]

Chapman wanted a speedy funeral. Frank Gilbert, a Southwark mortuary attendant, recalled that on the evening of the day that Maud died, Chapman came to see him and asked him to remove the body from the pub that very night, but was told he would have to wait to the next morning. Chapman was annoyed and wanted the funeral as soon as possible. On 25 October he told Gilbert 'Look here, I want a quick job made of it; not the body buried from my place, so as to make a fuss'.[63]

Dr Stoker was, as noted, suspicious of her death, in part because Bessie Taylor's death had been so similar to this one and also because death occurred so soon. He undertook the post mortem as promised, with Dr Cotter of Islington, who had been consulted over Bessie Taylor, and with Dr French. They found no obvious cause of death. Therefore part of the stomach was sent to Richard Bodmer, the borough analyst, with a note to the effect that an irritant poison such as arsenic might be present, and he did indeed find that there was an 'appreciable quantity of arsenic therein'.[64]

Bodmer received the jars containing the stomach on 24 October. There was a reddish gluey substance there. He applied Reinsch's test to detect arsenic. It proved positive. He also noticed that there were copper slips tinted purple. These suggested antimony. On the next day, he also conducted Marsh's test on the contents and it revealed the presence of both poisons, though there was far more antimony than arsenic.[65]

This was enough evidence with which to contact the coroner and the police. On 25 October Detective Inspector George Godley and detective sergeants Kemp and Neil went to the Crown pub and found Chapman serving behind the bar. Once the detectives had confirmed his identity with him, they asked if they could speak to him in private. The four men went to the billiard room, where Godley stated:

'Maud Marsh, who has been living with you as your wife, has been poisoned by arsenic and from the surrounding circumstances, I shall take you to the police station while I make enquiries about the case'.

Chapman replied, 'I know nothing about it. I don't know how she got the poison. She has been in Guy's Hospital for some sort of sickness'.

He was taken to the police station and later that day was charged by Godley with murder.[66]

After the arrest, the police searched the premises. They found £268 10s in gold and various denominations of notes, books and medicines and drugs, white powder and undertakers' bills for the burials of the previous 'wives'.[67] Neil wrote in his memoirs that they also found proof that Chapman was considering flight to France as he had noted boat train departures from Victoria.[68]

On 27 October at Southwark magistrates' court Chapman was charged with the murder of Maud Marsh by poison. Paul Taylor was the magistrate and evidence of the arrest and charge were given. Chapman denied the charge, and his money was used to fund his defence. He was remanded in custody and sent to Brixton Prison to await further court hearings.[69]

Dr Stevenson, who had investigated the victims of Mrs Winters and Dr Cream, was present at St George's Mortuary on 30 October, along with Dr Stoker and others, to conduct a full post mortem on Maud. The condition of the body suggested death by a metallic irritant poison. He already knew of Bodmer's work and the rumours of arsenic. He did not, however, believe that arsenic was the cause of death, but that she had died from antimony poisoning.[70]

In the meantime, Maud was buried at Queen's Road Cemetery, Croydon, on 5 November. It was a far grander affair than the previous funerals, with a procession begun at Southwark and led by a police inspector on horseback. There was a large floral cross 'From a devoted friend. G.C.', which was from Chapman himself. There was rain during the funeral service.[71]

There followed exhumations of Chapman's earlier 'wives'. On 22 November, Bessie's remains were exhumed by a Home Office order at Lymm. Dr Stevenson, his two assistants, Godley and a Southwark assistant undertaker, were among those present. The coffin had to be taken out as well as those of her parents on top of it. The body was in a fair condition and was identified by her brothers. The organs were removed and put into sealed glass jars for examination in London.[72]

On 9 December, the coffin of Mary Spink was removed from a common grave in St Patrick's Catholic Cemetery, Leytonstone. It was taken to a shed in the cemetery where Stevenson and two assistants extracted the organs that they would need to check for poison.[73]

Stevenson's investigation into the organs showed that all three women had been poisoned. He found 1.37 grams of metallic antimony in Mary's organs. Furthermore, there was emetic tartar in the liver. The body was saturated with antimony and he declared that this was a unique case in his experience. Moving onto Bessie Taylor, he said that in the bowels, stomach, liver and kidney he found 10.49 grains of metallic antimony. Tartar emetic, the soluble form of antimony, was found in these organs, amounting to 29.12 grains. He thought that a large dose must have been taken three hours prior to death.[74]

By 11 February, Chapman had been before the Southwark magistrates' court on seventeen occasions. The coroners' court had already named him as the murderer of the three women. There had been 500 folios worth of depositions taken in evidence. Chapman appeared in much better health at this time. The magistrates' court finally committed him for trial at the Old Bailey. Sydney, Chapman's solicitor, told the court that his client had pleaded not guilty and reserved his defence. The court then expressed their thanks to the detectives for obtaining the necessary evidence.[75]

The trial began on 16 March 1903 and lasted for four days. The judge was Mr Justice Grantham; the prosecution was led by Sir Edward Carson, MP, the Solicitor General, and the defence by Mr George Elliott. The charge was the murder of Maud Marsh, to which Chapman pleaded not guilty. There was some discussion as to whether evidence from the first two murders was admissible, but the judge allowed it. The prosecution examined the witnesses concerning the murder of Maud Marsh and then those for the first two murders. The defence put up no witnesses and the speech for the defence, which took place on 19 March, was very brief indeed. It began with an observation that the accused was a foreigner and that the jury must not find him guilty on account of any prejudice. Elliott also stated that there was no obvious motive for Chapman to kill Maud and that the jury should give him the benefit of every possible doubt. There was no attempt made to counter any of the evidence presented by the prosecution. There was also some criticism of Dr Rogers and Dr Stoker for not having identified the symptoms of poisoning earlier.[76]

The prosecution then made a final speech and a motive was, for the first time, put forward, though it was not part of the prosecution's job to do so: 'what is the use of seeking for motive when we have the actual fact of murder? In this instance there was the most ample motive, for the prisoner's was a history of unbridled, heartless and cruel lust'. The judge then gave a final summing up. It was clear that he thought the evidence pointed strongly to the guilt of the defendant. The jury was only absent for ten minutes. They returned a verdict of guilty.[77]

Chapman was sent to Wandsworth Prison following the trial. He was morose and reticent towards prison staff, though enjoyed talking about gardening and going to church services. He continued to plead his innocence, claiming that 'the whole of the evidence is a fabrication of the police', that he was orphaned at seven, was born in Michigan, USA, not Poland and that he was friendless. As to the three women, he claimed he 'has always done his best for the benefit of their health and not to cause any injury'.[78] He expected a reprieve, which could only be granted by the Home Secretary, but in this he was to be disappointed and was moody and depressed thereafter. Chapman was hanged at 9am on Tuesday 7 April by Billington and Henry Pierrepoint. Since there was no question of insanity it was not felt necessary to examine his brain at the inquest. He was buried by the grave of murderess Kate Webster.[79] He left his jewellery, worth £140, to the family of his second victim.[80]

Chapman did not seem obviously attractive to women, being described in 1903 as 'a wizened little man. His small ferrety eyes, high cheek bones, sallow complexion, and heavy moustache, make up a face which is not at all prepossessing. One wonders what attracted to him the women who went to live with him as his wives. He is anything but an Adonis'.[81]

The question to ask is why Chapman killed his victims. Mary had had money, but this had been used by Chapman to establish his hairdressing business in Hastings and then his publican ventures, so presumably there was little left and neither she nor his next two 'wives' left a will; in any case his last victim was from a poor family and had nothing to leave. He may have had a perverse delight in killing women, either because he hated women or he had tired of them and wanted another or enjoyed watching the suffering of others at first hand or because he enjoyed the power that poison gave him over them. Chapman himself gave no reason and made no confession. His recent biographer dismisses all the usual motives and concludes that he probably killed because of Munchausen's syndrome by proxy; he wanted sympathy and attention that he sought through the suffering of another. The biography lists the symptoms of this together with corroborating evidence from Chapman's experience.[82] It is also possible that he enjoyed wielding the power that his limited knowledge of medicine gave him, like doctors such as John Bodkin Adams and Harold Shipman.

It has been long surmised that Chapman was Jack the Ripper. Almost as soon as Chapman had been found guilty of murder, Chief Inspector Frederick Abberline, by then retired, propounded the theory to a journalist. He alleged 'I have been so struck with the remarkable coincidences in the two series of murders', before listing them. However, some of what he said was factually incorrect. Chapman did not have surgical knowledge, there had been no Ripper series of murders in America after he arrived there, and his wife Lucy had no knowledge of his activities during the Ripper months in 1888 (they were not even married until the next year).[83] Unsurprisingly, this statement was reproduced in many newspapers and so gained wide currency. George Sims, an amateur criminologist, disagreed, stating that 'the dissimilarity of method in the two series of crimes supplies conclusive evidence that they were the work of different persons. The Whitechapel murders were in the nature of furious butchery by a savage maniac, the recent poisoning case which has brought Klosowski to the condemned cell reveal a coldly calm criminal, whose scientific method was the refinement of cruelty'.[84] Neil, in his memoirs of 1932, also suggested that Chapman might have been the Ripper.[85] Adams, in the book on Chapman in the *Notable British Trials* series, also discusses the alleged similarities between Chapman and the Ripper.[86] Many writing subsequently have nominated

Chapman as being Jack the Ripper, though Chapman's recent biographer rebuts most of these.[87]

Who was right? Chapman was certainly in Whitechapel in 1888, and he had some limited knowledge of first aid, as an apprentice to a field dresser in Poland. He was known for violence towards women, he was a known serial killer of women and he would have matched the description of a low-class Pole that some thought the killer to be. He might also have been about the right age. Yet much of this would have applied to thousands of other men in London's East End at the time. It is usually said that the difference in *modus operandi* is the key reason why he could not have been the Ripper; the Ripper used a knife and Chapman was a poisoner and it is almost unknown for a serial killer to change his methods (although not entirely unknown, as we shall see in Haigh's case). The Ripper spoke English, yet it was noted in 1888 that Chapman could only speak Yiddish, Polish and Russian and probably had not been in England long enough to pick up much English. Nor did anyone note the Ripper to have had a foreign accent, as Chapman must have had in 1888. It would seem safe to say that he was not Jack the Ripper.

What Chapman was, however, was a man who poisoned his three so-called wives for motives which are not entirely clear. He was able to do so because he had a limited amount of medical knowledge and had acquired the means to kill, which was extremely easy as Mrs Winters and Dr Cream had found out. The killings initially went unnoticed by doctors, victims and others, and that may well have puffed up Chapman's vanity, believing he could continue to operate unscathed. One undetected murder was not enough for him and of course the more one kills the more likely it is that someone will notice, and that is exactly what happened. Had he not been stopped in 1902 it is likely he would have killed again.

As with Cream, a wax statue of Chapman was exhibited at Madame Tussaud's Waxwork Museum in London; evidence of the public fascination with celebrities both great and wicked. It remained until the fire there in the 1960s, but unlike those of some later serial killers it was not rebuilt.[88]

Chapter 5

The Brides in the Bath, 1912–14

The next case involves another man with a penchant to be much married; although unlike Chapman, he usually went through the formal ceremony. As with Chapman and Mrs Winters, the subsequent deaths passed by as natural and were thus reported as such in the press, but this was not another poisoning case. It has been dramatised on television at least twice and there has been a recent book on the case. Furthermore, since it involved the best-known pathologist and one of the most famous barristers of the period, it enjoys far more notoriety than some of the cases in this book. It is even referred to in several of Agatha Christie's novels.

George Joseph Smith was an East Ender, being born on 11 January 1872 at 92 Roman Road in Bethnal Green, London. His parents were George Thomas Smith, an insurance agent (in 1871), born in 1833 and Louise Smith, born in 1835. He was their third son, but the two parents were separated by 1881. Virtually nothing is known about his childhood and early life. This is partly because he said very little about it, in part due to the fact that he was scarcely trustworthy and reliable in what he said about anything, and partly because of his constant changes of name and address.

According to his first wife, Caroline Beatrice Thornhill, Smith fell foul of the law several times. In 1881, when living in Lambeth, he had been sent to a reformatory school in Gravesend, where he remained until he was sixteen. This evidently had no effect on him, because on returning to his mother's home he persisted in his thieving ways, and after he stole £7 from his lodgings, he was given a short prison sentence. Afterwards he lived with an aunt and stole from her. He also stole a bicycle from where he worked in 1891 and was caught and sentenced to six months in prison. He began living with a woman and persuaded her to find employment as a domestic servant and then steal for him from her employer. However, in 1896, known as George Baker, he was arrested after trying to sell a stolen watch. He was given a twelve-month sentence. It did not deter him from similar ventures and in September 1897 he had his female dupe steal a cash box containing £115. Taking this he left her and then went to Leicester.[1]

It was in Leicester that Smith met the woman who would be his first and only legitimate bride. We can be sure that Smith, under the name of George Oliver Love, married Caroline Beatrice Thornhill at Leicester on 17 January

81

1898 at St Matthew's Church. Smith was then working as a baker. His bride was a local girl, aged eighteen and employed as a barmaid in the opera house. He had wanted them to live together, but she insisted on marriage, which her parents opposed. They left for Islington in London after a few months, and it was in June 1898 that Smith induced his young bride to begin a life of crime (he did no work himself). She claimed he abused and threatened her before she did so. Posing as Mary Bright he found her employment as a servant in a variety of houses in different parts of London including Kensington, Croydon and Stoke Newington, as well as in Birmingham, and in the next year she stole £390 worth of goods, which her husband subsequently pawned. Typically she would work for two or three days in a house before absconding with valuables. The couple returned to Leicester in 1899 and ran a shop in Martin Street, though not for long. Caroline's parents could see something was wrong but she never explained what it was. At some point in 1899, Smith married another woman, this time in London, but her name is unknown. Bigamy and deceit did not worry Smith.[2]

Smith, claiming to be a writer, and his first wife arrived in Hastings on 15 August 1899 and stayed in a rented room on the High Street, leaving on 17 August without paying the rent. On the day they left the Revd Henry Maldon Burrows of Park Road found that he had been robbed of silver cutlery worth £20 and suspicion fell on the woman his wife had recently employed as a servant, known as Miss Mary Stone, who had also vanished. She then tried to pawn the goods in Eastbourne on 18 August, but was arrested (Smith fled the scene) and tried. The woman was Smith's wife and received two sentences (thefts in Brighton were also discovered) of three months with hard labour at Lewes Prison, but she would not divulge the whereabouts of her husband.[3]

When Caroline was in prison, it was found that she had committed other crimes of a similar nature in London in 1898–99. She explained that her husband had three women doing similar work for him, and was living with a woman, and so pleaded guilty and wept at the Old Bailey on 11 December 1899. She was not given another sentence and instead helped the police find Smith, perhaps because of the realisation that he was happy to abandon her and to live with another woman. He was arrested in Oxford Street, London, on 5 November 1900 and handed over to the Hastings police. Smith threatened his wife when he realised she had been the instrument of his downfall.[4]

On 8 January 1901, Smith, known as Oliver George Love, a journeyman baker aged twenty-seven 'of imperfect education', was sentenced to two years in gaol at the quarter sessions court at Hastings for the theft of cutlery and other items from the Revd Burrows, after pleading guilty. He was described as 'a young fellow of respectable appearance' who posed as a poet. Caroline Love, alias Mary Stone, was also charged. It was said 'he was deserving of very heavy punishment' and narrowly avoided penal servitude. It was also noted that he had been responsible for twenty-seven thefts in London, using a servant of Eaton Square, London to carry them out, and then he pawned the stolen goods; he had been running a gang of three women to steal for him. He also consorted with men who carried guns and was regarded as a dangerous character. He then went to Lewes Prison to serve his sentence.[5] Caroline wanted nothing more to do with her husband and she was worried when he arrived in Leicester looking for her. She reported him to the police and her brothers thrashed him. She left for Canada in 1906.[6]

Smith's movements for the next few years are unknown (a detective later noted that nothing is known from 1902–08) and he does not seem to have been identified in any criminal exploit, though it's hard to think that he led an honest life. Possibly he briefly emigrated, perhaps to Canada, or served in the army as he later claimed. Having at least two marriages behind him, and still being legally married, by 1908 Smith, who was proverbially workshy himself, decided to wholly live off women, as he had done previously, but this time he would try a new technique. From now on he would marry them, then steal from them. He was to marry at least another six women. Greed and a lack of scruples were to mark his life and he can be fairly termed a professional criminal.

Smith was clearly attractive enough to women to be able to persuade several, some of a higher social class than himself, to marry him after the briefest of acquaintanceships. Yet he had a minimum of education, was not intelligent and was mean with money. Smith had other attractions to offer and these have been the subject of speculation by commentators.

As far as is known, the next woman he was to cruelly deceive was Flora Walter, a widow whom he met at Brighton in June 1908. Assuring her that he was a man of means he suggested marriage, which she accepted, but he never went through with the ceremony. He insisted on seeing her bank book and suggested to her that as he was an antiques dealer they should pool their resources to build up the business. She withdrew £30 in cash, almost all her savings, and gave it to him. On 3 July they were in London, in a lodging house, and went to visit the Franco-British Exhibition. He left her there, and disappeared. Eventually she returned to their lodgings to find he had taken all her property, valued at between £50 and £60. She never heard from him again.[7]

Yet Smith did not always act in the same way with women. Shortly after this deception and theft, he was in Bristol, having opened an antiques business at 389 Gloucester Street, and advertised for a housekeeper. Edith Mabel Pegler, born in 1879 and who had worked in a chocolate factory, answered the advertisement. They were married at a registry office on 30 July 1908, Smith marrying under his real name, but describing himself as a bachelor aged thirty-three. For the next six years the couple travelled around various towns and cities in southern England: Southend, Bristol, London, Bedford, Luton and Croydon, trying to earn a crust through keeping a shop. Smith often left Pegler for periods of time, often months or weeks, when he was allegedly away on business, sometimes with 'a young fellow', but he never told her where he was and rarely sent her much money, often leaving her to exist on the breadline, or being forced to sell the business and return to live with her mother. Sometimes he would return with jewellery, women's clothes or other goods that he told her they could sell in the shop. He also told her that he was from Canada. However, despite these many lies, and his financial and personal neglect, Edith later admitted that Smith had been kind to her when he had been with her. She was to be his constant companion, though apparently unaware of his nefarious activities.[8] Although he lived with her intermittently for over six years she never had any children by him; whether this was because Smith was infertile we will never know, but there is no suggestion he made any of his other 'wives' pregnant either.

There was good reason for Smith to be deceptive. In June 1909 he met Sarah Annie Falkner, an unmarried woman, in Southampton. He called himself George Rose and again, as in 1908, introduced himself as an antiques dealer. He learnt she had £50 in ready money. He met her again in October and she soon agreed to marry him. They were married at Southampton registry office on 29 October 1909 and then took a train to London. They took lodgings in Clapham. As before, Smith talked of pooling their resources to establish an antiques business, as he had not enough himself. So she emptied her savings account of £260 and sold her £30 of stock. She had already given him her £50. By 5 November she had taken out her remaining resources, in gold and notes, and handed it over to her husband. On the same day they visited the National Gallery. Making an excuse, he left her there. She never saw him again until 1915, and on returning to their lodgings she found that all her possessions there had gone. In all, he had stolen property worth £400 from her.[9]

Bessie Constance Annie Mundy was born in Warminster, Wiltshire, in 1875 and was baptised there on 9 July 1875. Her father was a bank manager for the Wiltshire and Dorset Bank and she had one brother. From at least 1891 to 1901 the family lived at 42 Market Place, Warminster, and Bessie did not need to work to earn her living. However, in 1904 her father died and the household broke up. Her family did not think that Bessie was worldly enough to take care of her own financial resources, as 'she did not understand money matters at all' and so, in November 1905, with her consent, they put the £2,500 (about half her father's wealth) worth of securities left to her in her father's will in a trust. This would be administered by her uncle Herbert and her brother George. It would pay her £8 per month, enough to live on, with the remaining income accumulating in the trustees' hands. The capital could not be touched in her lifetime, even if she married and her husband wanted to obtain it. In doing so, the family believed they had made Bessie secure against any predatory fortune hunters.[10]

Unfortunately, Bessie, now cast adrift from her family, met Smith. Since her father's death she had lived at the rectory at Sutton Benger for 18 months and then in a series of boarding houses in the south of England. In 1910 she was at 100 Cromwell Road, Bristol. It seems she took up no profession, as she did not need to work to earn her living, nor took part in any church or charitable work. Her family saw very little of her. The situation for women like her is accurately noted by Sherlock Holmes in a story published in 1911:

> One of the most dangerous classes in the world is the drifting and friendless woman. She is the most harmless, and often the most useful of mortals, but she is the inevitable inciter of crime in others. She is helpless. She is migratory... She is lost, as often as not, in a maze of obscure pensions and boarding houses. She is a stray chicken in a world of foxes.[11]

In the summer of 1910 Smith was in Weymouth – as in 1908 and 1909 he haunted seaside resorts in the holiday season, when single women might reasonably yearn for romance, have their normal defences lowered and be susceptible to a stranger's persuasion. Smith passed himself off as Henry Williams, a bachelor and a picture restorer.

Bessie met him on the Clifton Downs and from 22 August 1910 she and Smith lived at 14 Rodwell Avenue, in two bedrooms and a sitting room owned by Maud and Frederick Crabbe. Maud noted his dominance over her: 'He would never let me speak to his wife alone... she always seemed afraid of him, and seemed incapable of opposing anything he said'. On 25 August Bessie married Smith at the Weymouth registry office. On the day after the wedding, the two went to see William Wilkinson, a solicitor of Weymouth, to see how they stood financially and asked for a copy of her father's will. Wilkinson later noted that 'It was Mr Williams who chiefly spoke to me'.[12]

Shortly afterwards, Smith began to press for what money he could obtain from his new bride. He ascertained that the income from the trust fund which had not formed her monthly income had been accumulating into a tidy sum. On 29 August, Smith wrote to her trustees to ask them to 'forward as much money as possible' and said that the banks were 'rather awkward'. The trustees were reluctant to comply with his wishes, but had no legal alternative, especially as Bessie wrote to tell them 'I am very happy indeed'.[13]

The couple met Wilkinson again on 1 September. He showed them the list of securities that belonged to Bessie as well as a copy of the will, as previously requested. Smith was asked about himself and his background and was very guarded in his replies.[14]

On the morning of 13 September, the newly-weds went to another solicitor's in Weymouth, Arthur Eaton, to receive the payment from the trustees. It amounted to £135 2s 11d. Eaton noted that Bessie was uncommunicative and seemed very much under her husband's influence. Bessie returned to the couple's lodgings later that day but her husband, taking the cash, never did. Instead both she and the landlord received letters from Smith. He told the Crabbes that his wife would stay at the guest house and would be able to pay their fee of 25s per month. He would see her later. What was more shocking was the letter to Bessie, which attempted to explain his departure with her money just three weeks after marriage: 'you have blighted all my hopes of a bright future. I have caught from you a disease which is called the bad disorder. For you to be in such a state proves you could not have kept yourself morally clean'. In other words he was accusing his hitherto virginal bride of giving him, a serial ladies' man, a venereal disease![15]

Bessie contacted her family and her brother came from Poole to be with her. He noted that she was unable to travel for two weeks, but thereafter she came to live with him for most of the remainder of the year. He was never to see her again. At the beginning of the next year she entered the Civil Service Institute in Bristol to learn book-keeping, typing and shorthand to enable her to gain work as a secretary. She was also, in 1911, a boarder at 7 Berkeley Square, Clifton, Bristol. At the beginning of the next year, an aunt recommended she stay at Sarah Tuckett's, a friend's house, called Norwood and located in the north Somerset seaside town of Weston-super-Mare. She arrived there on 2 February 1912.[16]

Twelve days later Bessie met Smith again. How and where is unknown and it has been remarked upon that this was an immense stroke of fate, but coincidences happen and Smith was often to be found at seaside towns on the lookout for unattached women. Despite his shoddy treatment of her in 1910, she was able to forgive him everything and later that day she returned to her lodgings and told Sarah Tuckett that they would be reconciled. The latter replied, 'I cannot stop you as you are 30'. Bessie's relatives were soon informed of this decision. Smith said that he had absconded with the money as he needed to pay pressing debts he had incurred, and that he had found what had been wrong with the venereal disease. 'Mrs Williams informed us that she is willing to forgive the past and that she has decided to live again with her husband'.[17]

The couple remained in Weston-super-Mare for a few weeks, lodging at 6 Walliscote Road. They then moved about, to 35 Wilmount Street, Woolwich, then to Ramsgate and Ashford. Bessie was very happy, writing to her uncle thus, 'Everything after all is happening for the best, and I am perfectly happy with my husband'.[18]

On 20 May the pair were in Herne Bay, another seaside town, on the north coast of Kent. Smith negotiated with Miss Rapley, a lettings agent, for the tenancy of 80 High Street, a two-storey house with three rooms on each floor. The annual rent, for this unfurnished house, was £18. Smith wanted to pay monthly and was pressed to supply references for his ability to pay the rent. He managed to skirt the issue and was unable to supply them. However, he had ready money to pay the first instalment of the rent and later to pay for furniture.[19] Smith dressed smartly, in a frock coat and silk hat, and wore a long gold chain and had a brass plate with his name and profession affixed to the house. Bessie recalled that he was very popular as well as being kind to her personally.[20]

On 25 June the couple visited a solicitor, Philip de Vere Annesley. They wished to draw up wills, each bequeathing all their possessions to the other. Draft wills were drawn up and they were finally executed on 8 July. Next day, Smith visited Adolphus Hill, an ironmonger of Herne Bay whom he had bought his furniture from, in order to buy a second-hand bath from him. It was five feet long and had a plug. He was told the price was £2 but this was too much. On the next day Bessie went to the shop and offered 37s for it and Hill accepted the price.[21]

The couple also visited Dr Frank French on 10 July. Smith wanted to enquire into the state of his wife's health because he told the doctor that he was particularly concerned after she had had a fit the previous day and then lost consciousness. Bessie told the doctor that she had not suffered such, but had only had a headache. Dr French prescribed bromide potassium. At 1.30am on 12 July Smith called on Dr French and implored him to come to their house as his wife was suffering from another fit. The doctor attended but could find nothing wrong with the young woman at all.[22]

The critical event of the next day can be told in Smith's own words:

> On Saturday morning, 12th July 1912, we both got up together at about 7.30. I went out for a stroll and got some fish. I returned at about 8 o'clock. No one was in the house, excepting my wife when I went out. I locked the front door when I went out. We always did that as the slam to latch was out of order. I went into the dining room and called for her, I called for her, then I went upstairs, looked into the bedroom, then the bathroom. She said the night previously, she would be having a bath that morning. She was in the bath. Her head was right down in the water, submerged. She had a piece of soap in her hand.[23]

Dr French was summoned and he and Smith took the body from the bath. The doctor knew that she was dead. Smith expressed his sorrow when contacting Bessie's relatives, 'Words cannot describe the shock I suffered in the loss of my wife'. There was an inquest on the Monday, when both the doctor and Smith gave evidence. The verdict was death by misadventure, caused by Bessie having an epileptic fit and then drowning. Her brother had wanted a more vigorous inquiry, writing 'I must insist that she died so suddenly a post mortem must be held before she is buried'. It was not.[24] A few newspapers reported the story, but it did not gain wide circulation. There was little reason to suspect foul play and it was not unknown for people to drown in their baths.

Smith agreed on a price of seven guineas for the funeral. He explained to the undertaker, 'After one was dead, it did not matter so long as it was carried out decently'. The burial took place on 16 July and there was no headstone. Smith then had to get out of paying more rent on the house, in which he was successful, and when discussing this with the lettings agent, told her 'Was it not a jolly good job that I got her to make a will?' which shocked her in its callousness. He sold back the furniture he had bought for the house and even managed to return the bath that had been bought without ever making any payment on it. He then left the district.[25]

Probate was granted on 6 September and Smith became the richer by £2,571 13s 6d. With this money Smith invested in property, buying seven houses between 31 October 1912 and 14 February 1913, for a total of £2,187. Unfortunately this venture was a financial failure, for between 1 August and 27 September 1913 he sold them for £1,435, realising a loss of just over £700. With the remaining money he bought an annuity of £1,300 in the North British Mercantile Company in early October 1913.[26]

Edith Pegler recalled that in the autumn of 1913 Smith met one Miss Burdett, a governess, and spent some time with her. Apparently he suggested she take out life insurance, but nothing ever came of it.[27]

It was in the late summer of 1913 that Smith met Alice Burnham in Southsea. Alice Burnham was the daughter of Charles and Elizabeth Burnham. She had been born on 28 March 1888, so was rather younger than Bessie. In 1901 they lived in a house in Aylesbury Road, Aston Clinton, a village in Buckinghamshire. Her father, Charles, was a coal merchant, born in 1855, the same year as his wife, Elizabeth. She was the fourth of five children, all born in the village. She was attending school aged three but had finished her formal education ten years later. By 1910 she had spread her wings and was living in a boarding house, Beach Mansions, St Helen's Parade, in the Southsea suburb of Portsmouth, from which she worked from 1910–13 as a sick nurse to a Mr Holt, a retired banker of 25 Granada Road, Southsea.[28]

Alice had some minor health problems, including rheumatic fever in 1899 and an operation in 1913. She was rather more worldly-wise than Bessie, having had to work for her living, and was not unknown to men either. Although she came from middle-class stock, as did Bessie, she was not particularly wealthy. She had just over £100, a combination of her savings from her work and from a contribution that her father had made to all his children.[29]

Again, as with Bessie, the exact circumstances in which Alice met Smith are unknown. He introduced himself under his real name, but claimed to be a bachelor and of independent means. The two arranged to spend a few days with her parents at their Buckinghamshire home at the end of October. She told them that they planned to get married in the next month (her two sisters already being married might have been a spur to Alice taking the plunge) and initially the suggestion was that the ceremony would take place at the parish church of Aston Clinton. Her father, however, did not like her intended husband and the visit turned sour.[30]

Relations between the older Burnhams and Smith worsened when Smith began writing to Alice's father, asking for the money that he was holding for his fiancée. At first Burnham demurred, but then Smith insinuated he was prepared to take legal action through a solicitor to claim what was rightfully Alice's. Burnham took legal advice too and soon realised that legally he was in the wrong. Therefore and with great reluctance, on 1 December he transmitted £104 1s 1d to Smith.[31] In a rare moment of candour, Smith told one Norman Dunham, 'He said he had never done any work and did not intend to do any'.[32]

Meanwhile, the couple had been living at 80 Kimberley Road, Portsmouth. They had married at the registry office there on 4 November. They had also consulted a doctor, Dr Harrold Burrows of Southsea. As with Bessie, Smith asked him to check his wife's health. Apart from childhood illnesses, there was nothing to report and she was a healthy young woman, though rather stout. They had also been to an insurance company and taken out a twenty-year endowment policy on Alice for £500. Alice paid the first premium herself.[33]

The couple then travelled to Blackpool for a holiday on 10 December. Initially they called at 65 Adelaide Road, and Susanna Marsden agreed to let them rooms there. Unfortunately there was no bath, so Smith demurred. Susanna suggested 16 Regent Road, so they went there and Mrs and Miss Crossley provided him with what he needed, charging 10s per week.[34]

On the same day as their arrival in Blackpool they called on one Dr George Billings, as Smith was concerned about his wife's health after the long train journey to the north. Smith said that Alice suffered from headaches. The doctor could find nothing wrong with her and thought she was a healthy young woman, but that she was tired. The Smiths took a bottle of medicine to remedy this.[35]

Smith gave his own account of what happened on the evening of 12 December:

> After which I took her for a walk and she appeared better. Later on I found she had made arrangements with the landlady for a bath. About 20 minutes after she entered the bath I called out to her and received no answer, and after acquainting the people in the house that something was wrong in getting no answer, I entered the bathroom and found poor Alice with her head and shoulders under water.

Drops of water appeared on the ceiling of the Crossleys' kitchen and they noticed these. When Smith appeared 'he looked so wild and agitated'. They called Dr Billings, who certified that Alice was dead. PS Robert Valiant also arrived and asked Smith to accompany him to the police station to make a statement, which he did. He wrote to Alice's parents to tell them: 'This is the greatest and most cruel shock that ever a man could have suffered. Words cannot describe my feelings. We were so happy together'.[36]

Despite telling her parents about his grief, Smith showed another emotion to others. Smith told the doctor 'I will bury her here as my means are limited', which the doctor thought 'appeared callous and in no ways disturbed'. He said to Mrs Crossley 'When they are dead, they are dead' and she asked him to find alternative accommodation, saying 'I won't have a callous man like you in the house'.[37]

Dr Billings conducted a post mortem on Alice, but as with the previous case there was no reason to suspect murder and he could find nothing to suggest that the death was not a natural one, but caused by asphyxia as a result of drowning in the bath. There was an inquest on the evening of the following day, 13 December, lasting a mere half an hour. It concluded that the deceased suffered from heart disease and was probably seized with a fit or faint and so drowned in the bath. Cause of death: accidental.[38] Again the death was reported in the press but gained only a limited circulation. Smith had a different name and killed in a different place, so he escaped scot free once again. No connection was made by anyone between the two deaths.

Earlier that day, John Hargreaves, a local undertaker, arrived at 16 Regent Road. Smith told him he wanted the burial 'done as cheaply as possible'. A public grave would suffice: 'Yes, that will do. A public grave – what they put any one in'. He also wanted it done as early as possible, but it could not be done on Sunday 14 December, so took place on Monday 15 December. He did not want anyone else to know Alice was being buried in a common grave, and he paid Hargreaves £6 3s 9d in all. The Crossleys, Mrs Burnham and one of Alice's brothers attended the funeral along with Smith. She was buried at Layton cemetery, Blackpool, and is in an unmarked grave, like Bessie Mundy.[39]

On 18 December Smith was in London at Kingsbury and Turners, solicitors, of 369 Brixton Road. He showed them the will of his late wife and the insurance policy on her life. It amounted to £604 less fees and probate was granted on 29 December. The next month Smith was able to cash in. By the year's end he was back with Edith in Bristol, then moved to Cheltenham in January 1914. During his months of absence he sent Edith only two one-pound notes, which forced her to sell the business and return to live with her mother.[40]

At the end of 1913, Smith and Edith were reunited and lived in London, Brighton and then Bristol. In June 1914, Smith, calling himself John Lloyd, a land agent, met Margaret Elizabeth Lofty in Bath, and told her that he was about to travel to Canada. Miss Lofty was born on 12 November 1876 at

Fournier Street, 2020.

The Ten Bells pub, 2020.

Christ Church, Spitalfields, 2020.

Plaque on Mitre Square, 2020.

Plaque for the grave of Annie Chapman (courtesy of Lindsay Siviter).

Church Street, Deptford (courtesy of Gareth Long).

Brockley Cemetery, (courtesy of John Coulter).

London nightlife, 1890s.

Dr Cream.

The Crown pub, Borough High Street, 2020.

George Chapman.

George Chapman and Bessie Taylor.

George Chapman and Maud Marsh.

White Hart pub sign, Whitechapel, 2020.

Wandsworth Prison.

George Joseph Smith.

Beatrice Mundy.

Alice Burnham.

Margaret Lofty.

14 Bismarck (now Waterlow) Road, 2020.

9/10 Gosfield Street, 2020.

187 Sussex Gardens, 2020.

Old Bailey.

John Haigh.

Onslow Court Hotel.

79 Gloucester Road, 2012.

John Christie.

10 Rillington Place.

The only remaining part of 10 Rillington Place; the wash house door.

PC Ledger.

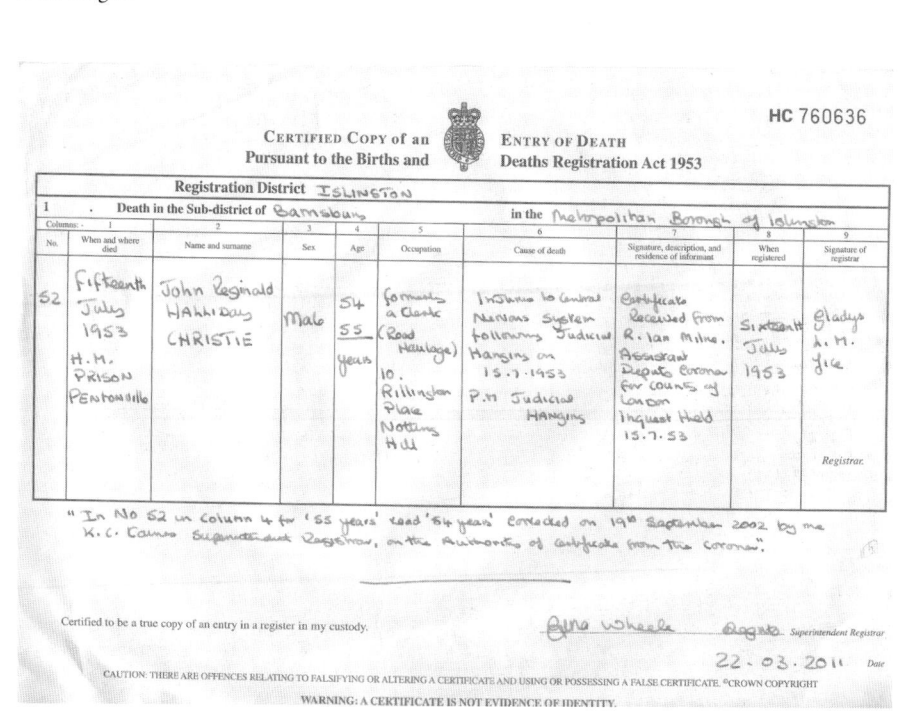

Christie's death certificate.

The Castle pub, Portobello Road, 2020.

The Bridge, Westfield Road, 2020.

The Portway, West Ham.

66 Old Compton Street, 2020.    46 Broadwick Street, 2020.

Monk Sherborne, Hampshire, and had five siblings. In 1881 she was living at Whitchurch Rectory, Whitchurch, Herefordshire, where her father was the rector, the Revd Fitzroy Lofty. In 1891, her father was retired and the family lived at 7 Ravenswood Road, Westbury, Bristol. He died in 1892 aged sixty-six. In 1901 and 1911 the family was living at 19 Woodstock Avenue, Redlands, Bristol, a nine-roomed house with two servants. Her mother, Elizabeth Sarah Lofty, was the householder.[41]

Margaret was of middle-class stock, like Bessie and Alice. She seems to have led a sheltered life, and did not need a full-time job. However, she did sometimes work as a paid companion to wealthy ladies in Bristol. Her love life, however, was a dismal failure. It seems, as far as her family knew, that she never enjoyed a romance until, at the beginning of 1914, she was engaged to be married. The notice of marriage was advertised and it was then found that William Gilbert, a railway clerk and her fiancé, was already married and so it was called off. Emily, one of her sisters, later said 'This seemed to worry my sister a good deal, and she spoke to me about it. As far as I know this was the only love affair she had ever had'.[42] It meant, of course, that she was very vulnerable to any plausible rogue that she might have the misfortune to meet. Aged almost forty it probably seemed to her and her family that she would never marry. However, as 1914 progressed, another sister, Elsie, claimed 'she was brighter and seemed happier'.[43]

Smith was not, of course, in Canada as he told the trusting Miss Lofty. In early September he was at Kinson near Bournemouth and spotted Alice Reavil, a servant from south London, aged forty-two, at the Royal Oak Hotel. She was on holiday. The two fell into conversation and he flattered her. He found that she had some money and told her he was Charles Oliver James, an artist with income from land in Canada, and he wanted to open an antiques shop in London. They very soon agreed to marry and that she would sell her goods to finance this business venture. The two married at Woolwich registry office on 17 September. Over the next few days she withdrew all her savings and sold her property, amounting to £76 6s, and entrusted it to her husband. They took lodgings in south London and on 22 September went for a walk in Brockwell Park. Excusing himself as needing the lavatory, Smith left his new bride, then went to their lodgings and stole her clothing. Alice died a spinster in 1959.[44]

Smith then returned to Edith at Weston-super-Mare, bringing with him women's clothes to sell in their shop. By November he returned to Bristol and was reunited with Miss Lofty. On 25 November she filled out a form for an endowment policy from the Yorkshire Insurance Company. The doctor employed by the firm, Dr George Henry Baker of Bristol, examined her on 29 November to make out a medical report for the insurance company. She seemed to him 'a perfectly healthy woman' and so an ideal candidate for a policy. Receiving this report, Thomas Cooper, a manager for the insurance company, suggested an endowment policy for £700 payable on death or on reaching 65 years, with an annual payment of £24 12s 4d. The premium was paid on 4 December and receipted a week later.[45]

On 8 December, Smith rented rooms at Dalkeith House, 4 Stanley Road, Bath, from Mrs Harrison Smith for 10s. He said he might need another bedroom for a lady friend. On 14 December Smith was in London and was arranging to rent rooms at 16 Orchard Road in Highgate. He gave the landlady's representative and lodger, Mrs Emma Heiss, a deposit of six shillings. He was insistent in asking whether there was a bath in the house. On being told there was, he insisted on seeing it, and though thinking it rather small, remarked 'I daresay it is large enough for someone to lie in'. He then returned to Bristol. Meanwhile the landlady, Miss Lokker, was concerned that the prospective lodger was unable to furnish any references.[46]

Back in Bath, Miss Lofty was engaged in subterfuge. On 15 December she told Elsie she was going out to tea. Later that day she wrote to her to say that she was off to Bristol railway station to meet her female employer to go to London for a day or two. She added 'Hope to see you soon... Do not worry. I am well and happy.' She wrote a similar letter to her mother, telling her that it had all been arranged very quickly. In reality, on this day she went with Smith to Dalkeith House and stayed two nights in separate bedrooms.[47]

The two left their lodgings on Thursday 17 December. Two days previously, Smith had informed the registrar of marriages at Bath that he wished to marry there. William Winckworth, deputy registrar, duly solemnised their marriage. Smith gave a false name, occupation and age, and claimed his father was John Arthur Lloyd, land agent. Miss Lofty, of course, gave her real details.[48]

The couple then took the train to London and reached 16 Orchard Road at 3pm. A lodger there told them they could not come in as the rooms they had booked were not ready, but to return in three hours. They did so and at six that evening the door was opened by Isaac Denninson, who was a detective sergeant. He told Smith that he could not have the rooms as he could not supply a reference. Smith said that he had paid a deposit, but Denninson was adamant that this would not do, so Smith remarked, 'This is a funny kind of house. I want my deposit back'. It was given to him and the couple left in search of new lodgings.[49]

They found them at 14 Bismarck (later Waterlow) Road, about a half mile away. Louisa Blatch let out rooms in her house and explained that there was a furnished bedroom on the second floor which they could have for 7s per week, with use of a sitting room. Later Mrs Lloyd asked about a bath and was shown the room in which there was one.[50]

Smith left his new bride for a short time and it might have been then that she wrote a letter to Elsie and her mother. She explained what was really happening, writing 'No doubt you will be surprised to hear I was married today to a gentleman named John Lloyd'. She then sung the praises of her husband: 'He is a thorough Christian man... I would do anything to secure the one I love, and I have every proof of his love for me. He has been honourable and has kept his word to me in everything. He is such a nice man, and am certain you would have liked him... I am perfectly happy'. Her only regret was her earlier deceit and that she had had him direct all his letters not to her home, but to the post office to be collected, and she claimed this was in case they moved house and she missed any of his correspondence.[51] Her landlady later observed, 'Mrs Lloyd seemed to be quite cheerful and happy when she was with me'.[52]

That evening the Smiths left the house and at 8pm were in the consulting room of Dr Stephen Bates of 31 Archway Road. Smith announced 'I have brought my wife to see you: she is suffering from a headache'. It had come on when they were at Highgate tube station. The doctor asked his wife a number of questions, which she did not answer. He then asked her 'Have you really a headache as your husband says?' Then she said yes. She failed to answer other questions and denied she had other symptoms. Eventually Dr Bates gave her a bottle of bromide to relieve the symptoms and told her to go home and rest. He suggested it might be influenza.[53]

On the next day, 18 December, Smith told his landlady that his wife was not feeling well. The landlady asked Margaret if this was so, but she did not answer. Smith said 'She is better. She is very well now except for a little headache'. The two went out that morning and went to a draper's, where Smith left her, returning at 11.30, and then they returned to their lodgings for lunch. Margaret took her medicine and then went out in the afternoon to the draper's. She also went to see Arthur Lewis, a solicitor of 84 Islington High Street, where she had a will drawn up, witnessed by Lewis and his clerk, to the effect that she left everything to her husband, who would also be sole executor. They then took tea. On this day she also called in at Muswell Hill Post Office and withdrew £19 5s 5d from her account, which she had arranged to do three days previously.[54]

Smith later explained what happened in the evening:

> She went upstairs to have a bath at 7.30pm. She appeared well. She was not depressed, but not extra cheerful. She was not complaining of pains in her head or chest. I played the harmonium for a quarter of an hour, and then went out at 7.45pm. I told her I was going out for a walk. I returned at 8.15pm... I enquired for her, and was informed by the landlady that she was not down. I shouted upstairs, but got no answer. I asked the landlady to come up and see... I then went from ground floor to first floor where bathroom was. The door was closed, and I don't think I had any difficulty in opening the door... I was anxious. I went to the door of the bathroom with the landlady. The door was not locked as far as I can remember. There was no light in

the room and I struck a match and lit the gas on the left hand side going in. I then looked straight at the bath and saw my wife under the water. The bath was about three parts full.[55]

Smith and the landlady took the body from the bath. PC Stanley Heath was on his beat when Mrs Blatch found him and he came with her to her house. He saw Smith with the body of a naked woman on the bathroom floor. He attempted artificial resuscitation, but to no effect. He reported this to the police station. Dr Bates arrived and saw that Margaret was dead. Smith told him that he hoped it was not suicide as he did not want to feel that his wife was insane. Two days later Dr Bates undertook a post mortem on the corpse and noted that there was some recent bruising on the left elbow.[56]

Smith needed to arrange his wife's funeral. As ever, he spared no time and no economy (Chapman had behaved in a similar way). On the day after her death, he contacted Frederick Beckett, a Highgate undertaker. Beckett came to 14 Bismarck Road and asked Smith if he wished to purchase a grave. Smith asked the cost. Beckett said it would be £4 2s 6d for a private grave. Smith said that was too expensive, and accepted the cheaper alternative of 9s 6d to be buried in a common grave. He then asked about the cost of a funeral and was quoted £7, which Smith negotiated down to £6 10s. On the next day, Smith went to Beckett's house and met his mother. He asked if it would be possible for Margaret to be buried the next day, but was told that cemetery regulations required 48 hours' notice of an interment. 'I think this sort of thing is best got over quickly', Smith said. She checked and confirmed that he would have to wait. As Smith turned to leave he said 'Some men would sit down and cry about it. What is the use of doing that?' Mrs Beckett thought 'he did not appear to be very upset about his wife's death... he appeared to be very callous about the whole matter'. The funeral took place at East Finchley Cemetery on 22 December. The Lofty family solicitor, Mr Kilvington, who met Smith, was also present.[57]

On the day before the funeral, Smith left the house in Bismarck Road and went to 14 Richmond Road, Shepherd's Bush, where Selina King let rooms. Smith paid a deposit of 2s 6d for a bedroom and returned on 23 December to explain he would return after Christmas. He then travelled back to spend the festive season with Edith Pegler in Bristol. She recalled him saying, when she mentioned she was about to take a bath, 'In that bath there [indicating the bathroom]? I should advise you to be careful of those things, as it is known that women have often lost their lives through weak hearts and fainting in the bath'. On 31 December Smith was back at Richmond Road and flitted between the two addresses in January 1915.[58]

The inquest into Margaret's death began on 22 December at the Islington coroners' court under Walter Schroeder, coroner for central London. Smith was the principal witness and gave his evidence as previously stated. Dr Bates gave evidence about the cause of death being asphyxia due to drowning. Mrs Blatch could not attend as she was unwell and it was not until 1 January that she could give evidence. The inquest concluded that death was due to misadventure. Dr Bates said that the deceased was depressed, suffered from pains in the forehead and had suffered from influenza and this, combined with the hot water, might have led to a fainting fit. The inquest was reported in several newspapers including *The News of the World*, a bestselling Sunday newspaper with a wide national circulation.[59] This was the crucial difference from the earlier murders: a death in London with a human interest story could be picked up by the regional press, but the converse was not true. Despite Smith having another name the modus operandi was the same and together with the greater press coverage he had inadvertently made a major error.

On 4 January Smith called on Arthur Davies, solicitor's clerk, of 60 Uxbridge Road, Shepherd's Bush. He showed Margaret Lofty's birth certificate, their marriage certificate and her will. He also showed Davies the insurance policy and asked for probate. Davies contacted the insurance company and probate was granted on 11 January. Smith was the gainer by £705 less fees.[60]

The report of the inquest in *The News of the World* was read by Charles Burnham. He spotted the similarity between the deaths of his daughter and this Mrs Lloyd. He contacted the police, enclosing copies of the relevant newspaper reports. He was not the only one to notice the pattern: Joseph Crossley of Blackpool did the same.[61] Detective Inspector Arthur Neil, who as a sergeant in 1902 had been with Inspector Godley when he arrested Chapman, received the cuttings and was to investigate them. He spoke to PC Heath, Dr Bates and Beckett. He became suspicious and reported this to the Assistant Commissioner of the CID, who was initially sceptical on the grounds that murder had never been committed in this way before. However, he allowed Neil to continue his investigations and Neil found the address in Shepherd's Bush of the solicitors Smith was dealing with. They would not give details of their client, so Neil had detectives take up quarters in a nearby pub run by a friendly landlord.[62]

On 1 February, after several days' surveillance, Neil, with two sergeants, stopped Smith on the Uxbridge Road at 12.40pm. Neil asked:

'Are you John Lloyd?'
'Yes'.
'You were married to Margaret Elizabeth Lofty on 17 December last and was found dead by you in a bath at 14 Bismarck Road, Highgate, the following morning [actually the evening], the 18th'.
'Yes, quite right'.

'You are also said to be identical with George Smith, whose wife was found dead in a bath under similar circumstances on 13th December 1913, at Blackpool, a few weeks after her marriage to you?'

'Smith? I am not Smith. I do not know what you are talking about'.

'I shall detain you and send to Aylesbury for witnesses, and if you are identified, you will be charged with causing a false entry to be made in the marriage register at Bath'.

'In that case I may as well say my proper name is George Smith and my wife died at Blackpool, but what of that, the entry in the register is not correct, but that is the only charge you can put against me'.

'The question of any further charges is a matter of inquiry'.

'Well, I must admit that the two deaths form a phenomenal coincidence, but that is my hard luck'.[63]

The police took Smith to Kentish Town police station and en route Smith told them that he had served for three years in the Northamptonshire Regiment. That evening Charles Burnham and Mrs Pinchin, a married daughter of his, came along. There was an identity parade to see if they could pick him out. Burnham hesitated in front of Smith. Smith then stepped forward and said 'I am Smith. He knows me. What is the good of fooling about?' Mrs Pinchin also identified him, also hesitantly. He was then charged with forging the marriage register, but told police, 'That is the only charge you can bring against me and that is what I am guilty of. My wife knew all about my first marriage and she suggested I should make a fresh start and say nothing about my former wife. I had told her how she died'. Neil then charged him with the murders of Bessie, Alice and Margaret Lofty. 'I have nothing to fear. My conscience is clear' he replied.[64]

On 2 February, Lloyd was charged at Bow Street magistrates' court with filing a false entry in a marriage register when he married Margaret at Bath the previous year. He admitted that his real name was George Smith.[65] He was sent to Brixton Prison, where he was seen by Dr Dyer. He reported, after several conversations, that 'He has always been quite rational, both in conduct and conversation, and shows no signs of insanity'.[66]

On the night of 3 February, Margaret's body was exhumed, following an application by the public prosecutor. The body was then taken to the Islington mortuary where it was examined by Professor Pepper, Mr Willcox and Dr Bernard Henry Spilsbury (1877–1947), a rising young pathologist.[67] The bodies of Alice and Bessie were also exhumed and examined by Spilsbury in the same month.

Neil conducted a very dangerous experiment with 'a very fine lady swimmer' to see how someone could be drowned in a bath. They found that it might be done by pressing down on the bather's forehead, though this resulted in noise and struggling. A surer method was achieved by pulling up the legs of the bather so the water rushed into mouth and nostrils immediately, rendering struggle impossible. In finding this out the woman fell unconscious and had to be revived.[68]

After a number of hearings at the Bow Street magistrates' court, Smith was committed for trial. Smith was put on trial at the Old Bailey for the murder of Bessie Mundy, with the first day being 22 June. The judge was Justice Scrutton and the prosecution was led by Archibald Bodkin. Supporting him was Travers Humphreys, who we will hear of again in this book. Sir Edward Marshall Hall was the defence barrister and he was one of the most well-known barristers at the time. In 1907 he had saved the neck of Robert Wood in the Camden murder case. Naturally Smith pleaded not guilty. The trial was an extraordinary event, taking place during a world war and lasting eight days, with over a hundred witnesses and twice that number of exhibits shown to the court. There was discussion as to whether other cases could be taken into account or not. Marshall Hall naturally argued that these should not be allowed. However, as in the cases of Cream and Chapman, the judge allowed it because it showed 'evidence of a system' of murder.

Most of the trial consisted of evidence given by the witnesses into the three deaths the defendant was accused of causing. Oddly enough, after Mrs Crossley gave her evidence Smith shouted in court 'This woman is a lunatic'. Spilsbury had been involved in the high-profile trials of Dr Hawley Crippen and poisoner Frederick Seddon in 1910 and 1912, giving evidence for the prosecution in both cases. He had not yet gained the prominence he was to acquire in the 1920s and 1930s, but he was clearly a rising star and will feature in two further chapters in this book. At this trial he spoke at length about how it would be perfectly possible for a man to murder his bride in a bath, and he withstood a lengthy cross-examination on this subject. He also stated that 'about the thighs and abdomen there was a condition of the skin known as goose skin. That condition occurs in some cases of sudden death, and perhaps more frequently in sudden death from drowning. It is a sort of corrugating of the surface, a roughening of the surface'.[69]

Marshall Hall, who did not call any witnesses nor put his client in the witness box, as was now permissible, did his best to counter the evidence against his client. He tried to suggest that the motive offered for the murder was weak and that the evidence for this particular death was limited. He recalled the fact that if Smith were guilty he would not only be criminal, but a monster. During the judge's summing up, Smith interrupted him on several occasions, which is almost unheard of. Smith said 'You may as well hang me at once the way you are going on' and 'You can go on forever; you cannot make me into a murderer.

I have done no murder'. He also raved at Neil 'That man's a villain, he ought to be in the dock with me'.[70]

The jury was not long in deciding their verdict, taking just 22 minutes. The foreman told the judge that they had decided that the defendant was guilty. Scrutton sentenced him to death and stated that there was no point in asking Smith to repent. When asked if he had anything to say, Smith thanked Marshall Hall and continued to protest his innocence; most prisoners say nothing.[71]

After the trial Smith was returned to prison. There was an appeal made to the Criminal Appeal Court, but this was turned down on 29 July. The condemned man was sent to Maidstone Prison on 4 August. He wrote many letters declaring his innocence. Smith also wrote to Marshall Hall and to Edith Pegler, whom he claimed was his true love. He wrote 'So an innocent man goes to his untimely end, a victim of cruel fate. God alone is my judge and the King of Kings'.[72] He said likewise to a visiting clergyman and even the deputy governor wrote 'He has within the last two days become, I believe, genuinely penitent', wanting to be confirmed and take holy communion with Edith Pegler. It does not seem this happened.[73]

On the last night of his life Smith was restless, as if resigned to his fate. On Friday 13 August, the chaplain visited him and at 7.30am John Ellis, the hangman, and his assistant Edward Taylor, entered Smith's cell to pinion him. Smith's steps faltered as he walked the 30 yards to the scaffold. He was hanged at 8am and then the prison bell tolled. Death was instantaneous and at the inquest it was noted that the sentence had been carried out humanely. A crowd of mainly working people gathered outside the prison gates and they agreed that the punishment was just.[74]

A happier footnote is that on the day of his death his widow, Caroline Beatrice Love, née Thornhill, was remarried in the town of her birth, Leicester, to Thomas Davies, a Canadian who had recently enlisted as a sapper in the Royal Engineers, and he survived the war.[75] She died in Canada in 1969.

Smith was motivated by money. Apparently he once told a detective, 'Money is the only thing worth living for'.[76] Another newspaper noted that 'Throughout Smith's amazing career, one motive has dominated his life. His ruling passion has been the love of money, the obtaining of it by any means, the retaining of it for his own benefit. Never in the whole annals of crime has such a callous criminal figured in the historic dock of the Old Bailey'.[77]

In all this, Smith had a great gift. This was 'a hypnotic personality which gave him a strange influence over girls and women'.[78] Marshall Hall wrote 'I am convinced he was a hypnotist' but Neil merely thought he was 'just like any butcher' and added in 1932, 'To this day it has always been a poser to me what women could see in a man of this type'. One of Smith's 'wives' agreed with Marshall Hall, embellishing his comment thus, 'He had an extraordinary power over women. The power lay in his eyes. When he looked at you for a minute or two you had the feeling you were being magnetised. They were little eyes that seemed to rob you of your will'. He could also be vicious, as a surviving 'wife' attested, 'Often he has beaten me black and blue. Often he locked me in a cabinet folding bed… Often he used to brag to me about his numerous women acquaintances. Once I met him with one of his victims and warned her to her face about him. She was greatly shocked and said she had always regarded him as a good religious man. That night he came home and thrashed me till I was nearly dead'.[79]

Smith's technique was always the same. He used his main asset, his charm, to convince women to do what he wanted with their assets and themselves. Initially he married women and took their savings. However, from 1912–14 he did far worse than that. He had three of his 'wives' insure themselves and make out their wills wholly in his favour. He persuaded them to give him all their money. He would then take them to a doctor and try to convince them that his new 'wife' to be was in poor health. He then married the woman, sometimes with false details, and then drowned them in a bath. He would bury them as cheaply as possible, sell their property and cash in on their insurance policies and any other monies they had. The inquest found the deaths to be accidental and Smith returned to his faithful Edith. No one was aware that he had carried out this process several times. It was only the fact that two men who knew of the previous drownings also read an account of Mrs Lloyd's fate that the police were alerted and took action, which was to bring Smith's serial killing to an end. He had killed three women and married eight; he may have married more, as we only know about those who came forward. It would be understandable if some did not admit to being humiliated and robbed.

One recent study of serial killings by Professor David Wilson attempts to examine the structural reasons for serial murder and claims that the socio-economic position of women prior to the First World War was the reason why these murders could occur. Yet predatory men are still preying on vulnerable single women a century later. It is a universal problem. In 2020 Richard Robinson, although not a murderer, was gaoled for bigamously marrying women and then persuading them to part with their savings and property to invest in his business, which took him around the country, where he saw other women. He used various names. He had been doing this since the 1980s and targeted women with modest savings, eventually leaving with their money to finance his own lifestyle.[80] As Molière once wrote, 'To inspire love is a woman's greatest ambition, believe me'.

Why did Smith not kill all the women he married? Had he insured their lives he would have made far more money than he did by robbing them of their savings and possessions. A recent author has pointed out those he killed were all from the lower middle class and those he spared were from his own class, suggesting the following hypothesis: 'A hierarchical society in which everyone was expected to know his place enraged George and he loathed those who considered themselves his superior'.[81] As for Edith, though he often treated her badly, he never made a penny from his association with her; he clearly needed the degree of female security and permanence he gained from her.

After Smith there were to be no more serial killers in Britain (that we know of) for over a quarter of a century. Why this should be is a matter of debate, for these were not untroubled times, with mass unemployment in some parts of the country, the growth of political extremism, as well as minority and coalition governments and the unprecedented royal abdication, not to mention the threat of war. It took another world war to help create the conditions for three serial killers, all from Yorkshire, to begin their deadly trade as London's fabric, both built and social, came under fire. Smith's infamy, though, was long lasting, and there was a statue of him in London's Madame Tussaud's Waxworks until at least 2012.

Chapter 6

The Blackout Ripper, 1942

Wartime London was a mecca for both servicemen of all allied nations and for prostitutes from across Britain. There was a high demand and a high supply and there was money to be made. Prostitution is always a dangerous business for those who take part in it, but many did so, soliciting on the streets of central London for passing trade. We have already seen that such situations can end horribly. This story is little known because the murders occurred during a world war, so press coverage was limited because paper was rationed and newspapers were smaller, and also matters to do with the war would normally be given greater coverage, resulting in other events being dealt with far more concisely. The killings took place over a very short time and thankfully were also dealt with very quickly. There were no loose ends as with Jack the Ripper. There has been only one book devoted to the topic, and although there never has been any explicit dramatization of it, an episode of *Foyle's War* appears to have been based upon it, as well as it being the basis for a novel.

The first murder did not portend the full horrors to come, however. On Monday morning, 9 February 1942, the dead body of a woman was found in a brick-built air-raid shelter at the side of Montagu Place, Marylebone, close to Gloucester Place. Harold Bachelor, a plumber, and William Baldwin, his assistant, saw a torch lying in the gutter nearby and on investigating saw a woman's leg protruding from the shelter. They then telephoned the police and at 8.51am a police car arrived with PC John Miles inside. His statement read:

> We saw apparently the dead body of a woman lying on her back with her legs drawn up, her head was inclined to the left and the lower part of her face covered with a scarf, her right breast bare and her clothing was disarrayed. Lying at her feet were her powder box and a box of matches. In the entrance of the opposite shelter there was a black torch. In between the shelter was a woman's hat.

PC Miles went to inform his colleagues at Marylebone police station and later returned to the scene. At 10.15am he found, lying on the pavement on Wyndham Place, a woman's black handbag which had been rifled and torn apart. This suggested that the killer went westwards after the murder as Wyndham

Place leads off from the west of Montagu Place, so perhaps he lived to the west or north-west of where the murder occurred.[1]

The woman had been strangled. She had been gagged over the mouth and nose by her own silk scarf. There was no sign of a struggle and no one heard anything. Possibly she was killed elsewhere and then dumped there from a car, but no one had seen or heard one. Detective Inspector Claire led the investigation.[2]

There was a sexual dimension to the case, too, which was not reported in the press. Not only had the victim's right breast been exposed, but her skirt had been pulled up and her underwear was pulled down. There were also blood smears on her underclothes. However, she was a virgin and had not been raped, but the way the clothing had been pulled about 'suggests that a sexual pervert was responsible'. Her wristwatch had stopped at 1am and the police assumed this was the time of her murder.[3]

Superintendent Frederick Cherrill (1892–1964), the well-known fingerprint expert, examined the body. He found marks on the woman's throat. Unfortunately there was no trace of the killer's fingerprints, though Cherrill thought he was probably left-handed. These marks were only bruises. Nor did the handbag and its contents yield any fingerprints except those of the victim.[4]

Initially the woman's identity was unknown and so the police advertised a description of her:

> Age 35, height 5ft 3in, medium build, dark brown hair, good teeth, stopped [filling] in right upper jaw, hazel eyes, oval face, straight thin nose, heavy eyebrows. Right middle finger near nail deformed, possibly result of crushing.
>
> She wore a single breasted raglan style overcoat, of biscuit colour mixture, green woollen hat, two pairs of light coloured cotton mixture stockings, imitation brown crocodile skin shoes, size 6½, brown velvet coatee, brown woollen mixture skirt with jacket to match having a three button front, green wool jumper, white vest and silk stockinette slip, knitted red and green mixture scarf and brown kid gloves.[5]

As it turned out, the woman was identified by her teeth, which had been worked on by a Newcastle dentist. The victim was Miss Evelyn Margaret Hamilton, who had been born in Newcastle on 8 April 1901, the second child of a draper's salesman and who, by 1939, lived at 6 Evaston Road, Durham, being employed as a retail chemist. She had been a student at Sunderland Technical College and then studied chemistry at Edinburgh University, graduating on 3 October 1928 before working for a Messrs A. Wilson, a chemist at Ryton, for twelve years. As someone who knew her at college stated, she was 'very well mannered and charming, the sort of person you remember years after you have met them'. On the other hand, a junior colleague claimed 'She was very unsociable and grumbling and did not speak to me except to give orders. She was very eccentric'. Evelyn had no interest in men but was an intellectual and a fervent socialist. At the time of her death she was living and working in Hornchurch, Essex. On death she had £209 1s 6d, left to her widowed mother.[6] Pointedly, perhaps, Detective Chief Inspector Greeno significantly stated that she was 'a respectable woman', as did Cherrill.[7]

Evelyn's job at the chemist in Hornchurch, which began on 1 December 1941, paid her £5 per week, but it came to an end after two months and casting around she found another position in Grimsby. On Sunday 8 February she left the Essex town for Grimsby via London, sending her luggage on ahead. She took the train to London and at 10pm was at Baker Street station. She then took a cab to 26 Gloucester Place, only a few minutes' walk away, but found that there were no spare rooms there. She then went to the Three Arts Club at 76 Gloucester Place and, arriving at 11pm, found a room there. There was no food there, so she went out on foot in search of supper. It seems that she went to Maison Lyon, Marble Arch, and was eating there at about midnight. The supper she had apparently included beetroot.[8] Presumably she walked southwards and then after eating walked northwards and either took a wrong turn along Montagu Place (where she was found) or was inveigled down there as 76 Gloucester Place is just after the junction with Montagu Place.

It was thought that robbery was the motive for Evelyn's murder, because her handbag had been rifled for its contents. It still contained her identity card, her ration book, her cigarette lighter, a nail file, a cigarette case, a powder compact and a black fountain pen.[9] There was no one who was known to have had any animosity towards her personally, so presumably her attacker did not know her prior to the murder. There was very little clue to his identity at all and so the crime might be virtually impossible to solve.

Unfortunately, this was not to be a one-off murder. The next woman to be killed was Mrs Evelyn Oatley. She had been born as Evelyn Judd in Earby, Yorkshire, on 5 April 1908 and had an elder brother, Herman. In 1911 they were living with the Tiernan family in a little house in Keighley, West Yorkshire. When she grew older she worked in a textile mill, of which there were many in the district. The family lived in the High Street and then in Grafton Road. In 1934 she moved to Blackpool and on 25 June 1936 married Harold Mollinson Oatley, four years her senior, at Fylde registry office. They had met in 1932. They did not have any children (before meeting Oatley Evelyn had an illegitimate child who was adopted and went to Canada). In 1939 the two were resident at 182 Ravensmead River Road, Thornton, in Lancashire. Oatley was a poultry farmer and Evelyn was a housewife.[10]

Evelyn probably found life as a farmer's wife in rural Lancashire tedious. She had lived and worked in London prior to her marriage, and returned there in April 1938 as she rented a bedsit on the first floor front at 153 Wardour Street in Soho, London, for 22s 6d per week, later falling to £1. There she was known as Nina and Lita Ward. It was claimed in the press that she was employed at the Windmill Theatre, but there is no evidence of this. Rather, it seemed that she earned her living by prostitution, though she was never convicted of soliciting. She often returned to her husband during the summers, but he last saw her on a trip to London, and she saw him off at Euston railway station on 3 February 1942. Though remaining on relatively friendly terms with her, apparently he had recently seen a solicitor, seeking a divorce as she wanted to remarry. He said his wife 'was fascinated with West End life and would not leave it'.[11]

Evelyn was seen alive outside the Monico restaurant, Piccadilly, at 11pm on Monday 9 February. Shortly afterwards, her neighbour, Ivy Poole, who lived in the room opposite, recalled her coming up the stairs with a man. The couple entered Evelyn's room and Ivy returned to her room and put the wireless on. It is probable she left the flat again that night.[12]

At 8.25 next morning, Charles Fuelling, employed by an electricity company, visited the house to read the meter and to collect the money due. He called at Ivy's flat and then at Evelyn's. He received no answer to his knock at the latter's door, so he tried it and found it was six inches ajar. He called Ivy and she entered the room and called out, 'Are you there, dear?', turned on the light and then saw Evelyn's naked body, lying motionless on the bed. She said 'Oh dear, she looks dead'. Fuelling left the building and ran to find a policeman.[13]

Fuelling found Inspector John Hennessay, and said, 'I am glad I found an officer'. Hennessay accompanied him to the room and later, in his report, wrote of what he saw:

> I flashed my torch and saw a woman (believed to be Evelyn Oatley aged about 26) on her back on a divan or single bed, in a transverse position. Her head was pointing north and was hanging over down the side of the bed. She was naked except for a slender garment which covered her breasts. I saw that her throat had been cut and a hand torch was wedged in her private parts. A tin opener was lying near the torch and her legs were wide apart.

There was a pillow on the floor beneath her head and a razor blade was a foot from one of her hands. Ivy told the policeman about seeing Evelyn with a man last night and added, 'I am a light sleeper but I did not hear any disturbance during the night'.[14]

As Hennessay did not have any colleagues with him, he asked Fuelling, whom he knew by sight, to go to nearby Trenchard House to bring additional officers, including the police surgeon and divisional detective inspector, while he prevented any public access to the room.[15]

Among those arriving was Superintendent Cherrill, who later wrote 'She was a ghastly sight. She had been the victim of a sadistic attack of the most horrible and revolting kind'. However, there was little disorder elsewhere in the room. Near the bed were interesting finds. One was a blood-stained tin opener, another was a pair of curling tongs. By the couch was her handbag, which had been emptied out. In this was a piece of mirror. Examining it, Cherrill found a thumb print. It had not been made by the owner. The tin opener, presumably the murder weapon, also bore the trace of a fingerprint. Both were left-handed. Unfortunately they did not match anyone with a criminal record whose fingerprints were on file.[16] The investigation was not advancing very much; the police needed to catch the killer before they could ascertain his identity and this was very much a chicken and egg situation.

Evelyn had been killed on the night of Monday/Tuesday 9/10 February by a man wielding a razor blade and then mutilated by a tin opener.[17] The wounds had also been probed by curling tongs which were now bloodstained. As with Evelyn Hamilton 'in addition to the murderer being a person of sadistic tendencies he is also a thief'. Evelyn was believed by those who knew her to carry £50–80 on her person and needless to say this was never found, though she left just over £470 to her husband.[18] Gladys Langford (1890–1972), a London teacher, noted in her diary, 'Two murders of women committed in the West End in 24 hours. I suspect a sex maniac maybe responsible for both'.[19]

There were apparently no murders on the next two nights, after two consecutive nights of murder, but two other women were accosted by the killer on the night of Thursday 12 February. Mrs Margaret Mary Heywood, a married woman living apart from her husband, was waiting to meet an army officer at the Brasserie Universelle. He was late, and while waiting she was accosted by a man in an RAF uniform. They went for a drink at the Trocadero. He said, 'I am not broke, I will just show you something' and showed her about £20–30, but she rejected his suggestions, though she did give him her telephone number, written down on a piece of paper. However, on leaving at 8.45 he said 'I want to kiss you good night. Aren't there any air raid shelters round here?' She replied 'I don't know of any and in any case I wouldn't go in one with you'. They walked along Windmill Street and Jermyn Street. It was on St Alban's Street near the Punch Bowl pub that he attacked her, kissing her and trying to pull her skirt up and 'as she resisted he put his hands up to her head as if he intended to kiss her but instead he gripped her by the throat so tightly that she lost consciousness'. Fortunately a passer by, 18-year-old John Shine, noticed what was happening and on shining his torch and making as if to intervene, Margaret's assailant fled.

It was about 9.45pm. The man left behind his gas mask and his would-be victim reported this to the police.[20]

Shortly after this, Margaret Heywood's attacker found, on nearby Regent Street, another woman, Mrs Catherine Mulcahy, alias Kathleen King, a 22-year-old prostitute. They went back to her flat at 29 Southwick Street, near Sussex Gardens, Paddington. They travelled by taxi. On entering the flat the light failed. The man wanted to spend a lot of time with her and despite earlier boasting of how much money he had, Catherine wanted to transact their business quickly so as to find another client. This attitude annoyed him and he wanted to take his time with her. He then tried to strangle Catherine. She fought back, freed herself from his grip and screamed. She rushed into the corridor, clad only in her boots, and Agnes Morris, a neighbour, recalled that she said 'Let me in. This man is trying to strangle me. Look at the marks on my neck. Fetch the police'. There were indeed red marks on her neck. Fearful of exposure, the man left, giving her ten £1 notes. It was about 11pm.[21]

The police issued a description of a man they wanted to question. It read as follows:

> Aged 25-26. Height five foot eight, fresh complexion, hair chestnut or medium brown wavy in front, frizzy on the crown, brown eyes, small mouth and thin lips, clean shaven, protruding chin, dressed in electric blue overcoat, with fine grey line and square check.[22]

Just as the panic was at its height, the killer was arrested, at 5.45am on Friday 13 February at St James' Close, because the respirator, with its owner's RAF number, 525987, had been left in the wake of the attack on Margaret Heywood. This made the owner very easy to trace and once he was, one of his living victims was able to pick him out of an identity parade; the other could only state he was an RAF man.[23] The man identified was Frederick Gordon Cummins, an RAF cadet pilot stationed in Regent's Park.

However, Cummins was more than a possible double murderer and double assailant. On the day of his arrest the police made two further shocking discoveries. The first concerned Mrs Margaret Florence Campbell Lowe, born as Margaret Burchett in Hawkes Bay, New Zealand, in about 1899, the oldest of the women to be killed and the only one with a child. By 1919 she had crossed the world and was working as a prostitute in London, where she received her first of three fines for soliciting (the second came in 1920). She left that business soon afterwards when she married Frederick George Lowe, a hairdresser, at Rochford registry office in Essex on 11 October 1921. They had a child, Barbara, born in about 1925. Margaret assisted her husband in his business in Southend. He died on 14 December 1932 in Southend. The two ran a boarding house at 21 Alexandra Street, Southend, in 1932–33. By October 1933 they had dispensed with this and Margaret moved to London, Barbara remaining in Essex to attend St Gabriel's School, York Road, in Southend. She would visit her mother every third weekend.[24]

Margaret lived at several addresses in London and, reverting to prostitution, acquired another fine for soliciting in 1938. On 27 October 1941 she lived at a flat at 9/10 Gosfield Street, paying a weekly rent of 25s. She had £215 3s to her name. She frequented Charing Cross Road, Oxford Street and Piccadilly. According to other women, she was known as 'the Lady' and 'the Pearl' because she was well spoken and did not associate with other prostitutes. Apparently she was handsome and well built. She also went by the name Peggy Campbell. However, once clients were back at her flat neighbours could sometimes hear arguments and the sounds of violence between them.[25]

In the previous week the police had called at her flat because she alleged that a Canadian soldier had attacked her.[26] Her neighbour, a Mrs Bartolini, recalled hearing Mrs Lowe enter her room with a guest on Wednesday 11 February, and heard the guest leaving in the early hours of the next morning.[27]

Mrs Lowe was last seen on the streets on Wednesday 11 February at 12.30am. She was near the Regent Palace Hotel on Piccadilly. Neighbours then heard her return at about 1.15–1.30am with a man. The latter was later heard noisily leaving at an unstated time. Maurice Wiseman, a neighbour and a tailor, noticed two days later that there was a parcel outside Lowe's door that had not been collected. He began to be suspicious and so called the police.[28]

He was not the only one to be concerned. A telephone call from Barbara, Lowe's 15-year-old daughter who had returned from evacuation, resulted in the police arriving at 4.30pm on Friday 13 February. DS Leonard Blacktop had been given a duplicate key to the outer door of the flats, but he found that the front door to Margaret's flat was locked. He found a key under the mat and then entered the room. He first noted, 'the room was a bed sitting room and in perfect order'. He went along the inside passage, all blacked out, and entered the kitchenette, the door of which was open. He went to the door of the middle room, which was locked. Knocking resulted in no response and, unable to find a key, Blacktop had to force it open.[29]

The room was in darkness, so he turned on the light. He then saw a bed in the room and on the bed was a body. The detective recorded:

> The bed clothes covered the body up to the neck and a pillow was covering most of her face... I removed the pillow and saw the woman's face and neck. I saw a tight ligature around the front and a frothy substance round the nose and mouth. The head was turned to the left and the face was cold. I concluded the woman was dead.

He sent for a police surgeon and a senior officer.[30]

As with Evelyn Oatley, what detectives saw was shocking. It was a scantily furnished room, with a single bed, chair, table, rug and carpet. On the black eiderdown at the foot of the bed were the woman's coat, skirt and jumper, clearly thrown aside by the owner. A hat was also nearby. The room had been ransacked. Cherrill wrote: 'But it was not these things which attracted my eye so much as the various mutilations which had been wreaked upon the dead woman and which were even more shocking than those inflicted upon Mrs Oatley'.[31] Cherrill did not state what was so terrible to his readers in 1954, but the police files relate that the killer had carried out a similar atrocity to what he had done to Evelyn. A candle had been inserted into her vagina. There was a five-inch cut across her stomach and a ten-inch wound on her right groin, presumably inflicted after strangulation.[32]

On the mantlepiece was a glass of beer and a candlestick, from which a candle had been torn. There were fingerprints on its base. There was also a bottle of stout in the kitchen, the contents of which had been poured into the glass. Again there were fingerprints on the bottle. These were important clues. The prints on the candlestick were those of a right-handed person, which led Cherrill to deduce that he was left-handed and had been grasping for the candle. Comparing the fingerprints taken at the previous crime scene he found that they were of different fingers but he deduced that the motive in all three murders was the same, and so it was one killer they were pursuing.[33] There were bloodstains on the blankets and these were removed the next day to the police laboratory at Hendon. Four bloody knives and a poker were also found.[34]

Detective Chief Inspector Greeno was the investigating officer and he was pleasantly surprised that the corpse had not been touched prior to his arrival. With him was the famous pathologist Sir Bernard Spilsbury. He said to Greeno, 'Have you seen the others?', to which the detective said no, he had only read about them. 'I have' said the pathologist, quietly. 'Are you thinking the same as I am?' said Greeno. A despatch rider stopped outside and brought in a message for Greeno, who thought that Spilsbury could probably guess the contents already.[35]

'Not another one?' asked Spilsbury. Returning the message to the envelope, Greeno said 'Yes. Another one. Sussex Gardens. Coming?' They were then driven to a two-roomed ground-floor flat at 187 Sussex Gardens, where they found the body of Mrs Doris Joaunnet, stabbed and strangled. The body was still warm and Greeno shuddered at the sight. Spilsbury said 'You've got a madman on parade here. When you catch him I would like to know if he's left-handed'.[36]

Doris Elizabeth Joaunnet had been born Doris Robson on 21 March 1909. As with Evelyn Hamilton she was from the north-east of England, the Leamington district of Newcastle-upon-Tyne. Likewise, along with Evelyn Hamilton and Margaret Lowe, she had gravitated at a young age to London and fell into prostitution. However, she did not walk the streets for trade like the others, or so she told her future husband. Rather, she entertained her men friends for money at her flat at 240 Edgware Road. It was in this way that she met the man she was to marry; they met in Oxford Street, which belies her previous comment.[37]

Doris had married Henri Alfred Joaunnet, naturalised as a British subject in about 1905, and a retired hotelier, thirty-four years her senior, at Paddington registry office on 4 November 1935. Her husband described her thus, 'My wife was five feet ten inches tall, very slim with fair hair and blue eyes. She was of a very happy disposition.' Initially they lived in a flat in Sussex Gardens and did not work as he had a private income from the profits of selling the business he owned, which provided them with an income of £10 per week. In 1937 they moved to Bournemouth and ran a café there that they bought. In the following year they lived in Gray's Road, Eastbourne, and in 1940 lived with Doris's mother in Harrogate. They returned to London in May 1941.[38]

It was at this time that the pair began to diverge, possibly because of the age difference. She wished to return to her former profession and they had rows. Eventually he agreed to give her a weekly allowance of £2 10s and a room in Sussex Gardens. In the autumn of that year he ran hotels in Haywards Heath and then in Farnborough, before returning to London on 1 February 1942. He was now the manager of the Royal Court Hotel, Sloane Square, and they rented a flat at 187 Sussex Gardens.[39]

Unlike the desperate women of 1888 who fell to the Ripper's knife, Doris did not need to be a prostitute. She had a home, a husband and a reasonable income. She chose her lifestyle and the risks it entailed perhaps because she liked the excitement, the power and the money it gave her. She claimed she knew 'lots of very nice class people' and had many of what she called 'men friends'. She was paid handsomely to whip some of them. She did not go into pubs and called herself Olga.[40]

Henri ran a hotel but also owned the flat and he had been sleeping at the hotel while his wife used the flat. On the night of the tragedy, Thursday 12 February, they had had supper together at the flat and they then walked to Paddington station. Henri explained: 'She wished me goodnight very sweetly and her last words to me were "Don't be late tomorrow, darling".'[41] It was about 9.30 and he got an Underground train to go to work, after advising his wife to go straight home.[42]

Meanwhile, Doris did not return to the flat. She went out soliciting on Sussex Gardens and the Edgware Road. She took at least one client back to the flat and then returned to look for another. A woman recalled that her last words to her at about 10.30pm were 'I am going to try and get off before I go home'.[43]

Her husband, who was very distraught, later related that on the next day, Friday 13 February:

> I returned to the flat at seven o'clock on Friday night and was surprised to see that the milk had not been taken in. When I got into the flat I shouted out 'Doris' but there was no reply. On going into the sitting room I found that the supper things from the night before were still on the table and the curtains had not been drawn. I was worried, and when I found the bedroom door had been locked I knew something was amiss. I could not get any reply, so I went to the housekeeper and we went for the police.[44]

PC William Payne and PC Cox were first to arrive, at 7.31pm. As the door was locked, Payne had to force it open using his foot. The room was all dark, so he switched on the light and noticed that the electric fire was still on. He saw that the two twin beds were close to one another and:

> there appeared to be the shape of a body under the bed clothes. I pulled the bed clothes but slightly and revealed the head of a woman. I pulled the bed clothes of the other twin bed and saw the apparently lifeless body of a woman [the same woman] naked except for a dressing gown... A tight bound stocking was round the neck, a circular cut ran round under the left breast, and the private parts appeared slashed over which was a pad.

He went next door to telephone Marylebone police station. Back at the flat, they found two preventatives [contraceptive devices] on the floor, as well as women's clothing. The clock had stopped at eight. There were also blood smears on the sheets of the bed where the body was not.[45]

It was clear that the killer had struck again. There was the body of Mrs Joaunnet, clad only in a dressing gown, which had been pulled open and with a tightly knotted scarf around her neck. She was lying across the bed. She had been savagely slashed in the stomach near the vagina and on the left groin, probably by the razor found in the room. There was no sign of a struggle. The woman's clothing was heaped on a chair at the foot of the bed. There was a clock which Cherrill claimed, contrary to PC Payne, had stopped at 4.45.[46]

Greeno searched about the flat for clues. There was a great quantity of dust and it revealed a number of tales to the detective. On the mantelpiece and the dressing table there were outlines showing items that had been taken recently. Greeno measured these. They might have belonged to a fountain pen and a comb. In the drawer was a broad roll of adhesive tape, out of which someone had cut a narrow strip. Greeno related in his memoirs, 'Not much in the way of clues, but we were starting'. He thought that one man was responsible for all the murders:

But where to start. Solving a murder is like doing a jigsaw. You have only to fit the pieces together – when you find them. That is where patience is needed, the careful plodding, the questioning, the screening and the sifting.

Of course, the killer had already been caught; possibly Greeno was being forgetful when recording his reminiscences nearly two decades later. Two of the victims were prostitutes and Doris was 'a part timer'. Therefore Greeno needed to look among them, the potential victims, for his next lead. He set up his headquarters, as he was now assigned to be in charge of the whole investigation, at Tottenham Court Road police station. He began a systematic tour of Paddington and Soho, asking prostitutes whether they had been attacked or if they knew anyone who had. As he later wrote, 'Speed was essential because the murderer might strike again at any moment'. He had killed on Sunday and Monday, Wednesday and Thursday, but not on Tuesday. Greeno wondered why there had been an interval.[47]

Fortunately evidence began to emerge. A cupboard door close to the bed yielded fingerprints, as did a hand mirror on the dressing table. The bedroom door also showed fingerprints.[48]

At least there was a prime suspect already in custody. Greeno saw Cummins at Brixton Prison. He admitted to being at the Trocadero on 12 February, having been out with RAF comrades between 6 and 9pm that evening in that vicinity, but not to attacking anyone. As to the gas masks, he said that there had been a mix up and another man had his and he had the other man's. The physical evidence went against him, however. His wristwatch had a piece of adhesive tape that exactly matched that taken from Doris's drawer. The gas mask with his name on it had traces of grit and cement dust which matched those in the air-raid shelter where Evelyn Hamilton's body had been found. He had a comb and pen that not only matched the dust outlines in Doris's room, but when they were shown to her husband he recognised them as being hers. There was also a scrap of paper with Margaret Heywood's telephone number on it.[49]

Greeno also searched Cummins' billet and found, in the bin, a green propelling pencil that friends of Evelyn Hamilton identified as hers. He also found there a pair of rubber-soled shoes. Greeno went back to Brixton and saw Cummins again. He asked him 'Why did you throw these away? Was it because you'd read something in the papers about our finding footprints in the snow?' There was no answer. The rubber soles fitted perfectly. Then there were the two pound notes that Phyllis' attacker had given her. Checking the issue numbers with those handed out on the recent pay parade, these matched those given to Cummins.[50]

However, despite all this evidence, Cummins had an alibi because of his pass book, which had to be signed when he left his billet and when he returned. This seemed to show that he had returned on the nights of the murders well before they had been committed. Likewise his mates in the barracks remembered him being in bed at relatively early hours. However the pass book evidence was weak; when a fellow airman returned, he told the corporal in the guardroom to cross Cummins off as well. This was a commonplace ruse at service camps. When Greeno brought it up with an officer, the latter said, 'For God's sake, what are you doing? You'll blow the whole place wide open'. Greeno replied, 'I'm sorry about that, but this is a murder case and that so called pass book is just a mass of lies'. As to his mates, one man recalled that after lights out he and Cummins got up and went out via the fire escape.[51]

The press was rather behind in its reporting, such was the relative speed of Cummins's capture. One newspaper posited the following theory:

> With the murder of two more women in the West End – the fourth murder in London in a week – the possibility arises that a 'killer' is at large.
>
> All the murders have been discovered in approximately the same area. The latest victims had both been strangled.[52]

Another newspaper did so too, after noting the number of murders in the previous week and that three had been by the same man. Reference was made to Jack the Ripper, who was stated as being a medical man, avenging his son's premature death from diseases he had contracted through his association with prostitutes, which was a favoured theory at one time, now long discounted by serious researchers and forgotten by others. The newspaper was confident that the killer would soon be found due to the police efforts.[53]

After Cummins's arrest he was associated with two previous unsolved murders in London. One was Maple Churchyard in 1941. Miss Churchyard was a 19-year-old clerk and was on her way home from Charing Cross to Tuffnell Park on the evening of 12 October 1941. Unfortunately she never arrived and the next day her body was found in the semi-derelict 225 Hampstead Road. She had been strangled and most of her clothing had been removed. There had been a scream at about 10pm that night which might have been her. No one was ever charged with the murder.[54]

The other was Edith Humphries, aged fifty, found dead in her home on Gloucester Crescent, Regent's Park, ten days later, having been stabbed in the head and then strangled. She worked as a cook in an Auxiliary Fire Station. It was thought that robbery might be the motive as jewellery was missing, but many of her valuables had not been taken.[55] However, Cummins was never charged with either murder, though subsequent writers have always included these in his tally.

What the police really thought has not been looked into. As to the Churchyard murder 'he could well have been responsible', but they were even less certain about the second, 'but in both it cannot go beyond the stage of assumption'. The local police found that Mrs Humphries's killer had entered her ground floor bedroom by means of an unfastened window, killing her while she was in bed, and this in no ways matches Cummins' modus operandi. Maple was a promiscuous young woman and possibly Cummins might have persuaded her to go to the ruined building for sex and might have robbed her of the little she had. But so might any other apparently personable young man.[56]

On 17 February, Cummins appeared at Bow Street magistrates' court before Mr McKenna. An hour before the hearing was to begin, there was a long queue outside the court and when the doors were opened, the public gallery was soon full. Cummins walked in in front of two prison officers. Greeno told McKenna that only formal proof of identity would be offered at the hearing. The public were afforded a look at Cummins, whose brown hair was brushed back and he wore an RAF overcoat. He sat with his hands clasped in his lap during the five-minute hearing. He was remanded until 20 February. McKenna asked if he had anything to say and he just replied 'No sir'. He stood up in the dock and bowed.[57]

At Bow Street magistrates' court on 26 March Cummins was committed for trial at the Old Bailey for the murder of Miss Hamilton.[58]

Cummins claimed he had alibis for the nights of the murders. He said that on Sunday 8 February he had visited his wife in their flat in Barnes. As he was broke, she let him have a pound so he could drink with his colleagues. He was at a pub near Baker Street at 9.15pm that night and returned to his billet between 10 and 11 as attested by a colleague. Yet he could easily have left by the fire escape when the others were asleep, and he could easily have engaged Evelyn Hamilton in conversation as he had a knowledge of chemistry and Newcastle-upon-Tyne. Finally, despite his being broke, on the next day he had £19, which could have been the result of robbing her (he claimed that an unnamed officer repaid a debt).[59]

Likewise, on the night of Evelyn Oatley's death, he had been out drinking with an RAF comrade, Aircraftsman Johnson, in Soho. At about 11pm the two men picked up two prostitutes, Molly Alven and Laura Denmark. Cummins went with the latter to her flat in 47 Frith Street and left at about midnight. He claimed he later met Johnson and they returned to their billet together, but Johnson said that this was not so.[60]

Cummins alleged that he had been drunk on the nights of the murders and that he had spent time with other women. On one instance, on 12 February, Mrs Doreen Lytton recalled meeting him at 2am in Piccadilly and the two went to her flat at 22 Polygon Mews. Although he gave her three pound notes, there was no sex, only conversation, and he left her unharmed at 3.45am. She recalled that he seemed rather drunk.[61] Neither of these accounts were helpful to his cause as the first finished before he could have killed Evelyn Oatley and the second took place after the murder of Doris.

The evidence against Cummins was strong. At Bow Street magistrates' court his fingerprints had been taken as a matter of course. On comparing these to the tin-opener found in Evelyn Oatley's room, the little left finger mark was there; on the mirror in her room was the print of his left thumb. The fingerprint on the base of the candlestick in Mrs Lowe's room had indeed been made by Cummins' right hand, as were those on the tumbler and the bottle.[62]

The trial at the Old Bailey began on 23 April. Justice Asquith oversaw it. Mr G.B. McClure led for the prosecution. Cummins was charged with the four murders and two attempted murders, but the focus was on the murder of Evelyn Oatley, because the evidence there was strongest. His prime evidence was Cummins's fingerprints on the tin-opener and mirror in Evelyn Oatley's room. Spilsbury gave evidence of strangulation.[63]

On 24 April the wrong document was shown to the jury and, fearing they 'might be prejudiced' because of it, Asquith dismissed the jury and empanelled a new one, to recommence the trial on Monday 27 April.[64] Apparently Cherrill had shown enlarged photographs of the fingerprints found at the murder scene and those of Cummins in order to see the similarities. Then, to his horror, Cherrill realised that he was showing the photographs of the Lowe crime scene, not Oatley's. He realised that there was an error and told the judge he had shown the wrong exhibits, so after legal discussions the trial was stopped and the jury was dismissed.[65]

Christmas Humphreys, son of the junior prosecuting counsel in the Brides in the Bath case and judge in the Haigh trial (see next chapter), was appointed as the new prosecuting counsel, and there was a new jury. The trial lasted two days. Cummins gave evidence in his own defence, denying he had ever been to Evelyn Oatley's flat, and claiming that he had been drunk that night but had returned to his billet. He added that the police had intimidated him into making a statement after he had been arrested, and accused Greeno of saying 'We have a rope around your neck'. John Flowers, for the defence, cited Laura Denmark, a defence witness, who stated that she had been with Cummins on the night of an alleged murder and he had been in every way gentlemanly, 'What could in a few minutes turn him into a homicidal maniac who senselessly killed and frightfully mutilated another woman?' On 28 April the jury discussed the verdict for 35 minutes before returning to give the judge their decision: guilty. Asquith remarked that the crime was 'a sadistic sexual murder of a ghoulish type'. However, when asked if he had anything to say, Cummins answered 'I am absolutely innocent'. He was sentenced to death.[66]

Cherrill later pondered a rhetorical question in his memoirs: 'You may wonder what manner of man this was who, night after night, set out to murder and mutilate women with such wanton savagery... One is left perplexed and horrified at the vicious cruelty which animated Cummins in his lust to kill'.[67]

There is little in Cummins' history to provide any clues as to his future activity. He came from a stable lower middle-class background. Cummins had been born in New Earswick, just to the north of York, on 18 February 1914. He had a brother and a sister and his father was a schoolmaster. He was the first but not the last London serial killer to have emerged from Yorkshire. Yet his background provides no clue as to what he would become. His father was the headmaster of an approved school for boys. Cummins attended the Llandovery Intermediate County School, Berrisbrooke, Carmarthenshire. The family moved to Harlestone, Northamptonshire, as his father took a new job there. From 1929–35 the family lived in the School House in Harlestone as his father was headmaster at that school. The family kept themselves to themselves and had few friends. Those who knew Cummins 'describe him as being a daredevil and always in mischief, but nothing of a serious nature' and local Quakers regarded him as 'an impulsive lad with a streak of phantasy in his make-up'. Here Cummins attended Northampton Town and County Secondary School for Boys on 15 January 1929 and left in July 1930. He then attended Northampton Technical School. His school record was poor, and at the college he was deemed to be a lazy student, but nevertheless he was awarded a diploma in chemistry.[68]

In August 1933 Cummins was employed at Messrs G. Barker and Co. Ltd of Northampton, a leather works, but was dismissed in September 1934 because he was seen as being inefficient at his job and unable to grasp the instructions he was given. Leaving the provinces he went to London. He then worked at a laboratory in Swiss Cottage, and at Messrs Reptile Dressers Ltd of Bermondsey Street as an assistant tanner and research assistant. On 11 November 1935 he joined the RAF as a flight rigger and in 1942 was trained to be a pilot. His father sent him allowances to supplement his pay. He was stationed at a number of bases during his six years of service: Felixstowe from 1936–39, Helensburgh in Scotland from 1939 to February 1941, and Colerne in April 1941. His conduct in the RAF was exemplary; he never complained, was very efficient at his job and was eager to fly. In October 1941 he was put forward as an aviation candidate and was then stationed at Predannack, Cornwall, as a cadet pilot. From 1 February 1942 he lived at a barracks for RAF pilot cadets at 27 St James' Close in the Regent's Park district of north London, sharing a room with a number of others.[69]

Cummins was married on 28 November 1936 to Marjorie Stevens at Paddington registry office in London but he and his wife had no children, as seems to be the case with several serial killers (including Smith and Christie).

Yet in 1942 he said 'Our six years of married life have been happy' and she said that he was 'cultured and well spoken... certainly not a sex maniac or a pervert'. Cummins claimed to his fellows that he had aristocratic connections and cultivated an upper-class accent; he was known as 'the Count' and 'the Duke' and spoke with a refined diction and acted in a polished manner. At one point he was known as 'the Honourable George Cummins'. He was a poseur. Corporal Vickery-Brown was impressed; to him Cummins was 'a well-spoken young man, appeared to be very well educated'. His flight sergeant said 'Cummins always seemed normal to me and was of a cheerful disposition'.[70]

It is possible that Cummins may have committed earlier crimes. There were the murders of two women in London in 1941 already alluded to. Then there were assaults on women in Bath and Colerne while he was there, but nothing could be proved against him.[71]

Cummins was fond of drinking to excess and enjoyed the company of women, as he had already admitted. Greeno wrote that his RAF colleagues deemed him 'a boastful type of person, very loose morally and having considerable influence over women'. Flight Sergeant Ball said that Cummins was always borrowing small sums of money from his colleagues and as for women, he 'seemed obsessed with them'.[72]

The police believed the motive for the murders was robbery. They deemed Cummins 'a cunning, boastful type of individual'. In 1941 he had worked as a barman at the Blue Peter Club in Bath and became friendly with the female owner, whose bedroom he had access to. He stole £35 worth of jewellery from her, but was never charged. Greeno wrote 'he could not carry on his high mode of living without money... resorted to robbery trying to cover up his crimes by murdering and mutilating the bodies of his victims to suggest the perpetrator was a madman'.[73]

Cummins certainly wanted a lifestyle in which drink flowed freely and he could enjoy the favours of women. This required an income he lacked. He had stolen to fund his habits previously and to kill to acquire more money was an extreme further step, but one he evidently took. Yet to ascribe his murders just to greed is insufficient. The mutilation and contempt he showed his three latter victims suggests a far more violent personality and a deep hatred of women: money may have been his primary aim, but he also spent time attacking their bodies after death, which he could do without interruption as he was indoors. Jack the Ripper had done likewise at Miller's Court, though his mutilations were far more severe than those inflicted by Cummins.

Following the verdict, there was an appeal. This was heard on 8 June, before three appeal court judges. They were shown the photographs of the relevant evidence. Denis Nowell Pritt, KC, was counsel for Cummins and he argued that the verdict was contrary to the weight of the evidence and that the judge had not given the jury emphatic enough warning over the stories in the press about the case, which he said biased the public against the defendant. Cummins himself smiled at the women at the back of the court. Sir Travers Humphreys was the senior judge present and he said that the evidence against Cummins had been overwhelming, especially the fingerprint evidence, and that the judge's summing-up had been impeccable. The appeal, therefore, was dismissed.[74]

Humphreys stated:

> There was no scamping the evidence in this case. Superintendent Cherrill was examined fairly fully in chief; he was fully cross-examined in the most minute detail by the learned counsel who appeared for the accused, and in order to make his points quite clear to the jury, counsel obtained permission from the learned judge to leave his place and go close to the jury-box, in order that he might point with a pencil to his copy of the photograph, so that the jury might see what it was he was referring to.[75]

After sentencing and the failure of the appeal, Cummins' family wrote to him and vice versa. They were convinced of his innocence, which he maintained, writing 'I am convinced that there is no justice in this country. I, who am completely innocent' and 'I shouldn't be punished at all'. His wife wrote 'we will go on fighting against injustice' and was adamant 'that nothing can alter my feelings for you and come what may I shall always believe that you are innocent'. They were convinced that 'John Flowers badly mishandled the case' and that 'We were up against the stonewall of unconscious prejudice'. The jury was 'such a collection of dimwits' Cummins and his family thought the fingerprint evidence was wrong, that he was drunk at the time of the murders, claimed there was no blood on his clothes and that another cadet was guilty. He claimed 'I was convicted on several so-called facts which are ridiculous'. On the other hand, while in Wandsworth Prison he wrote 'I am treated here with every consideration', enjoying the 15 cigarettes a day, better food than in the RAF and the facilities of the prison library.[76]

There had been discussion of Cummins' mental state, as this might alter his fate. In the RAF he was deemed 'quite normal and possessed of his full faculties'.[77] In Brixton Prison, before his trial, Dr Hugh Grierson, the medical officer there, concluded that 'the accused has been normal in conduct and rational conversation. At no time has he exhibited any evidence of mental disease'. Cummins denied any perversion or being sexually deviant.[78] There was a medical examination of Cummins on 19 June by Dr East, former Commissioner of Prisons, and Dr Hopwood, Superintendent of Broadmoor, to ascertain whether he was sane (if he was not he would be sent to Broadmoor). The report no longer exists, but presumably it agreed with the earlier reports.[79]

Alcohol played a part in these crimes. On all occasions Cummins had been drinking prior to the murders. Alcohol, in some cases, can reduce moral qualms that might inhibit criminal action, but in itself it does not cause violence. Alcohol played a part in Donald Hume's murder of Stanley Setty in 1949, and for Field and Gray in the murder of Irene Munro in 1920, and also for Peter Sutcliffe in his murders in 1975–1981, to name but a few.

We should also note that unlike Jack the Ripper in 1888, Cummins did not go out equipped to kill. He could be termed a 'disorganised' serial killer in that he used the weapons that were to hand, such as Evelyn Hamilton's scarf, Evelyn Oatley's razor and the ligatures available in Margaret Lowe's and Doris's rooms.

There were also letters petitioning Herbert Morrison, the Home Secretary, for clemency. These came from Cummins' father, naturally enough, and also from William Temple, the archbishop of Canterbury. The People's Common Law Society also petitioned him. Morrison, however, found no grounds on which he could recommend a royal pardon.[80] Cummins was executed at Wandsworth Prison (like Cream and Chapman) on 25 June 1942 during an air raid. Greeno later wrote 'I shed no tears for Cummins'.[81]

Cummins was likened to Jack the Ripper, and noted as being the worst killer since him. He had mostly preyed on prostitutes and had mutilated them after killing them. For instance, *The People* stated, as did many other newspapers, that he was 'the most notorious killer since Jack the Ripper'.[82] The term Blackout Ripper was not immediately used to refer to Cummins, but it was in use by 1954 when Cherrill titled his chapter about Cummins' crimes in his memoirs. Yet the police also noted 'This interesting but sordid series of murders has no parallels, so far as can be ascertained, in the history of the Metropolitan Police'.[83]

However, there was one crucial difference. Cummins made serious blunders in leaving his fingerprints all over two of the scenes of his murders, and to cap it all, left his gas mask behind during his attack on Margaret Heywood. With clues like these the detectives were able to track him down with relative speed and so bring his crimes to an end. The speed with which Cummins worked – four murders in four days – may also have proved his undoing as he showed extreme carelessness or/and arrogance.

Chapter 7

The Acid Bath Murders, 1944–49

On Saturday 19 February 1949, Mrs Constance Lane, the elderly widow of a solicitor, and resident at the Onslow Court Hotel in South Kensington, was a worried woman. She probably recalled the conversation that she had had on the previous afternoon with her friend, Mrs Henrietta Helen Olivia Robarts Durand-Deacon. They had been in the Tudor Lounge of the hotel just after 2pm on the previous day. Mrs Durand-Deacon said that she was going out to meet Mr Haigh and to go down to his workshop.[1]

Haigh was a fellow long-standing guest at the hotel, though considerably younger than most of the residents. His full name was John George Haigh, then aged thirty-nine, and he had a reputation as being an engineer and inventor with a workshop in Crawley, Sussex. He often chatted to Mrs Durand-Deacon in the hotel's dining room.

It seemed strange to Mrs Lane that Mrs Durand-Deacon had not dined at the hotel the previous night (nor had Haigh) and nor was she at breakfast the following morning. Mrs Lane approached Haigh at breakfast and asked him if he knew anything about the whereabouts of her friend. He said he did not. They had arranged to meet at the Army and Navy Stores. Apparently Haigh had then waited outside the shop for an hour, but there was no sign of Mrs Durand-Deacon. Mrs Lane then concluded 'Well, I must do something about it'.

She made enquiries at the hotel, but none of the staff could help her. Her friend was a lady of fixed habits; if she intended to visit friends and family elsewhere and be absent for a night from the hotel she would usually tell them. This was most unlike her. She had evidently left the hotel yesterday afternoon, as Mrs Lane had witnessed with her own eyes, but she had not come back. Why was this? The man whom she said she was to meet, and who had confirmed that he was to meet her, denied that he had seen her at all. It was all very mysterious.[2]

On the next day, Sunday 20 February, Mrs Lane's fears had not abated, for there had been no sign or news of her friend. Haigh asked her at breakfast for news of Durand-Deacon, but of course she had nothing to tell the concerned young man. She decided to report her friend's disappearance to Chelsea police station and told Haigh that she would do so after lunch. That afternoon Haigh said 'I think we had better go together to the Chelsea police station' and she agreed, 'I think so, too'. He said 'I will drive you there' and she readily consented to this. They arrived at their destination at 2.45pm.[3]

PS Leonard Dale was the duty officer and he recalled dealing with the two:

> Mrs Lane did most of the talking... but frequently appealed to Mr Haigh, who gave corroborations... I assured them that every possible enquiry would be made... Mr Haigh then said, 'You have written down Mrs Lane's news, but you haven't asked me for mine. I think you ought to take it'.

It is not illegal to go missing and adults often do so for many reasons which are unconnected to crime and so are no concern of the police. As DS John DuRose, attached to the Chelsea CID, wrote: 'Elderly people frequently go out and fail to return, for a variety of reasons'. At this time, the few women police were usually assigned to work concerning women and children, and this case was no exception. After checking a dozen hospitals and institutions and not having found that Mrs Durand-Deacon had been injured and was being treated there, it was necessary to seek her elsewhere.[4]

Who was the missing woman? Mrs Durand-Deacon had been born in 1880 into an upper middle-class family in Richmond, Surrey, soon moving to nearby Twickenham. In the 1900s she became a suffragette and was arrested for smashing shop windows in London. In 1918 she had married Captain John Durand-Deacon MC, a solicitor in civil life. She was also a Christian as well as a feminist. Her husband died in 1938 and she began to live in expensive London hotels, moving to the Onslow Court Hotel by 1943. She was very wealthy, with just over £36,000 (in 2021 this would be just over £1 million) to her name in 1949.[5]

On the morning of Monday 21 February, WPS Alexandra Maud Lambourne went to the Onslow Court Hotel to make routine enquiries. She spoke to Mrs Lane first, and then to Miss Alicia Robbie, the manageress of the hotel. WPS Lambourne also briefly met Haigh, and later reported 'apart from the fact that I do not like the man Haigh, with his mannerisms, I have a sense he is a wrong'un and that there may be a case behind the whole business'.[6]

Lambourne reported the case to Detective Inspector Alfred Webb, and he and DuRose went to the hotel. There they spoke to Miss Robbie, the manageress, who reported that Haigh had, in the previous week, been several weeks behind in paying his hotel bills and had been given an ultimatum to pay up or leave. However, on 16 February he had been able to meet his pressing debts. Otherwise Haigh was highly respectable. Webb began to think that this might not be a simple disappearance but a case of murder. DuRose agreed with his guvnor. Webb reported his findings to Detective Chief Inspector Shelley Symes and he told the two detectives to return to the hotel and take a proper statement from Haigh.[7]

The officers also checked at the Criminal Records Office, which listed all those convicted of crimes throughout Britain. There were some interesting findings there, for Haigh had a criminal record stretching back to 1934. In that year, working with two others in Leeds, he had run a hire purchase scam for those wishing to buy motor cars, taking money from clients but not delivering the goods. Within a few months all three were arrested, and, deemed the ringleader, Haigh received the stiffest sentence at the Yorkshire Assizes on 3 December 1934: fifteen months in prison.[8]

His next offences occurred in London, Surrey and Sussex in 1937. Here he sent out adverts alleging that he could provide customers with cut-price shares, but needed 25 per cent of their value upfront. The shares were non-existent, but he fraudulently acquired several thousands of pounds before he was arrested. At the Surrey Assizes on 23 November he was found guilty and was given four years in gaol.[9]

Released on licence in 1940, he drifted to London and once again his thieving tendencies came to the fore. He stole goods and acted as a receiver for other stolen items. On 11 June 1941 he was charged at Marlborough Street magistrates' court and as he was only out of prison on licence he was given a stiffer sentence of twenty-one months in prison with hard labour and was released in 1943.[10] However, none of these crimes featured any violence and it seemed that Haigh was basically a fraudster and a thief, or had been a few years previously.

It was on the evening of 21 February that Webb and Symes met Haigh at the hotel. Symes explained that he was investigating Mrs Durand-Deacon's disappearance. Haigh made a lengthy statement, explaining he was an engineer with a business in Crawley and that he had known Mrs Durand-Deacon for a number of years as friendly hotel acquaintances. He told them that they had been discussing an invention of his to manufacture false ladies' fingernails. She was interested in the project and agreed to come down to his business premises in Crawley to see his work. They agreed to meet on 18 February and would meet at the Army and Navy stores that afternoon. He then told them what had happened – that he had waited for her at the Army and Navy Stores until half past three – but that she had not arrived, so he had driven alone to Crawley.[11]

The police returned to interview Haigh on 24 February and he made a second statement. It was mostly a repeat of what he had already told them, about what he had done on 18 February in relation to Mrs Durand-Deacon. He added a little about his concern for her and asking about her on 18 and 19 February. He also added information about his engineering business and that he won substantial sums by betting on dogs and horses.[12]

The statement did nothing to reduce the policemen's suspicions, though there was nothing concrete they could act upon. DuRose wrote in his memoirs:

> He gave apparently straightforward answers to all our questions and nothing he said should be challenged... The three of us sat in such a way as to form a triangle, so that I was watching Haigh's profile during Webb's questioning, and Webb was watching his face and neck from the same angle when I put the questions. Thus we both noticed the very odd behaviour of his Adam's apple. Every time he answered a question he gulped to swallow saliva and his Adam's apple seemed to be flying up and down like a yo yo... The rapid action of his Adam's apple was not normal. It was an involuntary physical reaction bred of nervous tension while we were questioning him, and it clearly indicated that the man had something on his conscience.[13]

Webb and DuRose left the hotel and talked over the case. The former said 'Well, what did you think of that?' and DuRose replied, 'I think he murdered the old lady'. His superior agreed and they informed the superintendent of their views. He contacted his superiors and the investigation took another turn.[14]

On Saturday 26 February, DS Patrick Heslin of the Sussex Constabulary went with Edward Jones, a Crawley businessman, to a workshop Jones owned on Leopold Road, Crawley, which he allowed Haigh to use. Haigh had not returned the key to the padlock to Jones, so Heslin had to cut through the chain and force the padlock. Heslin described the scene, 'I saw a large square shaped leather case on a table in the far corner of the room. I also saw three acid carboys in the centre of the floor. There was a stirrup pump to the left of the room and a rubber apron'. He also saw a mackintosh and a pair of rubber gloves. The two then locked up and left.[15]

Heslin returned later that day. He took the leather case and a hatbox. Both contained some interesting finds. The former contained a British army service revolver, an Enfield No.2 Mark 1, and eight bullets. There was also a receipt from Cottage Cleaners, a dry cleaning firm on Reigate High Street, for a Persian lamb coat. Mrs Durand-Deacon had been wearing one when she disappeared. He also found passports and identity cards for Dr Archibald and Mrs Rosalie Henderson, and for Mr Donald and Amy McSwan and their son Donald William McSwan. Identity cards were still essential documentation for Britons to carry with them at all times in the 1940s, despite the war being over. It was odd that they should be there and not with their owners.[16]

The discovery of these items led to further police investigations. Symes and Webb went to visit Haigh for the third time. On this occasion he was taken down to Chelsea police station to make a statement, which he did at nine o'clock that night:

> I have been asked if I would give an explanation respecting two cases found by the police at Crawley in one of Mr Jones' store sheds at Leopold Road, Crawley.

The square with the initial H on it is the property of Dr Arthur [sic] Henderson, who used to live at 22 Ladbroke Square where his wife ran a guest house. I first met him when he advertised his address for sale and called upon him. He also owned a shop with flats above at No.16 Dawes Road, Waltham Green. I bought these premises from him and resold them. I remained friendly with Dr Henderson and his wife until they went to South Africa in 1948.

Just before they left England, they stayed at the Hotel Metropole, Brighton, and Dr Henderson, after he left the hotel, asked me to collect some cases he left there. This I did and took them to 16 Dawes Road. When he went to South Africa he left some cases, including the one I have mentioned, in my care. The case is locked and I do not know what it contained.

When I sold 16 Dawes Road I brought the case and other property to my garage at Manson Place and took the case down to Crawley a couple of weeks ago.

The other case, a thin attaché case, is my own property. It contains ration books, clothing coupon books, a pawn ticket for a typewriter, and a dry cleaning ticket for a coat belonging to Mrs Henderson. The ration books etc are in the name of McSwan and were left with me by her and Mr Donald McSwan and their son Donald when their family went to Africa in 1944 or 1945. I met the McSwans some years before this and had been on friendly terms with them. Their last known address in this country was Claverton Street, SW, I believe No.99.

I do not know what was in the case left me by Dr Henderson but I do know he had been an officer in the RAMC. This statement has been read by me and is true.[17]

What should have set alarm bells ringing was the fact that the passports of the five people who had allegedly gone abroad were still there. How could they have left the country and arrived in another without them? And if they had not emigrated, why had Haigh told them they had? Yet the police let Haigh leave the station at the day's end as their case against him was not yet complete.

On 27 February, Symes paid a visit to the dry cleaners, where Mrs Mabel Marriott, the manageress, explained that the coat had been deposited by a man at the shop on 19 February, the day after Mrs Durand-Deacon disappeared. The case had featured in the press, so the police had received a call from Messrs Walter Bull and Sons, jewellers in Horsham, to the effect that a necklace, earrings and a jewelled watch had been bought by them on 21 February from a man calling himself Mr McLean, of 32 St George's Drive, London. This jewellery matched that which the missing lady was wearing. The gun went to the Metropolitan Police laboratory, as did the coat, and it ascertained that the revolver had been fired recently.[18]

It was all looking very suspicious and the evidence was building up against Haigh. On the afternoon of 28 February, Haigh was standing outside the hotel he lived in, by his beloved Alvis motor car. Webb approached him and asked him to accompany him to the police station, though Haigh asked if he could visit his solicitor first. This would not do, so he went with Webb to the police station that he had been to twice already.[19]

Haigh had a lengthy wait as Webb's colleagues were in Crawley. He had some conversation with Webb in the meantime. When the others (Symes and Superintendent Barratt) arrived, they showed him the evidence that they had collected, such as the jewellery and the dry cleaner's ticket. Symes cautioned him and Haigh said 'It's a long story; it is one of blackmail, and I shall have to implicate many others. How do I stand about that?' and was told 'What you have to say is entirely a matter for you'.[20]

Symes and Barratt then left the interview room and left Haigh with Webb. They had another lengthy talk. Haigh remarked that a murder could not be proved without there being a corpse. He also asked what was the case if a man was found guilty of crime but was mentally deficient. Webb told him that he would be sent to the Broadmoor Institute for the insane. Seizing on this piece of information, Haigh then asked about the possibilities of release from there. Webb refused to answer. Passing over this, Haigh referred to the five people whose personal documentation had been found on the premises he used in Crawley and announced that they would never be found. He then made a lengthy statement: 'They just disappeared. No part of them still exists. No trace of any of them will ever be found... if I told you the truth, you wouldn't believe it; it sounds too fantastic for belief'. He was then cautioned and made a statement about not one murder, but six, but that was not all that was shocking about the statement. There was worse, much worse, as Haigh explained:

> I have already made some statements to you about the disappearance of Mrs Durand-Deacon. I have been worried about the matter and fenced about it, in the hope that you would not find out about it. The truth is, however, that we left the hotel together and went to Crawley together in my car. She was inveigled into going to Crawley by me in view of her interest in artificial fingernails. Having taken her into the storeroom at Leopold Road, I shot her in the back of the head while she was examining some paper for the use as fingernails. Then I went out to the car and fetched in a drinking glass and made an incision, I think with a penknife, in the side of the throat, and collected a glass of blood, which I then drank. Following that, I removed the coat she was

wearing, a Persian lamb, and the jewellery, rings, necklace, earrings and cruciform, and put her in a forty-five gallon tank. I then filled the tank up with sulphuric acid, by means of a stirrup pump, from a carboy. I then left it to react. I should have said that in between having her in the tank and pumping in the acid I went round to the Ancient Prior's for a cup of tea. Having left the tank to react, I brought the jewellery and the revolver into the car and left the coat on the bench. I went to the 'George' for dinner and I remember I was late, about nineish. I then came back to town, and returned to the hotel about half past ten. I put the revolver back into the square hat box.

The following morning I had breakfast, and as I have already said, discussed the disappearance of Mrs Durand-Deacon with the waitress and Mrs Lane. I eventually went back to Crawley, via Putney, where I sold her watch, en route to a jeweller's shop in the High Street, for ten pounds. I took this watch from her at the same time as the other jewellery. At Crawley I called in to see how the reaction in the tank had gone on. It was not satisfactorily completed so I went to Horsham, having picked up the coat and put it into the back of the car. I called at Bull's, the jewellers, for a valuation of the jewellery, but Mr Bull was not in. I returned to town, and on the way dropped in the coat at the Cottage Cleaners at Reigate. On Monday I returned to Crawley to find the reaction almost complete, but a piece of fat and bone was still floating on the sludge. I emptied the sludge off with a bucket and tipped it on the ground opposite the shed, and pumped a further quantity of acid into the tank to decompose the remaining fat and bone. I then left that to work until the following day. From there I went to Horsham again and had the jewellery valued, ostensibly for probate. It was valued at just over £130. I called back at the West Street factory and eventually returned to town.

I returned to Horsham on Tuesday and sold the jewellery for what was offered, at a purchase price of £100. Unfortunately the jewellers had not got that amount of money and could only give me £60. I called back for the £40 on the next day. On the Tuesday I returned to Crawley and found decomposition complete and emptied the tank off. I would add that on Monday I found that the only thing which the acid had not attacked was the plastic handbag, and I tipped this out with the sludge. On the Tuesday when I completely emptied the tank, I left it outside in the yard.

I owed Mr Jones, who, as I have said, is a co-director of Hurstlea Products, £50, and I paid him £36 on the Tuesday from the money I got from the jewellers. The revolver which the police found in Crawley in the storeroom is the one I used to shoot Mrs Durand-Deacon, and I took it down there in the hat box on the Saturday morning. Before I put the handbag in the tank I took from it the cash – about thirty shillings – and her fountain pen and kept these, and tipped the rest into the tank with the bag. The fountain pen is still in my room. She also had a bunch of keys attached to the inside pocket of the coat by a chain and a large safety pin. I discarded the chains of the cruciform and the keys in the bottom of the hedge in the lane going down to Bracken Cottage, when I went to stay with friends on the Wednesday. The keys themselves I inserted separately into the ground and also the cruciform.[22]

This seems a pretty comprehensive statement as to the murder of Mrs Durand-Deacon. However, Haigh had a lot more to say and this concerned the other five people. He continued:

The ration books and clothing coupon books and other documents in the names of McSwan and Henderson are the subject of another story. This is covered very briefly by the fact that in 1944 I disposed of William Donald McSwan in a similar manner to the above, in the basement of 79 Gloucester Road, SW7, and of Donald McSwan and Amy McSwan in 1946 [sic] at the same address. In 1948, Dr Archibald Henderson and his wife Rosalie Henderson, also in a similar manner at Leopold Road, Crawley.

Going back to the McSwans, William Donald, the son, whose address at that particular time, I can't remember, met me at the Goat public house, Kensington High Street, and from there we went to No. 79 Gloucester Road, where in the basement, which I had rented, I hit him on the head with a cosh, withdrew a glass of blood from his throat as before and drank it. He was dead within five minutes or so. I put him in a forty gallon tank and disposed of him with acid, as in the case of Mrs Durand-Deacon, disposing of the sludge down a manhole in the basement. I took his watch and odds and ends, including an identity card, before putting him into the tank. I had known this McSwan and his mother and father for some time, and on seeing his mother and father, explained that he had gone to avoid his 'Call up'. I wrote a number of letters in due course to his mother and father, purporting to come from him and posted in, I think, Glasgow and Edinburgh, explaining various details of the dispositions of properties, which were to follow. In the following year, I took separately to the basement the father, Donald, and the mother, Amy, disposing of them in exactly the same way as the son. The files of the McSwans are at my hotel and will give details of the properties which I disposed of after their deaths. I have since got additional ration books by producing their identity cards in the usual way.[23]

The McSwans were a family that Haigh had become acquainted with at the beginning of 1937, when he answered an advertisement for the job of managing the pin ball arcades owned by the junior McSwan. McSwan senior had been born in Scotland in 1878 and had moved down to Kent for employment in a hotel. There he met Amy, four years his junior, and they married. Their son, who was their only child, was born in 1911. McSwan served in the army in the First World War. Afterwards he worked as a clerk for the London County Council and lived in Pimlico, in south-west London. The son went into business, and briefly employed Haigh in early 1937, but they kept in touch over the next few years. Reuniting in 1944, the McSwans had by then acquired four properties in London and the elderly couple added to their pensions by the rents on these four houses. They had also built up savings and had invested some of their money, too.[24]

The younger McSwan had dabbled in the black market during the war and had been fined for receiving stolen goods. In 1944 he wanted to avoid conscription and so had to disappear. Haigh managed to do this for his 'friend'; only not in a way that his victim would have appreciated or predicted. He was last seen alive on 9 September 1944. His unsuspecting parents were never seen again after 2 July 1945.[25]

Haigh then talked about his next victims:

I met the Hendersons by answering an advertisement offering for sale their property at 22 Ladbroke Square. I did not purchase 22 Ladbroke Square. They sold it and moved to 16 Dawes Road, Fulham. This runs in a period from November 1947, to February 1948. In February 1948, the Hendersons were staying at Kingsgate Castle, Kent. I visited them there and went with them to Brighton, where they stayed at the Metropole. From there I took Dr Henderson to Crawley and disposed of him in the storeroom at Leopold Road by shooting him in the head with his own revolver, which I had taken from his property in Dawes Road. I put him in a tank of acid as in the other cases. This was in the morning and I went back to Brighton and brought up Mrs Henderson on the pretext that her husband was ill. I shot her in the store-room and put her in another tank and disposed of her with acid. In each of the last four cases I had my glass of blood as before. In the case of Dr Henderson I removed his gold cigarette case, his gold pocket watch and chain and, from his wife, her wedding ring and diamond ring and disposed of all this to Bull's at Horsham for about

£300. I paid their bill at the Hotel Metropole, collected their luggage and their red setter and took the luggage to Dawes Road. The dog I kept for a period at the Onslow Court Hotel and later at Gatwick hall, until I had to send him to Professor Sorsby's Kennels in the country on account of his night blindness. By means of letters purporting to come from the Hendersons, I kept the relatives quiet, by sending the letters to Mrs Henderson's brother, Arnold Burlin, who lives in Manchester. His address is in the Index book in my room. No.16 Dawes Road, I acquired by forged deeds of transfer and sold it to the present owner, J.B. Clarke.[26]

Dr Archibald Henderson had been born in Scotland in 1897 and attended Glasgow University, qualifying as a doctor after military service in the First World War. He had married well, but during his first marriage he met Rosalie Erren, born in 1907, who married Rudolph Erren in 1931, a German inventor and former air ace. The two began an affair. Mrs Henderson died in 1937 and Erren divorced his wife. Rosalie and Archibald married in 1938. Henderson was a captain in the RAMC during the Second World War but was never posted overseas.[27]

After the war the couple acquired property in west London and it was there that Haigh met them. The Hendersons had a tempestuous marriage; there were suspicions of adultery on her part and drunkenness and violence on his. They had an expensive lifestyle and partied hard; quite the opposite of the McSwans, who were careful with their money.[28] Haigh continued, 'The McSwan properties were also acquired in a similar way and disposed of and the particulars are in the file at the hotel. I have read this statement and it is true'.[29]

Haigh then signed his statement in the presence of Symes and Barratt. It had taken two and a half hours and Haigh slept the night in a police cell. Next day, Dr Keith Simpson (1907–87), an up and coming Home Office pathologist who had undertaken numerous murder cases in the previous decade, was summoned by the police to go to the workshop at Crawley where Haigh killed his last three victims. The police also searched the basement of 79 Gloucester Road, though as Haigh had vacated it nearly four years previously after the last of the McSwans had been disposed of, very little was found there. It was at Crawley where the vital evidence, if any, was to be found.

Dr Simpson described what happened in his bestselling memoirs. While he was travelling to Crawley in a police car with Chief Inspector Guy Mahon, Symes and his secretary, Miss Jean Hunter Dunn (later his second wife), he thought over what he might find there, later writing 'I did not have any great hope of finding much beyond residual acid sludge, but on the way down I pondered on what parts of the body might conceivably have escaped destruction'.[30]

Once there, examining the yard around the workshop, Simpson found a gallstone. He then found another. There was also eroded bone among the sludge. 'These were exciting discoveries' he noted, but there was too much of the greasy mass to examine in situ. He had Mahon box up 475 pounds of greasy residue and earth and had it taken to Scotland Yard. Inside the workshop he found red spots on the wall. These were photographed and the plaster on which they were found was carefully removed.[31]

Dr Holden and Superintendent Cuthbert spent the next three days with Simpson examining these finds. The gallstones were human. The bones were those of a left human foot and they fitted one of Mrs Durand-Deacon's shoes. The red spots were blood. Apart from the animal fat in the sludge, there were the remains of more bones, showing that there had been the body of an elderly woman; remains of a red handbag confirmed this. Most important of all were the intact dentures that were found. When Miss Helen Mayo, Mrs Durand-Deacon's dentist, checked her records, it was found that the dentures matched them. Simpson concluded, 'Haigh's labours had been in vain. The remains of Mrs Durand-Deacon were identified as surely as if her body had never been given an acid bath'.[32]

Haigh was charged with murder on 1 March and was sent to Lewes Prison on remand until his trial. There were a number of appearances at the magistrates' court at Horsham and crowds flocked to see him enter and leave. He was especially popular with women and he revelled in the attention that was being showered on him. He remarked in a letter to his parents that only his idols, Churchill and Princess Margaret, would garner more adulation than himself.

While at Lewes Prison, Haigh asked if Webb, with whom he clearly thought he had a rapport, could visit him so he could make a statement. Webb drove down and on 4 March took another lengthy and almost as shocking a statement as he had heard a few days earlier at Chelsea police station:

> About two months or more after (the February following, I believe) the young McSwan, I met a woman of about 35 years of age, 5ft 7in, slim build, dark hair, no hat, wearing a dark cloth coat, and carrying a dark envelope-type blackish handbag, in Hammersmith, somewhere between the Broadway and Hammersmith Bridge. I had never seen her before. We stood chatting by the bridge for about twenty minutes, and then I asked her if she would walk back to Kensington with me. She agreed to do so. We walked back as far as High Street, Kensington, and then took the Underground to Gloucester Road. From there I invited her round to what I called my flat. That was 79 Gloucester Road (basement). She came with me to that address, where I duly tapped her on the head with a cosh, and tapped her for

blood. She had next to nothing in her handbag, and I disposed of her body in the same manner as in the other cases.[33]

This woman was never identified; assuming she even existed. It is possible that Haigh made the confession to strengthen the impression that he had vampiric tendencies and was insane. To continue with the statement:

> Similarly there was the case of a youngish man, about the autumn of the same year. He was aged about 35, about my own height and build, brownish hair, wavy, wearing a dark brown double-breasted suit, I believe blue. I met him at the Goat public house, High Street Kensington, about 6 or 6.30 in the evening. I had seen him before in the Goat, about a couple of months previously, and had a drink with him. On the present occasion we had a drink or two and a snack in the snack bar. I talked to him about pin tables and asked him to come down to the basement at 79 Gloucester Road, which on this occasion, I described as a workshop. He came with me and the same thing happened as before. He had no jewellery and no more than a pound in money.[34]

This victim sounds a lot like McSwan junior: a young man with an association with the Goat pub. As with the woman just mentioned, there is no evidence that this man ever existed. However, Haigh had stopped using the basement at 79 Gloucester Road by July 1945 and so the story is undoubtedly fiction. We now carry on with the statement:

> Between the late summer and autumn of last year (1948) I was down in Eastbourne, quite apart from the time when the car was stolen and found over the cliff. On the front, near the Mansion Hotel, I met, that evening, about 8pm, a girl, who later told me her name was Mary. She was shorter than myself, black hair, she was not English – probably Welsh – wearing a white and green summer dress, white beach shoes, carrying a light coloured handbag. Later the same evening we went to Hastings together, and had a meal at a café on the sea front in the old part of the town. I later took her back to Crawley in my car (the Alvis). We went to the shed at Leopold Road, where I hit her on the head with the cosh, tapped for blood, and put her in a tub, but left her there until the following morning. The tub was one of those I used for the Hendersons which probably explained why one of the tubs you found was almost eaten away. The following morning, I returned to Crawley, where I pumped sulphuric acid into the tank containing the woman's body. I tipped the sludge out the following morning into the yard. The girl had little or no property, but I do remember a small bottle of scent (in her handbag) about which Inspector Mahon asked

me the other morning and for which I could not account. The man I have mentioned called himself 'Max' and I should think he came from the southern counties. I think I might add here that although the newspapers were connecting the loss of the Lagonda car at Beachy Head with a possible murder committed by me, this is not the case, nor had I anything to do with a body they say was found on the beach at Beachy Head a week after the car was found. Neither have I had anything to do with the disappearance of any persons other than those I have already mentioned. The Eastbourne girl calling herself Mary did not live in Eastbourne, but whether she was there on holiday or for employment, I would not know. I have read this statement through and it is true.[35]

There is no evidence that Mary or the other two people ever existed, or that Haigh killed them. There are good reasons to suppose them entirely fictitious. Firstly, Haigh never gives enough information to prove or disprove their existence. Second, Haigh was acquainted with his known victims for some months, at least, before their murders. Third, there was evidence found in Haigh's hotel room and the workshop about his known victims and there was none for the others.

Haigh was put on trial at the Sussex Assizes, held at Lewes Court House on 18 and 19 July. Sir Hartley Shawcross was the Attorney General and he led the case for the prosecution; Sir David Maxwell Fyfe was the defending counsel and Sir Travers Humphreys was the judge. The prosecution argued that this was 'an exceedingly simple case of a carefully premeditated murder for gain'. Haigh was being tried for the murder of Mrs Durand-Deacon and he pleaded not guilty. Over thirty witnesses were brought forward by the prosecution. They showed that Haigh had a strong need for money, being overdrawn with his bank for £83 and owing the hotel £32. There were witnesses to his purchasing sulphuric acid just before the murder and others who testified to him having sold Mrs Durand-Deacon's jewellery after her disappearance. The Persian coat and jewellery were identified as belonging to the dead woman. That she was dead was proved by Dr Simpson and Miss Mayo. Maxwell Fyfe did not contest this evidence and very little cross-examination occurred.[36]

Instead the defence rested on the MacNaughton Rules, dating back to 1843 and enabling a defendant, if they could be shown to be mentally ill, to avoid the death penalty. These rules stated that if the accused could be shown to have not known what he was doing, or to have not been aware that it was wrong, then he would be incarcerated in an asylum.

Haigh did not step into the witness box. Instead his counsel spoke for him and the single defence witness was Dr Henry Yellowlees, a psychiatrist. He argued that Haigh was suffering from an advanced form of paranoia which had its origins in his strict religious upbringing and the conflict with his being then exposed to the High Anglicanism of Wakefield Cathedral. His solitary boyhood and his lack of interest in sex were also offered as proof for his confused mental condition. These factors led him to having nightmarish dreams as a prelude to murder, where he was directed by a higher power. The dream which caused Haigh the trouble was described by Dr Yellowlees:

> He goes out into a forest and sees before him an entire forest of crucifixes. These gradually turn into trees, which have branches stretching out at right angles, appear to be dripping with dew or rain. As he gets nearer he sees that it is blood that is dripping from the tress, not water. One of the trees gradually takes the shape of a man who holds a bowl or cup beneath one of the dripping trees, and collects blood which comes from it. As this happens he sees the tree getting paler in colour, and he himself feels that he is losing strength. Then the man in the dream, when the cup is full, approaches him, offers it to him, and invites him to drink it. He says that he is unable to move before them and the man recedes and he cannot get to him and the dream ends.[37]

However, in Shawcross's cross-examination of Yellowlees, the latter had to admit that Haigh, who was his sole source of information about his mental state, might have been lying to him, that he had been aware enough to know that his deeds were punishable by law, and that he knew the gravity of his actions. On the second day of the trial, the speeches were all over and the jury took a mere seventeen minutes to decide their verdict. This was that Haigh was guilty and he was sentenced to death. He had nothing to say to the verdict.[38] Gladys Langford recorded in her diary: 'he has tried to pretend he is mad. He seems to have modelled himself on Ronald True [murderer in 1922 who was sent to Broadmoor]'.[39]

Haigh was sent to Wandsworth Prison. He did not suggest to his barrister that they appeal, but there was a medical enquiry to ascertain his mental health. He was found to be sane. During his last weeks of life he wrote a lengthy autobiography, to be published after his death in *The News of the World*, as a quid pro quo for the newspaper paying his defence costs. It stressed his vampiric motivation for murder, as well as his love of animals. Haigh was hanged by Albert Pierrepoint on 10 August 1949 and 500 spectators came to see the death notice being posted on the prison gates. His waxwork statue then appeared in his own clothes, which he had donated, in Madame Tussaud's Chamber of Horrors, next to that of sadistic double murderer Neville Heath.

Haigh, an only child, had been born on 24 July 1909 at Stamford in Lincolnshire but by 1911 was living in Outwood, near Wakefield in Yorkshire. His father was a mining engineer. His parents were members of a puritanical Protestant sect called the Plymouth Brethren and they tried to shield their son from worldly pleasures. He was a bright lad and obtained a scholarship to the prestigious Wakefield Grammar School and sang in the choir at Wakefield Cathedral. He did not make friends and abhorred sport. However, despite his intelligence, he was lazy and left school in 1926 without any qualifications, subsequently undertaking a number of clerical jobs. In 1934 he married Beatrice Hamer and she gave birth to a daughter, Pauline, whom she gave up for adoption and whom Haigh never saw nor cared about. From then on, Haigh had little interest in sex, but from 1944–49 he had a platonic friendship with Barbara Stephens, who was half his age. He had a great interest in classical music and posed as an engineer and director of the non-existent Union Group Engineering Ltd. He was a snob and, unlike most serial killers, voted Conservative.[40]

All his life Haigh desired money and the power it would give him. He was not interested in honest toil, earning relatively little and living the humble life as his parents did. He had a fascination for sports cars, good clothes and the lifestyle of the rich. Unfortunately his legitimate earning power was limited as at school he did not want to put in the hard work and long hours necessary for success. Cleverness in itself was not enough.

This led Haigh into a world of crime, beginning in at least 1934. Initially he was successful, but as already noted he was arrested, tried and gaoled on three occasions. It seems that when he was in Lincoln Prison in 1942–43 he started experimenting on field mice, to see how they dissolved in acid. In Chelmsford Prison in 1940, according to a former fellow inmate, he said 'Who could tell if a murder had been done if a person completely disappeared? Only the murderer would know and if he kept his mouth shut he would be safe'. Another prisoner recalled discussions with Haigh when the latter spoke about acid, he 'never heard so much talk about sex and the disposal of humans'. Haigh said 'without a body they could never do anything about' a murder. The convict added 'He always maintained that in his case it would be a case of corpus delicti'. This Latin phrase means the body of evidence needed to convict a defendant, but Haigh, with his little learning proving dangerous, thought it concerned the necessity to have a physical corpse to prove murder, which is not the case.[41]

Haigh never explained why he decided to use acid to dispose of his victims. He is usually credited with having read about a French criminal, George Sarett, known in the British press in the 1930s as the 'acid bath murderer', a name later applied to Haigh. Sarrett killed for gain and destroyed the corpses in acid, but was arrested and executed in 1934. However, popular thrillers also featured acid baths being employed by villains. In the Agatha Christie novel *One Two Buckle*

My Shoe, published in 1940, Chief Inspector Japp discusses with Hercule Poirot the fate of a missing woman and wonders if she could have been dissolved in acid. In *Bulldog Drummond*, published in 1920, an acid bath is used to dissolve a corpse.

In the 1940s, therefore, Haigh made the leap from the non-violent crimes of embezzlement, fraud and theft to that of calculated murder. Haigh was able to get away with his murders because of the war and also because of the way his victims lived their lives. He could explain the disappearance of William Donald McSwan to his parents by saying that he had gone into hiding to avoid military service, which was entirely plausible in wartime. Afterwards, the relative social isolation of his victims played into Haigh's hands. McSwan had no close friends to enquire after his whereabouts. Nor did his parents when they disappeared in 1945. One of William McSwan's siblings recalled in 1949 that they had not seen him since 1929 and had last heard of him in 1932. Some had not seen him since their father's funeral in Scotland in 1916. Apparently he was of 'a very reserved disposition'. Philip Paige, an artist of Sevenoaks, was Amy's brother and he said his brother-in-law was a recluse. He had not heard from his sister since 1945 (not surprisingly as she was killed in that year). He later said, 'We used to write to each other regularly and the letters she sent me were all in the most affectionate terms. When her letters stopped suddenly some three years back, I was afraid something I wrote had offended her, and I hastened to make amendments, but still there was no reply'. He ceased writing and did not investigate. Mrs McSwan's sister had not seen her since their parents' funeral in 1924. It is presumed they were relatively friendless too, despite living in a populous part of London. So when they disappeared, their relatives would have little or no cause to even notice, let alone make any enquiries.[42] Likewise with Dr and Mrs Henderson. There were, therefore, no reports to the police that any of these people had disappeared.

Haigh was able to deflect the few questions that were asked. He arranged a power of attorney with a firm of solicitors in Glasgow to allow him to dispose of the McSwans' assets. Armed with this legal document he was able to prevent suspicion. If anyone asked him, he would tell them that the McSwans had emigrated. No one asked for any evidence.

However, the disappearance of the Hendersons led to concern from the manager of their shop in Fulham, and more importantly from Arnold Burlin, Mrs Henderson's brother. However, Haigh's powers of forgery, noted since his schooldays, were used to the full. He knew plenty about the Hendersons and forged letters from them to himself, showing that they were still alive, and explaining why they had left their normal haunts and were on the move, so could not be contacted. Finally there was a letter about their emigration to South Africa, leaving Haigh their property as payment for an earlier loan. Burlin was concerned, but he lived in Lancashire and had a business to run as well as being married with a child and having an elderly mother to look after. He was geographically distant and preoccupied with other concerns so could not spend too much time and effort in finding his sister.

Once dead, Haigh could then sell his victims' assets, which were considerable. The McSwans owned four houses in London; 9 Grand Drive, Raynes Park, 106 Kenilworth Drive, Wimbledon and 15 Wimborne Way and 122 Churchfields Road, both in Beckenham. All these were sold by Haigh. He also sold the McSwans' War Bonds and stock, emptied their bank accounts, took what money he could find and sold their property; one buyer being Barbara's father. In all, about £5,375 was gained by Haigh. He wanted the money to pay for his stay in the high-class Onslow Court Hotel, a Lagonda sports car and also to indulge in gambling on horses and dogs.[43]

By 1947 his expenditure had been so high that he had little money left. Attaching himself to the Hendersons, he chose them as his next victims. They were richer than the McSwans. Their deaths netted Haigh the sale of their shop at Dawes Road, as well as jewellery, savings and much more. He even sold some of Mrs Henderson's clothing to Barbara. In all he gained £7,771. He kept their dog and Dr Henderson's gold-rimmed spectacles. By February 1949 the money (worth nearly half a million pounds in today's money) had all been spent, mostly on gambling, and he needed yet another source of income to meet his debts and pay his hotel bill, so Mrs Durand-Deacon had to die.[44]

Haigh's appearance and outward personality were crucial to his initial success. He was very smartly dressed in tailor-made suits. He was ingratiating and pleasing to his victims. An early employer wrote 'he had charm. I had to like him'. A colleague observed 'We all found him charming and so did all our connections'. Two Crawley residents recalled that he was 'always very kind and friendly towards me as a young lad' and another said 'very charming, very friendly, easy to talk to, very pleasant'.[45] Barbara recalled 'the most charming man I ever met... he was always kind and gentle – everything that a man of culture should be'.[46] She said that Mrs Durand-Deacon 'seemed to think the world of John [Haigh]' and that the old lady thought that 'Haigh was an infinitely kind, considerate and generous young man'.[47]

Haigh planned his murders carefully, by ordering sulphuric acid (10 gallons in the case of Mrs Durand-Deacon) from industrial suppliers prior to each murder. Once having killed a victim he would strip them of any valuables, place them in a specially treated oil drum and then use a stirrup pump to feed the acid into the drum. The process of dissolution would take several days. If he was at his Gloucester Road address, he would then tip the sludge down the drain; at Crawley he tipped it out into the yard outside the workshop (there was a fence around it to prevent prying eyes). He learnt on the job; for his first murder he nearly choked on the fumes as the acid reacted with human flesh, but for his later murders he wore a gas mask (taken from Dr Henderson) and rubber gloves to protect himself from the acid and the fumes.[48]

However, Haigh had a superiority complex, as many serial killers do. Having killed five times already and not been suspected, he had no doubt that he could carry on. Yet in the case of Mrs Durand-Deacon she was missed almost immediately by her friend Mrs Lane. Mrs Lane contacted the police and they found clues. Haigh had left the documentation from his first five victims and the dry cleaners' receipt at the workshop in Crawley. He had not entirely destroyed his final victim. These failings led to his arrest. And once her disappearance was reported in the press, Arnold Burlin, Rose's brother, read about it and contacted the police, as had similarly occurred in the Brides in the Bath murders.

Haigh's letters to his parents and his autobiographical writings in prison shed light on his character. He did not see himself as a common criminal and looked down on both his fellow convicts and the prison officers, remarking after his trial, 'I have no desire for protracted conversation below my intellectual level'. He complained that his victims were not his real friends and that he would do anything for his real friends. He claimed to prefer animals to people, telling a doctor, 'if I were driving a car and was in a situation where I had to choose between hitting a man or a dog, I should always choose the man. I think the doctor was a little surprised'. He likened himself to both Christ and Hitler, claiming that he was the victim of religious intolerance.

Haigh certainly felt no remorse. In prison, psychiatrists noted, 'He shows no remorse… He is quite unconcerned with the rights and feelings of others'. Of the Hendersons, Haigh wrote, 'But we were never great friends. I never had any great affection for any of my eventual victims'.[49]

Haigh was a psychopath, but not a sadist. Unlike most serial killers he cared nothing for power, sex or cruelty. In this he was like Smith (whom he admired), as well as being like him in another respect: mean with money. Money was what he wanted and that is what he got. He had no empathy for his victims and disliked the word murder. So, in this, he was a very typical serial killer. He had killed more people than any known British serial killer so far in the twentieth century and had disposed of the bodies (or tried to) in a novel manner. The term 'Vampire Killer' was used for him, but he is better known as 'the Acid Bath Murderer'.

Chapter 8

The Christie Murders, 1943–53

Ten Rillington Place in Notting Hill was already known as a house where murder had been committed when Beresford Brown moved in as a tenant in 1951. In December 1949 police had found the strangled bodies of 20-year-old Beryl Evans and her daughter, Geraldine Evans, aged thirteen months, in the outhouse in the backyard. Beryl's husband, Timothy, was subsequently hanged for murder. Yet everyone needs a roof above their heads and otherwise the house fitted the bill. Certainly, with post-war housing shortages, there was no lack of tenants, despite the crowded condition of the little house and the high rents demanded by the landlord.

When Beresford Brown entered the little kitchen, which adjoined the back garden, he had no idea that he was about to make a terrible discovery that would cause reverberations on a national scale. As he later stated:

> I was going to fix some shelves in the kitchen and knocked the wall first above what appeared to be a door and then just at the top of it appeared to be hollow. I then took a torch and tore the top corner of the paper away. I shone my torch through the hole I had made and saw the back of somebody's body. I called another tenant and we fetched the police.

Ivan Williams, a fellow tenant, left the house and found a public telephone box at the corner of nearby St Mark's Road. It was about five o'clock that evening when he made the call and then went back to await the police's arrival.[1]

PC Leslie Siseman was one of the first policemen on the scene. Entering the kitchen, he saw a little more of what Brown had found: 'I could see the body of a woman in a sitting position back to the opening with her head and shoulders hunched'.[2] This was clearly murder. Chief Inspector Albert Griffin of F Division, from Hammersmith police station, arrived to take charge and he summoned Dr Francis Camps (1905–72), a pathologist. They were to make worse discoveries.

The small recess in the kitchen yielded not just one corpse, or even two, but three. Camps reported of the corpses that:

One was on its back with the legs vertical against the back of the cupboard. It was wrapped in a blanket, tied round the ankles with a piece of wire, and the torso covered with earth and ashes.

Another body, also wrapped in a blanket and tied round the ankles with a sock, was lying on top of the other in a similar position and also covered with earth and ashes.

The third body was sitting in an upright position and kept in that position by her brassiere, to the back of which was tied the end of the blanket from the feet of the middle body.[3]

Veteran policemen were shocked at what they had found. But the house had not yielded up all its secrets, as Dr Camps explained:

Later that night I examined the front room on the ground floor and noticed some loose boards in the middle of the room. I lifted the boards and completely buried in earth and rubble was another body wrapped in a blanket.[4]

The police initially had no idea who the corpses were, though the first three were young women and the last to be found was a middle-aged woman. However, the man who might well be able to assist them was the previous tenant of these ground-floor rooms who had left the house on 20 March, destination unknown. The police therefore issued a description of John Reginald Halliday Christie, which was circulated to the newspapers and published on the following day:

Aged 55, height 5ft 9in, slim build, dark brown hair thin on top, clean shaven. Sallow complexion, long nose, wearing horn rimmed spectacles, dentures, top and bottom, walks with military bearing. Wearing a dark blue herring bone suit, brown leather shoes, fawn belted raincoat, and brown trilby hat.[5]

On the following morning the four corpses were taken to Kensington mortuary so that Dr Camps could perform post mortems on them. His findings revealed that of the three bodies found in the kitchen recess, two had died in January and one in early March. All three had been gassed and raped, but the cause of death was strangulation. Each wore a type of diaper. One of the victims had an extremely large amount of alcohol in her body, another had a little, and was also found to be six months pregnant. The woman from the front room had been dead for rather longer. She had been strangled as well, but neither gassed nor raped. All but the most recent corpse had had their faces covered. Thankfully the identities of all four victims were quickly ascertained.[6]

First there was Kathleen Maloney, born in Plymouth in 1926 and an orphan by the age of three. She had drifted into a life of prostitution while in her teens and had continued in this lifestyle for the remainder of her life. Her relatives did not want to know her. She had lived chiefly in London and then Southampton, giving birth to five children, and had a long record of petty crime. In 1952 she moved to London and also made money by posing naked for photographers. She often frequented pubs near Paddington station to pick up clients. She had last been seen just after Christmas but no one had reported her as missing.[7]

The second victim was Rita Elizabeth Nelson, born in Belfast in 1927. Her parents had separated and she had a record of petty crime, including prostitution and theft. She had had a baby and had spent time in a mental hospital. In October 1952 she came to London with her cousin. Eventually she rented a room in Shepherd's Bush. Although she was pregnant again, she had a variety of brief menial jobs. Her landlady reported her missing to the police at Hammersmith police station on 19 January.[8]

The third victim was Hectorina Mackay Maclennan, born in Glasgow in 1926. In 1948 she and the rest of the family joined her father in London, living in Kensington. She had two children with a man in the Burmese Air Force. Unlike the two young women mentioned previously there is no record that Hectorina was involved in prostitution, nor did she have a criminal record. Like them, though, she had a number of menial employments. In 1951–52 she was childminder for Alexander Pomeroy Baker's children and he left his wife for her. He had not seen her since 6 March 1953 but had not reported her missing, because she was often known to disappear for various periods of time.[9]

Finally, the older woman was Ethel Christie, née Simpson, the wife of the missing tenant. She had been born in Halifax in 1898 and had married John Christie there in 1920. They were childless and had separated in 1923, reuniting a decade later. She had worked in a secretarial capacity but became a housewife when reunited with her husband. Neighbours in the street knew her well and knew that she had complained about being harassed by the new tenants at 10 Rillington Place. No one had seen her since before Christmas; her husband had told neighbours that she was with relatives in Sheffield.[10]

Meanwhile, a search of the premises continued and spread to the back garden, which was strewn with rubbish. On 27 March the search there began to unearth human bones. Three days later it was possible to reassemble these into two human female skeletons, though one was missing its skull. It seemed, therefore, that six women in all had been killed and concealed at the house, but the identity of the two skeletons, who clearly had lain there for some years, was initially unknown. One clue was that the skull in the garden showed indications that dentistry in central Europe had taken place.[11]

More strange discoveries were made. One item found in the back garden was a small pastille tin in which were four clumps of female pubic hair. It was never ascertained who these belonged to. Certainly they were not from any of the four bodies found in the house. The tin belonged to the former tenant, Christie. There was also a square glass container with a screw top lid and two rubber tubes emanating from it.[12]

More pressing was the need to locate the missing former tenant. It was soon found that after leaving the house on 20 March he had gone to a men's hostel called Rowton House in north London, signing in under his own name. However, he left there on 24 March. His relatives in the north of England were contacted, but to no avail. There were numerous sightings of him, not only in London, but throughout Britain and even abroad.[13]

The newspapers were able to have a field day with these murders and reported them with great prominence – except *The Times*, which only had a few paragraphs tucked inside, not giving it top billing. *The Daily Mirror* had headlines such as 'Three women dead in house of murder' and later 'Race against time to trap horror killer'. *The Sunday Pictorial* followed suit; 'Another Body is found' and 'The House of Death yields new secrets'. More dramatically *The News of the World* referred to 'the Ripper of Rillington Place', (a clear comparison to the Jack the Ripper murders of 1888) and claimed he was worse than murderers John Haigh or Gordon Cummins.[14]

There was also concern that there might be more murders, and this was encouraged by the press. *The Sunday Pictorial* claimed 'the sex strangler of Notting Hill may strike again' and that the murderer was 'one of the most dangerous of modern time murderers'. One theory argued he was mad and motivated by the phases of the moon. Since there would be a full moon on 30 March, then that might be when he would kill again. No woman was safe.[15]

The dénouement when it came was an anti-climax. At about nine o'clock in the morning of 31 March, PC Thomas Ledger, on his regular Putney beat, saw a man who looked homeless. Unshaven and unkempt, he stood by Putney Bridge, looking at a barge being loaded. Ledger recalled, 'I saw a man leaning over the embankment with his hands resting on the wall itself. He was unkempt. I first noticed he was wearing glasses and from a side view thought he resembled the man Christie'. Ledger approached the man and asked:

'What are you doing, looking for work?'
'Yes, but my employment cards haven't come through yet'.
'Where are you from?'
'Paddington'.
'What is your name and address?'
'John Waddington, 35 Westbourne Gardens'.
'Have you anything on you to prove your identity?'
'Nothing at all'.

Ledger asked the man to remove his hat and he complied. It was then that Ledger knew that the man before him was the man that the police were searching for. Summoning two other constables, they took him to Putney police station and he accompanied them without any fuss.[16]

At 9.15am they arrived at the station. It is probable that Christie was pleased to be there, as he had not eaten for four days and had been wandering around London since leaving Rowton House a week previously. After eating breakfast, Inspector Edward Kelly asked him, 'Are you John Reginald Halliday Christie?' and he agreed that he was. Christie was then told that he would be taken to Notting Hill police station where he would be charged with the murder of his wife. To this he said nothing. Kelly searched him. In his wallet was his identity card, his rent book, his marriage certificate, National Insurance papers, his St John Ambulance card, his trade union card, his ration book and a news cutting about the trial of Timothy Evans, in which he had been a witness for the prosecution. His only money was a halfpenny, a threepenny piece and a bent florin. He was grateful to his captors, later writing 'I wish to state that I am grateful to the police in charge for the kindly way in which I have been treated at Putney Police Station. There has been no act of any kind to force me to say or do anything'.[17]

Later that day, at Notting Hill police station, Griffin took a statement from Christie, which gave the latter's version of events as to the deaths of the four women whose bodies had been found in the house. He said:

> My wife had been suffering a great deal from persecution and assaults, from the black people in the house, No.10 Rillington Place, and had to undergo treatment at the doctor's for her nerves. In December, she was becoming very frightened… and was afraid to go about the house when they were about, and she got very depressed.
>
> On December 14 I was awakened at about 8.15am. I think it was my wife moving about in the bed. I sat up and saw she appeared to be convulsive. Her face was blue and she was choking. I did what I could to try and restore breathing, but it was hopeless. It appeared to be too late to call for assistance, that is when I could not bear to see her so. I got a stocking and tied it round her neck to put her to sleep.
>
> Then I got out of bed and saw a small bottle and a cup half full of water on a small table near the bed. I noticed that the bottle contained two pheno-barbitone tablets and it originally contained 25. I then knew she must have taken the remainder. I got them from the hospital because I couldn't sleep. I left her in bed for two or three days and didn't know what to do. Then I remembered some loose floorboards

in the front room. I had to move a table and some chairs to roll the lino back about half way.

Those boards had been up previously because of the drainage system. There were several of these depressions in these floorboards. Then I believe I went back and put her in a blanket or sheet or something and tried to carry her. But she was too heavy and so I had to sort of half carry her and half drag her and put her in that depression and cover her up with earth. I thought that was the best way to lay her to rest. I then put the boards and lino back. I was in a state and didn't know what to do, and after Christmas I sold all my furniture.[18]

Christie appeared emotionally affected by having to recount the death of the woman he had been married to for 32 years and was crying. Yet some of his account was deceitful and self-serving; his wife had not been taking the pills that he claimed she was and the law does not recognise mercy killing by an allegedly loving husband. He then went on to the deaths of the three women found in the alcove in a like manner. According to him:

One evening I went up Ladbroke Grove to get some fish and chips for the animals. I had a dog and cat. On the way back, on Ladbroke Grove, a drunken woman stood in front of me and demanded a pound for me to take her round the corner. I said 'I'm not interested and I haven't got money to throw away'. I'm not like that. I haven't had intercourse with any woman for over two years, my doctor will tell you that. She then demanded 30 shillings and said she would scream and say I had interfered with her if I didn't give it to her. I walked away as I am so well-known round there and she obviously would have created a scene. She came along. She wouldn't go, and she came right to the door still demanding thirty shillings. When I opened the door she forced her way in. I went to the kitchen, and she was still on about this thirty shillings. I tried to get her out and she picked up a frying pan to hit me. I closed with her and there was a struggle and she fell back on the chair. It was a deck chair. There was a piece of rope hanging from the chair. I don't remember what happened, but I must have gone haywire. The next thing I remember she was lying still in the chair with the rope round her neck. I don't remember taking it off. It couldn't have been tied. I left her there and went into the front room. After that I believe I had a cup of tea and went to bed. I got up in the morning and went to the kitchen and washed and shaved. She was still in the chair. I believe I made some tea then. I pulled away a small cupbord in the corner and gained access to a small alcove. I knew it was there because a pipe burst during the frosty weather and a plumber opened it up to mend the pipe. I must have put her in there. I don't remember doing it, but I remember pulling away the cupboard because it came away in two pieces. I slung her clothes in the bedroom. She started to undress before she picked up the frying pan. I put the small cupboard back. It wasn't a fixture.[19]

Let us pause for a moment to analyse this account of murder; almost certainly that of Kathleen Maloney, killed in early January 1953. Christie portrays himself as an innocent victim, as a man simply out to eat his dinner and then accosted by a drunken prostitute. Quite why he is unable to brush her off or ignore her is questionable. She then invades his home, begins to strip and then threatens to assault him with a frying pan. Again it is Christie who appears as the innocent victim, merely trying to defend himself. However, he omits to say what the pathologist had found out; that Kathleen had been gassed to render her unconscious, and had been raped just prior to her death. It is also noteworthy that Christie has a lapse of memory, which is convenient for him. To return to his statement:

Some time after this, I suppose it was February, I went into a café at Notting Hill Gate for a cup of tea and a sandwich. The café was pretty full, there wasn't much space. Two girls sat at a table and I sat opposite at the same table. They were talking about rooms, where they had been looking to get accommodation. Then one of them spoke to me. She asked me for a cigarette and then started conversation. During the conversation I mentioned about leaving my flat and it would be vacant very soon and they suggested coming down to see it together in the evening. Only one of them came down. She looked over the flat. She said it would be suitable subject to the landlord's permission. It was then that she made suggestions that she would visit me for a few days. She said this so that I would use my influence with the landlord as a sort of payment in kind. I was rather annoyed and told her it didn't interest me. I think she started saying I was making accusations against her when she saw there was nothing doing. She said that she would bring somebody down to me. I thought she meant she was going to have some of the boys down to do me. I believe it was then that she mentioned something about Irish blood. She was in a violent temper. I remember she started fighting. I am very quiet and avoid fighting. I knew there was something. It's in the back of my mind. She was on the floor. I must have put her in the alcove straight away.[20]

This is his description of the murder of Rita Elizabeth Nelson, who was six months pregnant, though her death cannot have been after 17 January when her landlady found her missing, and it probably took place on the 14th. Again, as with Kathleen Maloney, it is the woman who makes the advances, it is she who asks for a cigarette and makes conversation. Christie paints himself as a passive victim, both here and at his home, where it is the woman who makes suggestions of a sexual nature and then when these are virtuously rebuffed, becomes violent. His violence towards her, as noted by the pathologist, is not mentioned. She just drops dead. The final victim's death was then recounted thus:

> Not long after this I met a man and a woman coming out of a café at Hammersmith. If I remember rightly, I had been to sign on [for National Assistance benefits] that day. The man went across the road to talk to a friend and while he was away she said they had to give up their diggings at the week-end. He was out of work. Then I told her that if they hadn't found anywhere I could put them up for a few days. They both came up together and stayed a few days. They said they had been thrown out of their digs. I told them they would have to go as he was being very unpleasant. He told me that police were looking for her for some offence. When they left the man said that if they couldn't find anywhere could they come back for that night. The girl came back alone. She asked if he had called and I said 'No' but I was expecting him. She said she would wait, but I advised her not to. She insisted on staying in case he came. I told her she couldn't and that he may be looking for her, and that she must go, and that she couldn't stay there alone. She was very funny about it. I got hold of her arm and tried to lead her out. I pushed her out of the kitchen. She started struggling like anything and some of her clothing got torn. She then sort of fell limp as I had hold of her. She sank to the ground and I think some of her clothes must have got caught round her neck in the struggle. She was just out of the kitchen in the passageway. I tried to lift her up, but couldn't. I then pulled her into the kitchen onto a chair. I felt her pulse, but it wasn't beating. I pulled the cupboard away again and I must have put her in there.[21]

This was the murder of Hectorina Mackay Maclennan, which had taken place on 6 March, after she and Alexander Baker had stayed at Christie's rooms from 3–5 March. As with his earlier statements, Christie's victim is the aggressive and unreasonable one and she is the one who initiates violence. As with Rita she just dies without Christie doing anything to her – there is no mention of his gassing, raping and strangling her.

Christie was charged with the murder of his wife by Griffin at the police station at 3.30pm that afternoon. Next day he was brought before the West London magistrates' court and so began a number of appearances in this court as a prelude to trial at the Old Bailey. Witness statements were given on these occasions and eventually a date for the trial was set. Christie was, in the meantime, as a prisoner on remand, placed in Brixton Prison.

Who exactly was Christie? John Reginald Halliday Christie had been born in Halifax on 8 April 1899, the sixth of seven children of Ernest John Christie, a carpet designer at a local mill, and Mary Hannah Christie, née Halliday, his wife. Much of what is known about his childhood comes from Christie himself, in a newspaper interview published after his trial, and so is open to doubt. He claimed that he had a strict upbringing from a father whom he respected but feared, and a loving mother. He went to All Souls Church, sang in the choir, was in the Scouts and attended school, where he did reasonably well, leaving in 1913 to work in a cinema. A neighbour later recalled that he was, 'An ordinary, quiet boy. There was nothing extraordinary about him at all'.[22]

Christie was a member of the St John Ambulance Brigade, like his father, and had certificates to show his skill in First Aid. He was also a lover of animals and cared for the animals of others. He was a keen amateur photographer and in later life an active trade union representative who voted Labour. Despite his high IQ, his intellectual tastes were low brow, reading the *Daily Mirror* and *The News of the World* as well as Westerns and thrillers. He was a chain smoker and was constantly visiting his doctor. Although he was a loner, he was not without a sense of humour and could be an interesting conversationalist when he chose.[23]

During the First World War Christie served as a private in a battalion of the Nottinghamshire and Derbyshire Regiment. Posted to France in April 1918 he was injured in July by a shell and mustard gas, so spent most of the remainder of the war in hospitals. He was never blinded, however, despite later claims that he was, but his vocal cords were affected and he was able to claim a wounds pension for two years after the war's end. He was deemed to have had a good character when in the army. In 1919 he was employed as a clerk at Sutcliffe's mill in Halifax and married Ethel Simpson in 1920.[24]

Christie had a criminal record dating back to 1921. In that year he was employed as a temporary postman in Halifax. He began stealing cheques and postal orders to the value of over £700 from the letters he was entrusted with delivering. Arrested, he appeared before the magistrates' court and was sentenced on 12 April to three sentences, each of three months, to run concurrently; the sentence was light because it was a first offence and he bore a good character (allegedly teaching at a Sunday School). Two years later he was in trouble with the law again. He was staying in bed and breakfast accommodation in Halifax without having the money to pay his bill. This time, at the same court, on 15 January 1923, he was put on probation for a year.[25]

Christie left Halifax after stealing from his parents and after a brief spell in Manchester he gravitated to London where he would spend the rest of his life.

He joined the RAF at Uxbridge and also worked in the Empire cinema there. Bad health led him to leave the service. He returned to a life of crime, stealing a bicycle outside a school and taking money and other items from the Uxbridge cinema he used to work in. Arrested in Southall Park, he was sentenced at Uxbridge court on 22 September 1924 to nine months in Wandsworth Prison for theft, this time with hard labour.[26]

Later Christie was employed in a number of jobs, including as an electrician and a lorry driver. In 1929 he was living with Mrs Maud Cole and her son at 6 Almeric Road, Battersea. It seems that he was out of work on 1 May when the two had words. Christie struck her on the head with her son's cricket bat. He claimed that it was an accident, and that he had merely been practising his cricket, but the court deemed it 'a murderous attack' and he was sentenced to six months hard labour at Wandsworth Prison.[27]

Christie then took another job as a lorry driver and it was then that he committed his fifth crime, stealing a motor car belonging to the company. He was apprehended in Buckinghamshire on 23 October 1933 and tried to evade responsibility. As in 1924 he was taken before the Uxbridge magistrates' court and found guilty of theft. He was sentenced to three months in prison, spent in Wandsworth, as before.[28]

Christie was reunited with his wife in about 1934 and they lived together thereafter, firstly at 23 Oxford Gardens in Notting Hill and then from at least 1937 in rooms at nearby 10 Rillington Place, eventually acquiring the three rooms on the ground floor in 1938. Christie was employed as a foreman at the Commodore cinema in Hammersmith and is not known to have committed any crimes in these years.[29]

During the first years of the Second World War, Christie was employed as a war reserve constable at Harrow Road police station, where he seemed to be quite efficient, gaining two commendations. However, he also had an affair with a female colleague and saw prostitutes at this time. At the end of 1943 he changed jobs and began to work at Ultra Electric Ltd on Western Avenue, Acton, west London, being employed as a despatch clerk and a driver. In 1946 he was once again employed in the postal service, despite being sacked after his conviction for theft in 1921. In 1950 he was employed as a clerk for British Road Services, a post he held until December 1952 when he quit his job.[30]

To return to the murders, the two skeletons in the back garden were eventually identified. The headless victim was Muriel Amelia Eady, who had been born in 1912. She had lived in Acton and then moved to her aunt's house at 12 Roskell Road, Putney. By 1944 she was employed on the assembly line at Ultra Electric Ltd. She was last seen by her aunt on 7 October 1944 and was assumed to have been killed in the bombing.[31]

The other was Ruth Fuerst, born in 1922 in Austria, who had fled Nazi persecution to arrive in Britain in 1939. She had numerous jobs and lived in various places in England during the next few years. In 1942 she had a baby by a Cypriot waiter, who was adopted. In 1943 she was employed in a munitions factory and lived in a room at 35 Oxford Gardens, not far from Rillington Place. She had been reported missing in August 1943.[32]

On 5 June, having been told about the two skeletons in the garden, Christie made another statement:

> When I was in the Police War Reserve I met an Austrian girl in the snack bar at the junction of Lancaster Road and Ladbroke Grove. I was off duty at the time and I used to go into the snack bar to see if I could find a man who was wanted for theft. It was in the summer of 1943. I was living in the ground floor flat of 10 Rillington Place, and my wife was away in Sheffield. The only other person living in the house was a Mr Kitchener who lived on the first floor. The Austrian girl told me she used to go out with American soldiers and one of them was responsible for a baby she had previously. I got friendly with her and she went to Rillington Place with me for two or three times.
>
> I have seen photographs in a newspaper recently of a girl named Ruth Fuerst. I could not recognise the photograph but I remembered that her name was Fuerst. I do not recognise the photograph now shown to me. She was about twenty four, I think. She was very tall, almost as tall as me, and I was five feet nine inches. She was dark. She told me she lived in Oxford Gardens. One day when this Austrian girl was with me in the flat at No.10 Rillington Place, she undressed and wanted to have intercourse with me. I got a telegram whilst we were there, saying that my wife was on her way home. The girl wanted us to team up together and go right away somewhere together. I would not do that. I got on the bed and had intercourse with her. While I was having intercourse with her, I strangled her with a piece of rope. I remember urine and excreta coming away from her. She was completely naked. I tried to put some of her clothes back on her. She had a leopard skin coat and I wrapped this round her. I took her from the bedroom into the front room and put her under the floorboards. I had to do that because of my wife coming back. I put the remainder of her clothing under the floorboards too.
>
> My wife came home in the evening. My brother in law, Mr Waddington, came with her. Mr Waddington went back home the next day and during the afternoon my wife went out. I think she was

working at Osrams. While she was out I pulled the body up from under the floor boards and took it into the outhouse (the wash-house). Later in the day I dug a hole in the garden and in the evening, when it was dark, about ten o'clock I should say, I put the body down into the hole and covered it up quickly with earth. It was the right hand side of the garden, about half way along towards the rockery. My wife never knew. I told her I was going to the lavatory. The only lavatory is in the yard, I buried all the clothing in the garden.

The next day I straightened the garden up and raked it over. There was an old dustbin in the garden with holes in it which I used for burning garden refuse. When I was burning some rubbish, I got the idea into my head to burn the clothing, and what I could pull out I put into the dustbin and burnt it. Months later I was digging in the garden, and I probably misjudged where it was, or something like that. I found the skull and put it in the dustbin and covered it up. I dug a hole in the corner of the garden and put the dustbin in the hole about 18 inches down. The top of the dustbin was open, and I still used it to burn any rubbish.[33]

As with his earlier statements, Christie tries to put the blame on his victim; it is she who is making unreasonable demands on him, which he cannot comply with. It should be noted that he also implies that Ruth was a prostitute, at least part-time, and being paid by the wealthier American servicemen, and that she had a baby by one of them. The latter fact is untrue and probably the first; she had no convictions for prostitution and if she was making good money from the GIs it seems odd she would need to turn to Christie to make ends meet, so he was probably slurring her character to make himself look less bad. However, unlike the earlier statement he is explicit that he killed her and explains how. To continue with the statement, however:

> I was released from the War Reserve in December 1943, and started work at Ultra Radio, Park Royal. I got friendly with a woman named Eady, who was about 30. She used to live at Putney. I took this woman and her man friend to Rillington Place and introduced them to my wife. They came several times together and had tea, and on one occasion we all went to the pictures together.
>
> On one occasion she came alone. I believe she complained of catarrh, and I said I thought I could help her. She came by appointment when my wife was out. I believe my wife was on holiday. I think I mixed some stuff up, some inhalants, Friar's balsam was one. She was in the kitchen, and at the time she was inhaling with a square

scarf over her head. I remember now, it was in the bedroom. The liquid (inhalant) was in a square glass jar with a metal screw top lid. I had made two holes in the lid and through one of the holes I put a rubber tube from the gas into the liquid. Through the other hole I put another rubber tube, about two feet long. The tube didn't touch the liquid. The idea was to stop what was coming from smelling of gas. She inhaled the stuff from the tube. I did it to make her dopy. She became sort of unconscious and I have a vague recollection of getting a stocking and tying it round her neck. I am not too clear about this. I have got them confused. It may have been the Austrian girl I used the gas on. I don't think it was both. I believe I had intercourse with her at the time I strangled her. I think I put her in the wash house. That night I buried her in the garden on the right hand side nearest the yard. She was still wearing her clothing.[34]

This statement is quite illuminating as it is a description of how Christie committed this, and his last three murders. It also shows how he lured his victim to his house.

As if all this was not enough, Christie made another statement to the police concerning another murder he claimed he committed. This took place in November 1949 and the victim was his fellow tenant, Beryl Evans. Christie alleged that she wished to commit suicide and he agreed to help her in return for sex. He went to her room and, so he said:

I got on my knees but found I was not physically capable of having intercourse with her owing to the fact that I had fibrositis in my back and enteritis. We were both fully dressed. I turned the gas tap on and as near as I can make out, I held it close to her face. When she became unconscious, I turned the tap off. I was going to try again to have intercourse with her but it was impossible. I couldn't bend over. I think that's when I strangled her. I think it was a stocking I found in the room. The gas wasn't on very long, not much over a minute, I think. Perhaps one or two minutes. I then left her where she was.[35]

This is clearly an inaccurate account, for several reasons. The post mortem examination on the corpse revealed no tell-tale marks of pink on the skin which is evidence of gassing. Nor did an exhumation in 1953. Christie makes no reference to the blows found inflicted on the body either; the four corpses found in the house showed no such signs. Had there been an attack of this nature Beryl would have cried out and at that time the house was full of people; workmen and Ethel Christie. Without gas it is hard to see how such a physically weak middle-aged man of sedentary occupation could have killed a young woman fighting for her life and it is impossible that he could have done so silently. This assumes that Beryl was even in the house at the time for there is good evidence that she was out with her baby in the pram as is common for young mothers.

Peter Thorley was Beryl's younger brother and a frequent visitor to see his sister at 10 Rillington Place. Apart from enjoying tea and sticky buns, playing cards and discussing contemporary events with the friendly Christies, he enjoyed seeing his elder sister and his niece Geraldine. She told him that her husband was a drunken, violent lout who often knocked her about so much that Peter was very worried about his sister's safety. She even gave him her wedding ring on the grounds that her husband would just sell it to buy booze. He has no doubts about Evans's guilt, which has been backed up by those who have carefully investigated the case.[36]

Yet Christie, like Haigh, probably felt the need to add to his 'body count' in order to seem insane and thus save his own life. Adding more victims to his total would not complicate his case and could even help it. As he said, 'the more the merrier'.

Christie was tried for the murder of his wife at the Old Bailey on 22 June 1953 and the trial lasted for four days. His barrister, Derek Curtis-Bennett, was paid for by *The Sunday Pictorial* in return for an exclusive story by Christie. As in the case of Haigh, the defence did not lead with a plea of not guilty, but one of guilty but insane.

This was a high-profile case which attracted immense public interest. The Attorney General led the case for the prosecution on the charge that Christie murdered his wife. Numerous witnesses came forward and were questioned to establish that there was a great deal of circumstantial evidence to show that Christie had indeed committed the crime.

Gladys Langford followed the trial, noting that 'The evidence of the court shows Christie to have been a most bestial man... I shouldn't be surprised if the jurors will be so nauseated by the accounts of Christie's doings that they will find him guilty and turn down the plea of insanity. He is clearly not normal and if hanged will be of little loss to the community'.[37]

The prosecution showed that Christie had concealed his wife's death from family and neighbours. He had taken money from her bank account but otherwise acted rationally. Under examination he was asked, 'You knew perfectly well at the time that you had done something wrong, and that you must not be found out if you could help it?' He replied with a typically evasive and hazy answer, 'Well, I do not know'. He was then asked, 'Christie, if on 14th December when you killed your wife in the bedroom, there had been a policeman there, you would not have done it, would you?' His answer scuppered his case, 'I don't suppose so. That's obvious'.[38]

Dr Jack Hobson, psychiatrist at the Middlesex Hospital, then gave evidence for the defence, arguing that Christie had been suffering from mental disease since his wartime injuries in 1918. Two psychiatrists were put up by the prosecution to rebut Hobson's arguments, arguing that he was 'a highly abnormal character, rather than a victim of disease'. After the closing speeches and the judge's summing-up, the jury retired to consider their verdict. They were away from the court for 80 minutes and so, unlike the jury at Haigh's trial, there was clearly some debate over the verdict. On the jury's return the foreman gave the unanimous decision that Christie was guilty. When asked if he had anything to say, Christie said nothing.

Once Christie had been found guilty, his fate was sealed. There was, as with Haigh, no appeal. He was, however, questioned by John Scott-Henderson, a barrister who was conducting an enquiry concerning a possible miscarriage of justice over whether Timothy Evans had killed his wife and child. As Gladys Langford wrote 'it seems unlikely there could have been two stranglers in one house'. Christie refused to give a straight answer. He was also questioned over a child murder, that of Christine Butcher in Windsor in 1952, which he denied having anything to do with. Christie seemed to have a very limited knowledge that he had done anything wrong; writing a note to his wife's relatives, he put 'an apology for any trouble I may have brought about'.[39]

Christie was hanged by Albert Pierrepoint at Pentonville Prison on the morning of 15 July 1953. A huge crowd waited outside the prison to see the notice of execution be attached to the prison gates. His corpse was buried in an unmarked grave in the prison grounds and a waxwork of him appeared at Madame Tussaud's Waxworks, and one was still there until at least 2012. Rillington Place was renamed Ruston Close in 1954 before its demolition in the 1970s. The site today, rebuilt and remodelled, is known as Bartle Road.

Three further questions are worth asking. Why did Christie commit the murders? How did he do so? And how did he evade the law for nearly ten years?

Christie did not commit his murders for monetary gain, nor for any personal reason. He was not a sadist, for his victims (other than Ruth Fuerst and Mrs Christie) were unconscious when he strangled them. The roots of his murderous desires seem to stem from his adolescent years, as he described in his story in *The Sunday Pictorial*. The teenage years are when most people first become attracted to the opposite sex and perhaps have their first sexual experiences. These are often difficult and embarrassing times. This was certainly the case for Christie. As with his fellows in Halifax he was certainly eager for sexual encounters.[40]

Unfortunately when he did meet a girl willing to have sex with him, he was unable to perform. This story got about his fellows and he was a laughing stock and was known as 'No Dick Reggie'. This humiliation made him feel inferior and created in him a hatred for women. Christie stated 'all my life since I have had this fear of appearing ridiculous as a lover' and said he was 'doubtful of my own sexual capabilities and these fears became very real doubts'.[41]

The other facet of Christie's nature was a fascination with death. As a boy of eleven, when he had seen the corpse of his maternal grandfather, David Halliday, laid out on a table prior to burial, he had an awe and pleasure in seeing the body: 'I was not in any way worried or perturbed'. Christie stated, 'all my life I never experienced fear or horror at the sight of a corpse. On the contrary I have seen many and they hold an interest and fascination over me'. His war service in 1918 and his police service during the Blitz would have led to him seeing numerous dead bodies of those who had died violently.[42]

Thus Christie had a fascination for sex and death. What he wanted was power over women; power that he was unable to exert in any other way. His jobs were all of a lowly nature, despite his intelligence. He certainly enjoyed the murders, writing that after his first, 'She looked more beautiful in death than in life' and 'I remember as I gazed down on the still form of my first victim, experiencing a strange, peaceful thrill'. He may have killed originally on the spur of the moment, but finding he liked murder he could not desist and would continue. After killing Muriel he wrote, 'Once again I experienced that quiet, peaceful thrill. I had no regrets'.[43]

Christie often tried to portray himself as essentially peaceful and gentle, writing 'I gave them a merciful end, the mob should remember that', but in other words he comes across as quite the opposite. He wrote of the drunken Kathleen Maloney, 'if ever a woman deserved to die, you do'. When in prison, he wrote 'You can't help feeling that women who gave you the come on wouldn't be so smug if helpless or dead' and 'Animals and birds are my friends. Women, well, that's different'.[44]

Doctors interviewed him and studied him. As one psychiatrist remarked, his crimes were 'committed to ward off acute feelings of fear produced in him by women'. Dr Matheson, a prison doctor, wrote 'He has, I think, to render a woman with whom he was going to have intercourse, unconscious before he began, lest he prove impotent and again subject to jeers and have it revealed once more that sexually he was not a normal man. Having done it [murder] once and not been found out it tempted him to repeat the act'.[45]

The only exception to this general rule was when he murdered his wife. Christie wanted to kill again but after the coming of peace in 1945 his wife remained at home for most of the time, preventing him bringing anyone back to kill. Sadly, Ethel's days were numbered and after her death he wrote, 'After she was gone the way was clear for me to fulfil my destiny', which is putting it too strongly, but the sentiment is clear.[46]

So how did Christie kill? Christie's statements to the police on 31 March do not provide an adequate explanation of his technique for murder. There are, however, other clues, from women who survived their visits to number 10, from the pathologist and from Christie's own later writings.

Christie did not look threatening. He appeared smartly dressed, respectable and polite. There was nothing in his looks to denote danger. Secondly he was intelligent and had enough of a smattering of knowledge about medicine and the law to impress the average laywoman. He played on these strengths to lure women back to his home, always when his wife was absent (or dead), working on their needs which he claimed he could fulfil, such as ill health in the case of Muriel Eady. He wrote 'My knowledge of medicine made it possible for me to talk convincingly about sickness and disease and she readily believed that I could cure her'.[47] He went to places such as snack bars, cafés and pubs where he could meet women. He met Ruth Fuerst, Kathleen Maloney and Rita Nelson in such places.

The evidence of Mrs Forrest is also important in understanding his technique. He told her at the Panda café in March 1953 that he could cure her migraine as he was a doctor who had been struck off for abortion. They arranged for her to visit him, but she failed to make the appointment and when he saw her again she said she was no longer interested.[48] When he met Mary O'Neill, he invited her back to his flat with promises of money but insisted 'Come along just after dark. I don't want anyone to see you. And don't tell anyone you are coming'. Fortunately once there she told Christie her husband knew where she was, so Christie 'got up and muttered to himself'. She left, unmolested.[49] Not every woman he approached went along with him. Kathleen MacAllum was approached by him and he offered her accommodation but she said 'I walked away as I did not like his looks'. Another potential victim declined his offers, 'I was suspicious of him' she later said.[50]

Gas was crucial to Christie. Physically weak, he needed to render his victims unconscious before he could use them as he would and then kill them (contrary to popular opinion, judging by the evidence of his last three victims Christie was not a necrophile, 'a man who enjoyed sexual intercourse with the dead' as Gladys Langford put it). Quite how he persuaded his last two victims to inhale is another question, for though Kathleen was drunk, the other two were not and this is impossible to answer satisfactorily, though without doubt they were gassed, despite being sober. Christie claimed he would sit his victims down in the deckchair in the kitchen and, as in the case of Rita Nelson, sitting nearby 'I removed the clip on the gas tube... I could see her eyes going a bit strange soon after... When they started getting overcome that is when I must have strangled them'.[51]

Finally, we turn to how Christie could commit murder for so long undiscovered. Christie's first two murders took place during the Second World War, as had Haigh's first three. Murder in wartime was less likely to be detected (especially if there were no corpses to be located) because the police had many more tasks in upholding the numerous wartime regulations, dealing with the general increase in crime and the fact that bombing caused thousands of fatalities. Furthermore, with the young adults of the population being liable to be called up on war-related service, disappearances at short notice were not uncommon. Unless there was any suspicion of foul play there was no reason to think that an adult's disappearance (which is not in itself an offence) needed an investigation. The disappearances of Ruth and Muriel were reported, but little or no action was taken and there is no evidence that Christie was even suspected. It is unlikely that either woman told anyone where she was going.

The fact that these murders took place in London gives them an anonymity that might not have been the case elsewhere. In 1939 London had a population of over eight million people, a number it would not again reach until the twenty-first century. Some of that population was very transient, with people arriving, often for work, moving about the capital, and then leaving. None of Christie's victims were born Londoners; one was Irish, one Scottish, one Austrian and the English victims were all from the provinces.

Also none of the victims came from stable backgrounds. None lived in a family unit and many lacked permanent employment. This meant that if they disappeared they would not be missed and might not even be reported as missing. Ruth lived by herself and had had numerous addresses and employments over the past four years. Kathleen was an orphan and unmarried. She had gone to London, but had not put down roots in her life as a prostitute and she had no fixed abode. Rita was from Ireland; she had a cousin and a sister in London but only saw the latter once and lost touch with her cousin after arriving. She had several short-lived menial jobs. Hectorina had left her family to live with Alexander Baker, who had left his wife; her brother said that he knew nothing of his sister's private life. No one reported the disappearance of Ethel, Kathleen or Hectorina. Ethel's family in Sheffield did nothing about her silence following her lack of communication in December 1952, though she had corresponded with her sister for many years. Unanswered letters were not followed up and because there was no telephone at Rillington Place, there was no easy way to keep in touch. Sadly no family members came to check.

Therefore, when these six women disappeared, no one knew that Christie had any involvement in their deaths at all. Furthermore, since he was able to conceal the corpses in his back garden, under the floorboards and in the cupboard in the kitchen, no one knew that murder had occurred – as in the case of Haigh's victims. No body means no murder investigation in these cases. Of course corpses decompose and smell, but Christie attempted to cover his tracks by liberally using Jeyes disinfection liquid. He had few visitors and for those who did come and noticed the smell he told them that this was because of the insanitary habits of the other residents of the house, an explanation they accepted. Neighbours kept themselves to themselves and failed to notice women arriving but never leaving. Even fellow inhabitants of 10 Rillington Place minded their own business and were not noticing people. Franklin Stewart told police 'I have not heard any knockings or unusual noises in the house'. Ivan Williams told them likewise, 'I have only met Christie on one occasion, and have no idea who may have visited him, or who was supposed to live with him. I have never heard any suspicious noises from the flat or anything to cause suspicion'.[52]

Christie once wrote that he aimed to kill ten women; he killed six in all, from 1943–53, the same as Haigh and the same (probably) as the killer in the next chapter. He was self-righteous and conceited. Yet his end became inevitable. Out of work and having sold all his and his wife's possessions, he could not remain at 10 Rillington Place forever. He had satisfied his lusts by first disposing of his wife and then, master of the three squalid rooms, went on a killing spree, killing three women in less than two months. But it could not last; he would have to leave the place and when he did it would not be long before his victims' corpses were found and when they were, he would be hunted down. He ignored what his reason must have told him would be the long-term result, preferring to indulge his desires in the short term. Killing and disposing of corpses in one's own property is a short-term solution as there are unlikely to be any witnesses in either event, but to leave them there means eventual discovery; doing the same deeds elsewhere is dangerous in the short term but safer in the long term, as seen in Chapter 1 and in the next chapter.

Chapter 9

The Thames Nudes Murders, 1964–65

The last of the accounts of undisputed serial murders in this book is perhaps one of the least well known, despite it being the most recent and with a renaissance of books on the topic in the present century, contrasting to just one in the twentieth. Compared to some of the other cases retold in this book, there have been no TV dramas or films about the murders, though the finding of a naked woman's body in the Thames at the beginning of Alfred Hitchcock's film *Frenzy* (1970) is a clear reference to these crimes, as is the case of a woman found in the river near Hammersmith Bridge in 'The Female Factor', an episode of *The Professionals* (1977). The real murders were the work of another unknown serial killer, usually referred to as Jack the Stripper or the Thames Nudes Murderer for reasons which will become obvious. No one was ever officially charged with the killings, though there have been a few theories about the killer's identity, none, thankfully, as outlandish as those offered for his Victorian counterpart.

The 1960s are often looked back upon nostalgically, especially by those who did not live through them. Football success, fashion, films and music all combine to give the decade a glamorous gloss, added to the general prosperity of the era. Underneath the sheen, however, there was, as ever, a sordid world of vice, made easier for customers who had access to motor vehicles. There was a constant supply of young women coming to London who became involved in the vice trade and who were easy prey for violent men as they plied their illegal (street prostitution was outlawed in 1959) and risky trade. The press in 1964–65 referred to prostitutes as 'vice girls' and, euphemistically, as 'good time girls', compared to the term 'unfortunates' employed in the previous century.

This chapter has been the most difficult to research, for two main reasons. The most important is that though there are forty existing police files on the murders, which are held at The National Archives, these are all closed until 2050 (those for the solved Haigh and Christie murders were opened for public access in 1992). This is not just because the murders were unsolved. It is also because many of those mentioned therein (as suspects for the killer or being questioned as associating with prostitutes or as being prostitutes or criminals themselves) are still alive, or could be. Secondly, the newspaper coverage is limited. This is because newspaper reporting was much reduced compared to their heyday in the nineteenth century or even in the 1930s. Nor was there any official report into the way the police (mis)handled the case, as there was following the Yorkshire Ripper killings of 1975–80. What follows is based on what newspaper coverage there is and other contemporary accounts that have been published, but it must be remembered that most of the evidence for these crimes is withheld and much that follows must be tentative, based on a limited amount of information.

The undoubted series of killings began in early 1964. George and Douglas Capon were brothers in their early twenties who lived at a house in Yeldham Road, Hammersmith, and on the afternoon of Sunday 2 February 1964 they were at the London Corinthian Sailing Club on the Thames in Hammersmith. George recalled: 'My brother and I had gone down to the sailing club early to get the rescue launch ready for the afternoon's sailing. We were both in the launch bailing it out. The launch was lying in the mud by the old pontoon which we don't very much use now. It was low tide. Then Douglas noticed the body wedged under the pontoon. We could see all of the body except the head. When we phoned Scotland Yard it was exactly 1.15. A policeman and a flying squad car arrived together. They got the body out of the river in a tarpaulin boat cover and it was about two hours later before a coffin arrived to take the girl away. I was pretty churned up about it'. Barbara Robinson, a Putney diarist, recorded, 'Body found!'[1]

The body was that of a young woman wearing nothing but a pair of tattered tights, and panties, later found to be her own, were stuffed in her mouth. Initially it seemed that death had been due to drowning and that she had been in the river for two or three days. One of the Capon brothers said 'She could have come down on the previous tide on Saturday. It was a really high tide and when that happens everything moves'. It was not certain at first who she was and where and why she had been killed.[2]

The woman was soon identified as Hannah Tailford (in the *Professionals* episode mentioned above the character emulating her is similarly named Ann Seaford), born on 19 August 1933 in Heddon on the Wall, Northumberland, the youngest daughter of at least four children of retired miner William Tailford and his wife, Anne.[3] She was also known as Anne Tailford, Teresa Bell and Anne Taylor. Since 1956 she had lived in London, latterly with Alan Lynch, aged thirty-three, an ex-billiards hall manager and now unemployed, at 37 Thurlby Road, West Norwood. She had a three-year-old daughter, Linda, and an eighteen-month-old baby, Lawrence, the latter by Lynch; Linda was by a previous boyfriend. Lynch met her when he left the Merchant Navy. He said that she worked in cafés as a waitress in the daytime until 9pm but did not usually return home until 6am. She had spoken of suicide and had asked her child if they wanted 'a new mummy'. Hannah also had a criminal record: five charges for theft and three for prostitution, the last of which occurred in January 1963. She also allegedly took drugs, 'purple heart tablets', but Lynch denied this, saying 'She never took drugs'.[4]

Lynch, who went into Lavender Hill police station on the evening of 4 February, later went to Hammersmith police station for questioning. He had a fairly casual attitude to Hannah's lifestyle, 'I did not care what she did at night as long as she returned to look after our baby during the day when I was at work.' He then described when he last saw her, 'On that Friday I gave her a few pounds and told her not to pay the rent. She didn't come back. I went to all her usual haunts during the next week and failed to find her. But then something happened last Saturday which made me give up the hunt and cease to worry. She had already told me she was having an affair with a man in Shepherd's Bush and intended to get married. Then on the following Saturday a man came to collect her clothes. There was another man she spoke of who lived in Kent. I know the man in Kent was a keen photographer and Hannah had told me he liked taking special pictures'. Presumably these were pornographic (Christie also took photographs of nude young women).[5]

Two weeks prior to Hannah's death she had been seen on four occasions near Charing Cross railway station by Arnold Downton, a railway shunter, and his wife. He remarked 'On the last one we saw her two days before she was found. She said she had been roaming about all day long and felt like committing suicide'. Detective Inspector Frederick Debonall elaborated on her nocturnal activities, 'She was especially known to go in cars' and then would go to Duke's Meadow by the riverside in Chiswick, 'a place known to be frequented by prostitutes for this kind of thing', and where Elizabeth Figg's dead body had been found in 1959. He added 'There is little doubt that this woman was sexually perverted... She used to go to parties where sexual orgies took place'.[6]

Lynch elaborated on these parties, saying 'She used to tell me quite a lot about these activities and the people she met with and in the hours I was with the police I gave them all the names I could. I have told the police there is more in this mystery than an ordinary murder'. He added 'She also told me of a diplomat who ran wierdie parties [orgies?] at a fashionable address in the West End'.[7] An *Express* journalist alleged she was involved with a foreign diplomat based in Kensington, who then left London, but returned later. He was cleared.[8]

Lynch was also going to try and investigate the matter, 'I have a lot of friends in clubs and establishments all over London where the police do not go and I have got all my friends making enquiries to try and get to the bottom of the mystery'.[9] It is not known what progress he made on this.

An inquest was held at the West London coroner's court, which concluded on 22 April. After evidence was taken, Gavin Thurston, the coroner, stated, 'you haven't enough evidence to say this was definitely murder. But then who would strip herself completely naked in the middle of January and jump into the river?'

Suicides have been known to remove their clothes before jumping into the river, so this is not inherently impossible. And there were no marks on the body. She had drowned, after all. The jury returned an open verdict.[10] One theory was that she had been drowned in a bath prior to being dumped in the river.[11]

Dr Robert Donald Teare (1911–79) was the Home Office pathologist who undertook the majority of the post mortems on the victims. He was one of the three leading pathologists working in London after 1945. He had performed the post mortems on Beryl and Geraldine Evans who were murdered at 10 Rillington Place in 1949 and been a leading defence witness in the trial of Donald Hume in the subsequent year. A colleague referred to him as 'a solid, likeable man with a good sense of humour, competent both in the field and the witness box'.[12]

The next victim was Irene Lockwood, alias Sandra Russell, who was found under Barnes Bridge, near Duke's Meadows on 8 April. She was believed to have been wearing a fur ocelot coat when she was last seen in a Chiswick pub on the previous night, but when found dead she was, as with Hannah, naked. She, too, had died from drowning.[13]

Irene had been born on 29 September 1938 at Walkeringham, Nottinghamshire, and came to London in 1958. She was living in a flat at 16 Denbigh Road in Notting Hill and paying £12 10s per week as rent. She may have had another flat elsewhere.[14]

It was believed that she had been taken to the river bank in a car, stripped of her clothing and then thrown in. She had perhaps been in the river for three days before being found in Chiswick.[15] This time the death was definitely believed to be murder. She had been found close to where she had probably been killed.

There was speculation that blackmail may have been involved in her murder and that of Hannah Tailford. Irene was a close friend of Vicki Pender, a prostitute who was strangled in her flat in Finsbury Park in 1963. Her killer had been convicted and gaoled shortly afterwards. Vicki would lure men to nude parties where photographs would be taken and she would then blackmail them and sometimes she was beaten up because of it. Irene was also possibly involved in this racket and the men behind it may have killed her and Hannah, perhaps because they demanded additional money from the victims.[16]

Detective Chief Inspector Frank Bridge, operating from Shepherd's Bush police station, was in charge of the case. He appealed to the public for information.[17] This was a sure sign that the police lacked any credible clues or suspects.

The death of Irene Lockwood posed the question as to how, or if, the two deaths were connected. After all, they had both been found near the same stretch of the Thames. Did the two know one another? They were prostitutes. Both apparently used the same coffee stall at Charing Cross station. Both were naked when found and none of their clothes had been located.[18]

On 22 April Archibald Kenneth, a middle-aged caretaker of Holland Park lawn tennis club on Addison Road, Kensington, who had also served twenty years as a soldier, was at Notting Hill police station. He was charged with the theft of a hearing aid worth £30. He had been drinking earlier that afternoon with a friend who said that he was tearful and seemed depressed. Kenneth told the police that it was 'more serious than that'.[19]

He revealed that on the evening of 7 April he had been on a pub crawl and was drinking in the Windmill pub on Chiswick High Street. It was there that he met Irene Lockwood. The two began a conversation and they left the pub and walked along Devonshire Road to the river. She asked him for money. He recalled, 'I must have lost my temper'. He took her by the throat and pushed her against a wall. She fell to the ground, presumably unconscious. He then removed her clothes and pushed her into the river. Taking her clothes home, he burnt them. He admitted 'Yes I did it, but I was drunk'.[20]

The police took the confession seriously and he was charged with murder at Acton magistrates' court. There were a number of hearings and at the first thirty people watched Kenneth being brought in. It was found that Irene plied her trade in Bayswater and Queensway, a major red light district. She shared a room with Maureen Gallagher. She stated that a man called Kenny had once come around to see Irene. However, he had been tall, young and dark. This Kenneth was a short, stocky and grey-haired 54-year-old. It was not the same man.[21]

Dr Teare, who undertook the post mortem, noted that none of what Kenneth had said was inconsistent with his findings. Yet none of what he found supported it either. Even so, the prosecution thought that there was enough material to have him sent to the Old Bailey on a murder charge and a date in June was set. His defence was reserved, said his legal aid barrister.[22]

After a 55-minute hearing, the case was thrown out of court. Kenneth admitted that his story was merely fiction, born out of him being depressed. He said now that he had never met Irene nor ever been to the pub in question. He was upset because he risked losing his job and the flat that came with it because he had stolen from the club he worked at. He claimed, 'I know now what a fool I was to confess'. It had been a harrowing ordeal and he was glad it was over, though he had lost his job through it as he feared.[23]

There is another reason why Kenneth could not have been the killer. Later in April, when he was under lock and key, there was another murder. The corpse of the third victim, Helen Catherine Barthelemy, was found on 24 April 1964 in an alleyway to a playing field off Swyncombe Avenue, on the border of Brentford and Ealing, rather further from the Thames than the two earlier victims. Christopher Parnell, an 18-year-old groundsman resident in Northfields Avenue, Ealing, was one of the first to see the body and he told the local newspaper, 'When I arrived around 8am I was told there was a stiff in the alley way.

I saw the body. It was face downwards with head on arms. She had black hair. My guvnor and I looked round the sports ground for clues, but didn't find any'.[24]

The woman was naked and had died of asphyxia. Again, there were no marks on the body. Two days before her death, two teeth had been knocked out, as had occurred with Gwyneth Rees, who will be discussed later. Helen, originally from Grimsby, had lived in a house in Talbot Road, Willesden, and had not been seen for some time. Dr Teare was the pathologist on the case. The inquest was opened at Ealing town hall (like Elizabeth Figg's) but was adjourned for a month.[25]

Unlike the two previous victims, Helen may not have been killed near where she was found and this suggests a shift in the killer's modus operandi. If she was killed on 20 April, when she was last seen alive, then the killer must have stored her body somewhere for two or three days before disposing of it, and this was to provide a clue. Flecks of white paint were found on her body. This suggested that she had lain for some time in a garage or workshop. Of course there were hundreds of these in London. Searches were made but without any result.[26]

Helen Barthelemy, alias Helen Paul, Teddie Thompson and Teddie Paul, was the youngest victim so far, born on 9 June 1941 in Ormiston, East Lothian, having been convent educated in Scotland. Her mother was Mary Thompson, now living in Grimsby; she had not seen her daughter for four years and did not know her whereabouts. She had previously worked in Blackpool as both a waitress in a hotel and as a stripper on Blackpool's Golden Mile. At Liverpool Assizes on 10 October 1962 she had been sentenced to four years in prison after she was found guilty of being involved in luring Friend Taylor, a young chef, to the beach for robbery at the hands of others, of £22 10s (he was also badly beaten up), but this sentence was quashed on appeal (had it not been Helen might still have been alive) in the next year as being too severe. Helen had always pleaded her innocence. She was also fined £20 for being involved in a brothel in March 1962. She had arrived in London in August 1963 and rented a room on the ground floor at 34 Talbot Road, Willesden. She was a prostitute and striptease artiste. As with Irene she was tattooed.[27]

Helen maintained her links with friends in Blackpool, as in early April she had rung Mrs Alex Paul, part proprietor of a boarding house and café in Chapel Street, Blackpool. She told her that she had been in hospital after a car accident.[28]

Helen was last seen alive by 28-year-old Mrs Ivy Williams, who had known Helen for three months. She recalled, 'I last saw Helene at ten o'clock on Monday night [20 April]. I know Helene had a visitor in her flat, but I don't know if it was a man or a woman. Helene had gone out to get some fish and chips for her visitor'.

She then left in a hurry, without washing up the crockery and left the door to her room open. However, she was later seen leaving a club with a black man.[29]

It is possible that she might have been the woman seen with a man near a blue Ford van on the towpath at Hampton by a married couple who, assuming they were lovers, quickly passed by. Helen was not choosy as to her clients, but one helpfully gave the police a list of names of those men she knew.[30] Helen was last seen wearing a black jumper with a long neck and sleeves, a tight-fitting dark grey or black skirt, a fawn tweedy mix overcoat with leather collar, and black calf length boots.[31]

It was thought that the killer might have been intending to put the body into the Thames but was disturbed and drove off, placing the body where it was found. It was clear by now that the killer had a car or van at his disposal.[32] Dr Teare conducted the post mortem and concluded that death was due to asphyxia.[33]

Police thought that the killer might have attacked but not killed other prostitutes, so they put out an appeal: 'Police wish to interview any prostitute who has been made to strip and has been assaulted. The identity of any woman wishing to give information to the police will not be divulged and if she telephones Shepherd's Bush Police Station Tel. No. Shepherds Bush 1113, stating she wishes to give information, a member of the special squad of male and female officers will meet her when and where she wishes or she can communicate by letter or telephone to the murder squad at New Scotland Yard'.[34]

Another technique to gain information was that detectives went undercover; the men in jeans and sweaters and the women in miniskirts and high heels, to hunt the killer. Others went to the clubs in Paddington and Notting Hill, showing club owners the photographs of the victims in an attempt to jog their memories.[35] House-to-house questioning also went on in Brentford.

Various motives for the killings were discussed. One was that the killer was a man who hated prostitutes. Another was that he was 'a monster' like John Christie. Or was this the work of a 'vice ring', enacting their revenge on any girl who disobeyed them? One ran a booking service and sent out the girls to the customers. A variant on this was that it was the work of a gang who frequented clubs used by prostitutes. If the latter became pregnant, the gang would fix up an appointment with a back-street abortionist and demand fees in advance from the girl. The abortionist worked on the guarantee that if anything went wrong the girl would be disposed of. It was described as 'an insurance scheme' for the abortionists. It was claimed that all the girls found murdered so far in this sequence had also been apparently pregnant.[36]

By now the newspapers were listing these three murders and ones from 1959 and 1963 as part of the same series. From now on with each new murder a brief summary of the previous ones would usually be listed alongside. The police files at The National Archives include these two in their series of files on the 'Thames Nudes Murders'.

It is not agreed when these murders began, which is similar to the case of Jack the Ripper. Some claimed that Elizabeth Figg, found dead on 17 June 1959 on Duke's Meadow, Chiswick, which overlooks the Thames, was the first victim. She had been strangled and partially unclothed (her handbag, shoes and underwear were missing). There was no obvious motive for her murder. She had been born in Bebington, Cheshire, in 1938, and had been a prostitute who lived in north London, working in Bayswater, but had been driven to Chiswick, either alive or dead and her body put there in the early hours of the morning. The inquest was held at Ealing Town Hall, in the Queen's Hall. Her pimp was questioned and so was the last man known to have seen her alive (a client), but there was no evidence that either were implicated in the crime. It became another unsolved murder, but this was, at least at first, only an apparent one-off.[37]

Then, on 8 November 1963, the remains of Gwyneth Rees, alias Tina Smart, Tina Dawson and Georgette Rees, aged twenty-two, were found in the Barnes council rubbish dump at Townmead Road, Mortlake, not far from the Thames, just across from where Elizabeth had been found, though she was not identified by name until 26 November. The five feet three inches tall woman was dark haired and was originally from Barry in south Wales, born in August 1941, but lived in Stepney, London, from 1959–63, with a brief return to Wales in the summer of 1963. She had then been living in a basement flat at 27 Warriner Street, Battersea, from 8 August to 12 September 1963. She was well known in both the West End and the East End and around the Angel, Islington. She was naked and was another prostitute, though the inquest was not able to state a cause of death, as the body was decomposing when found, and so whether this was murder or not is unclear. It was also thought that she had been in the water for some time. If so, the motive and method were unknown, let alone the identity of the perpetrator. Several young men were questioned about her at Richmond police station and a dossier of her London life was composed. Whether these two victims were linked is another question. It seems less likely that Elizabeth was, on the grounds that serial killers do not usually leave so long a gap between their killings, although the killer might have been in prison/hospital or abroad; for Gwyneth it is less uncertain because the police and public did not have to wait too long for another prostitute's corpse to be found in west London. A man called Terry from Notting Hill was sought in connection with her death.[38]

Meanwhile, in 1964, the killings continued. It was on an Acton street that the body of the next victim, Mary Theresa Fleming or Turner, born in Scotland on 16 September 1933, separated from her husband, was found on Tuesday 14 July 1964, three miles away from where Helen had been found and again some distance from the Thames. George Heard, a 34-year-old chauffeur who lived at 53 Berrymede Road, Acton, left home at ten to five that morning. He happened to look towards the driveway of No.48 and saw what he thought was a tailor's dummy. On close examination he realised it was not and so he called the police. Number 48 is right at the end of the cul-de-sac.[39]

It was assumed a car had dumped the body in the road. Heard had heard a car outside between 2 and 3am and later heard a car door slam. Mrs Dove at No.47 thought there had been a car outside at 2.30. But it was not uncommon to hear cars in the road in the night, though it was not a through road. The local newspaper headline ran 'Stripper strikes in W4' but in reality the killing had taken place elsewhere. The fact that the street has a W4 postcode has led most commentators on this crime to incorrectly assume that the corpse was found in Chiswick (Elizabeth Figg and Irene Lockwood were found dead in Chiswick), not Acton. Yet it is clear by a perusal of a map or electoral register that Berrymede Road is in Acton not Chiswick. The body was not identified for a few days. As with the previous victim, specks of white paint were found on the corpse. She was naked and had been strangled.[40]

Mary's last known address was a ground-floor one-bedroom flat at 44 Lancaster Road (very near to Rillington Place) in Notting Hill; she had previously lived in a flat with two other girls in Leighton Road. She had several convictions for prostitution.[41] She was the mother of Veronica, aged two, and David, nine months. She was last seen alive in Queensway, Bayswater, early on Saturday morning, 11 July and was known to be missing later that day when there was no one to look after the children. As with Helen, she was Scottish and aged thirty-one when she died.[42] Also her body was clearly stored somewhere for two days prior to being taken to where it was found, and it was not concealed.

Mary was last seen wearing a grey blouse and a heavy blue and grey two-piece suit. She also wore a red suspender belt, lace bra and panties, new dark nylon stockings, cheap white plastic shoes, and was carrying a plastic black and white handbag.[43]

By this time the press were referring to the killer as Jack the Stripper, a clear comparison with the Victorian serial killer of Whitechapel who had also preyed on prostitutes in 1888. There was an unfortunate jokey reference to this phrase in June in a newspaper reporting that a young teacher in Acton had received a sheep's carcase from her farmer father in New Zealand and that the parcel leaked blood: 'Could it have been Jack the Stripper's sixth victim?' the newspaper asked.[44] I recall referring to this nom de plume in a crime talk in 2006 and it raised unintentional laughter from the audience, so I had to state that this killer was no laughing matter.

Ten weeks were to elapse before there was another killing. Then on 25 November the next victim was found in wasteland behind Kensington High Street (where Kensington Central Library is now located). This was the most central location in which any of the women had been found. This was Frances Brown, also known as Margaret McGowan, Frances Quin, and Alice Sutherland, yet another woman from Scotland, who had been born in Glasgow on 3 January 1943. She had convictions for prostitution. Unlike the previous two victims, no white paint was found, but she had been stripped and died of asphyxia. She was the fifth woman to die. She had given evidence at the high-profile trial in the previous year when Stephen Ward (1912–63) was on trial as part of the Profumo scandal. Ward had picked up Frances and Vicky Barrett when they were soliciting and took them back to his flat where they were introduced to an Italian artist called Lazzalo. They had posed for him.[45] Ward was a society osteopath accused of living off immoral earnings and before a verdict could be reached he committed suicide. He had been involved with Christine Keeler, John Profumo MP and Captain Ivanov, a Soviet diplomat, which led to Profumo's resignation for lying to Parliament over his affair with Christine and weakened the government.

Frances had three children, aged between five months and six years. One lived with their grandmother in Scotland and one had been adopted.[46] She had lived in Leighton Road, Kentish Town (as had the previous victim) for two years and her last address was 16a Southerton Road, Hammersmith. She was a prostitute working in Notting Hill and Bayswater. She was naked and had been dead for perhaps four or five weeks when she was found by Dennis Sutton of Kensington's Civil Defence Corps, though it is impossible to know when she was put there, as unlike Helen and Mary she was not in open view. Apparently Sutton first saw her head and then found the remainder of her body. It was hidden under rubble and a dustbin lid off Hornton Road in Kensington.[47]

Mrs Kay or Kim Taylor, a machinist of Pembridge Crescent, Notting Hill, may have been one of the last to see Frances alive about five weeks before her body was found. They spent the day together and drank at the Warwick Castle pub, 225 Portobello Road, Notting Hill, on 23 October. This pub was also a haunt of Mary Fleming; both also drank at the Kensington Park Hotel. At 11pm they picked up two men in cars on the Portobello Road. The two women entered a car each; Frances taking the first one. Mrs Taylor recalled 'We were going to follow the first car, but we lost sight of it in the Bayswater Road and did not see it again'.[48]

Frances was last seen wearing a green two-piece suit with a dark fur collar on the jacket, a plain white linen blouse and a blue and white check petticoat, red and pink panties, dark stockings and black suede shoes. She carried a light blue plastic handbag and wore blue gloves. Her jewellery consisted of a silver cross around her neck and a gold ring set with a small pearl and two blue stones.[49]

Important evidence emerged from a woman known as Beryl X, who was presumably Kay Taylor, who had been with Frances as they emerged from the pub to meet their clients. The car that Frances went into was a dark grey Zephyr or Zodiac. The man was aged between thirty and thirty-five; was five feet eight, stocky, with brown hair and a full face. He was clean shaven and spoke with a

London accent. He wore a light tan suede driving jacket with a sheepskin collar and a white shirt. A photofit picture of the man was compiled by the police and published in the press. The women had agreed that if they parted they would meet again outside the Jazz Club in Notting Hill, but tragically Frances never arrived.[50] Of course, it does not follow that the man Frances went with was her murderer; they may have transacted their business and then Frances found another punter who did kill her, as occurred with Helen Rytka, killed by the Yorkshire Ripper in January 1978. Understandably the first man who picked her up would be reluctant to come forward knowing that he would be likely to be charged with murder. However, he could have given crucial information and may have even seen the man and car which picked Frances up.

The man's companion was driving a new grey car too, make unknown, and was aged thirty to thirty-two, five feet ten, medium build, oval face, thinning brown hair. He was wearing a light grey two-piece suit and a white shirt.[51] It is presumed Frances died on 23 October, after she was last seen.

At the resumed inquest on 24 February 1965 the police had to admit that they had no real clues to the murderer's identity. This was despite lengthy interviews and statements taken from thousands of people. Detective Superintendent William Marchant said 'But I regret to say that at the moment there is no real suspect for the death of this woman... There have been certain other deaths in the past 12 months which quite likely have a bearing in the death of this case'.[52]

It was over two months later that there was another murder. Bridget, or Bridie, Esther O'Hara was born in Dublin on 2 March 1937 and married Michael Joseph O'Hara, a scaffolder of 41 Agate Road, Hammersmith, in 1962. She was the eldest of a family of thirteen of Mr and Mrs Matthew Moore of Emmet Buildings, Watling Street, Dublin. The couple had separated in December 1964 but had been reunited just prior to her death. She was last seen alive by him at 9pm on 11 January 1965, when she left home. She said she was going out to call on a friend in Brook Green but never did, and was later seen leaving the Shepherd's Bush Hotel on Shepherd's Bush Green at closing time. It was believed that she had gone with a man in a vehicle and had been killed that night.[53]

Many of Bridget's associates were Irish. She was well thought of, one saying 'Most of us knew Bridie. Some of us knew her simply as O'Hara. She was a heck of a nice girl. Any one of us had only to say we were short of money, smokes or beer and she would help us out'.[54]

Bridget had been missing for 36 days when on the night of 15 February, Gerry Marcangelo, who with his brother Roger ran the Bridge café on Westfield Road, north Acton, was out walking his dog. They went near an electricity sub-station on the Heron trading estate, which is very close to the café. Gerry recalled 'That night the dog would not come away. I had to pull her off'. He did not investigate what his Alsatian was so interested in until the following day.[55] As with Frances, Bridget's body had been concealed and it cannot be known when it was placed there. To be exact, the body was under a blanket of grass and thistles in a two feet space between a store shed on Westfield Road and part of the Central Line railway between North and West Acton stations. It had been covered by a tarpaulin. Leonard Beecham, a factory employee, found the corpse at about 11am. He had walked over the service road off Westfield Road to the Surgical Instruments Company's store shed and happened to look around. At first he thought it was a tailor's dummy.[56]

Police thought that the killer was building up a 'Black Museum' (akin perhaps to that at Scotland Yard, now called the Crime Museum) of items belonging to his victims. This would include their clothes and jewellery, such as cheap plastic handbags, high-heeled shoes, frilly panties and pink G-strings. This would be in a place somewhere near where the murders were occurring.[57] It is not uncommon for serial killers to retain the belongings of their victims as souvenirs so that they can relive their crimes.

When Bridget disappeared, she was wearing a wide octagonal-shaped wedding ring, a cheap white metal half hoop engagement ring with four stones, of which one was missing. She wore a loose fitting grey tweed coat with a herringbone pattern with three buttons on the front. There was a scarf of the same material with a black fringe. She had a black skirt and a fawn cardigan with a red and black mottled blouse. She was not wearing anything when found dead.[58]

Initially the cause of death was unknown, as was her identity. Mrs O'Hara was the last known victim of this unknown murderer. It was noted that the industrial estate where her body had been found was the same place as the factory where the now long-dead serial killer Christie had worked in 1944–45. Up to now Detective Superintendent Frederick Baldock had led the enquiries, based at Brentford police station, and had 150 detectives working with him.[59]

Dr Teare had undertaken the post mortems on all the victims to date. Now it was the turn of Dr David Bowen, pathologist at St George's Hospital. He found that, as with the earlier victims, death was due to asphyxia. The inquest was then postponed from 18 February to a later date.[60]

Shortly after this murder, the police took a man from Brook Green to question at a police station and then searched a garage there. They took a box of clothes from it.[61] It seems he was a receiver of stolen goods, though, not a killer.

Baldock thought that 'The property may be intact or may have been destroyed. Anyone known to have been burning ladies clothing we would like to know about. Outdoor clothes more than indoor clothes, or about the remains of a fire'.[62]

On 22 February the police visited a West End club and spent an hour interviewing a 20-year-old hostess. She told them about a man she had entertained a month ago. He was a prosperous Scottish businessman, aged between forty-five and fifty, grey haired, probably married and a frequent visitor to London. He was well known at West End clubs. The hostess later said 'I had only been at the club a few days when he came in with a friend and asked me to sit with him. I have not seen him since'. Another member of staff said 'This man often entertained hostesses and took them home after the club closed. He is a good spender'.[63]

Anthony John Holland, aged twenty-nine, used to live in Hammersmith and was named as a man the police wanted to interview.[64] He was later questioned and presumably released without charge.

The police made their usual appeals to prostitutes for information. They also decided to have a woman (never named; a young housewife), who looked like the victim, to dress in the same type of clothes (made especially by a seamstress) that Bridget had worn in order to try and jog people's memories. She then paraded in a police yard to be photographed by press photographers for publication. No one was allowed to speak to her.[65]

All the victims were prostitutes who had come to London from other parts of the country, three from Scotland. All were young. None had been killed where they had been found. Many had several aliases. All were short in stature, between about five feet and five feet two inches in height. Dr Bowen added that they all frequented late-night cafés and clubs, solicited their clients from among 'late-night kerb crawlers' and concluded 'their deaths were all attributed to forcible suffocation during violent oral sex'.[66]

All the victims had been found in different police divisions and so different divisional forces had taken over their investigation. Detective Inspector Frank Ridge was in charge of the Tailford enquiry; Superintendent Davies, the Lockwood investigation; Superintendent Maurice Osborn the Barthelemy killing; Detective Superintendent William Baldock the O'Hara case. It was not until 1965 that all these murders came under the purview of one man, Detective Chief Superintendent John DuRose, who as a detective sergeant had played a part in the John Haigh investigation sixteen years earlier.[67]

Police also tried to trace the killer by noting registration numbers of cars which were seen in the red light districts in Bayswater, Shepherd's Bush and Notting Hill where prostitutes were thick on the ground and where men seeking their services 'kerb crawled' to pick up women. Cars which were seen more than three times in each district were stopped for questioning. This was known as flagging. How accurate the officers were in taking down the numbers of cars using notebooks at night is another question (in West Yorkshire in the 1970s they did so by speaking into mini tape recorders). It was very time consuming in terms of manpower and failed to locate the killer, as was also the case in Yorkshire in the next decade. [68]

By this time the police had a clue. The bodies of Helen and Mary had yielded evidence which the first two victims in 1964 had not, as they had been immersed in water. Dirt found on the two later bodies was found to contain traces of the paint used on cars, which would have been put on by high-pressure spray guns. This suggested that the bodies had been stored in a paint spray shop, perhaps, or a garage. There were many industrial estates in west London; the biggest being that at Park Royal, which straddles Acton and Brent.[69]

The police headquarters for the investigation was at Shepherd's Bush police station. DuRose had 600 officers working on the case, including Special Patrol Group men as well as uniformed officers. 'I wanted the whole of west London flooded with police and it was', DuRose wrote. Percy Hoskins, a journalist, wrote, 'There has never been a bigger one in the history of Scotland Yard. They gave du Rose everything they had to give, in spirit and cheerfulness and devotion to duty – a duty that as far as the women police decoys were concerned was highly dangerous and unpleasant – while John du Rose… was an inspiration to them all'.[70]

According to DuRose, writing in his memoirs in 1971, his policy was, in part, to wage a psychological war against the killer, who, he was sure, would be paying heed to anything in the press about his crimes. According to the detective, 'In this war of nerves important clues were leaked in day to day bulletins covering our activities in many areas. The original number of suspects was given at twenty, but these were gradually scaled down until it was revealed that of the three that remained, one was known to be the killer… Without a shadow of a doubt the weight of our investigation and the inquiries we made about him led to the killer committing suicide'.[71]

There is no doubt that the police worked hard in all these cases. In 1966 it was noted that in all 120,000 people were questioned and 4,000 statements were taken. House-to-house questioning took place over 24 square miles of London.[72]

Yet, as Baldock noted in 1966, police were still interested in six people, despite the huge manhunt having been called off in the previous year. They were not necessarily suspects, he told the press. 'There are six persons who we haven't really cleared. There are further enquiries and the situation is being carefully watched… But we have not discovered any person who can throw any light directly on the case'.[73] Police continued to take statements and make reports about the case until the end of August 1965, and for Gwyneth Rees until 1986.[74]

The inquest on Bridget was resumed nearly a year after her death. This was at Hammersmith on 16 February 1966 and veteran coroner Harold Broadbridge was summoned out of retirement to oversee the inquest, because he had begun the hearing at the Ealing coroners' court (now defunct following a reorganisation of the courts) a year before. Dr Bowen gave the medical evidence. He declared that there was some evidence of discolouration and post mortem changes in the body. There were marks of grazing on the left side of the neck and the face. 'She had been partly dressed at the time of her death. She must have lain in a prone or semi prone position for some time after her death and before the rest of her clothing was removed'. However, he was uncertain about the cause of death, 'due to asphyxia due to pressure on the face and neck, more in the nature of suffocation than strangulation'. Such pressure could have been the work of fingers or material.[75]

Baldock then made a statement: 'We haven't any evidence as to where the body has been. There have been certain developments, but nothing authentic or definite'. It was then up to the eight-man jury to decide how Bridget had met her death and that was not difficult. They conferred for less than a minute to decide it was a case of murder by person or persons unknown.[76]

It is usually stated that after Bridget's murder no other murder was ascribed to the same killer (after 1888 two murders were noted as being possibly by the Ripper). However, a trawl through the lists of files at The National Archives reveals that on 28 January 1970 the body of 20-year-old Mrs Ann Smith, from Tooting, strangled, battered and raped, was found in a ditch on the Epsom Downs in Surrey, though she was killed elsewhere. She was thought to have been involved in a 'vice ring'. Some of her clothing was missing. The police apparently linked this to the Thames Nudes Murders – and later to the Yorkshire Ripper. The case was never solved.[77] Geographically it would seem that the association with the Yorkshire Ripper is unlikely; there is no evidence that Sutcliffe killed anyone in the south of England at this time, and the lengthy study on the case by Michael Bilton does not link him to it. On balance, though, the former suggestion seems very unlikely, too, as with the case of the 1889 and 1891 Whitechapel murders for the unknown Victorian killer. It was five years later, with a different modus operandi and a different geographical location, so quite why the connection was made is unknown; perhaps the missing clothing and her occupation led the police to consider the possibility.

The big question, of course, is who was the killer? Some witness statements did describe men seen with the victims or near the places their corpses were placed. Shortly before Helen's body was found a van was seen quickly leaving Sywncombe Avenue. This was similar to one seen near Berrymede Avenue on the morning of Mary's corpse being found there. In the latter case the driver was seen; a young man, smartly dressed. The last man seen with Bridie was described as being a young man too.[78]

Over the years there have been a number of suspects. The man favoured by DuRose committed suicide shortly after the murders ceased. This man worked as a security guard on the Heron trading estate. He was found gassed to death in his garage after leaving a note for his family which merely stated that he couldn't stick it anymore. It is not known why he killed himself. However, more recent research has uncovered his identity and the fact that he was apparently in Scotland at the time of one of the murders, so presumably unless he was working with another man he must be stated as being innocent.[79]

Percy Hoskins, crime reporter on *The Daily Express*, endorsed DuRose's opinion. He considered that the murders had been solved even though the man suspected could not be charged as he was dead. Hoskins was a friend of DuRose and had an uncritical admiration for Scotland Yard and so perhaps this coloured his assessment of the case's conclusion. Not everyone has agreed with this verdict, however, and the majority view is that these murders remain unsolved. Sir Richard Jackson, Assistant Commissioner: Crime, 1953–63, noted in 1966, 'The killer has not, at the time of writing, been detected'.[80]

DuRose's suspect has been subsequently identified as Mungo Ireland (1920–65), who lived in Notting Hill in the late 1940s, then in Hammersmith and by 1962 he resided in Putney, finally living at 132 Westleigh Avenue. He therefore had a good knowledge of the part of west London where the murders occurred. The suicide theory may in part be because in 1959 an influential book by Daniel Farson about the Jack the Ripper stated that the serial killer ended his murders by committing suicide by drowning himself in the Thames towards the end of 1888, although later authors have rebutted this and serial killers rarely if ever kill themselves.

Barbara Tilley was a female detective sergeant during the enquiries and recalled in 1978 that, 'I think everyone had their own ideas as to who was responsible. Nothing was ever proved'. Apparently she thought that it was a famous man who later committed suicide.[81]

The first book on the topic rejected DuRose's theory and posited that a man from the north of England with a harsh father who had gone onto serve in the army and then the police, who had ultra-moralistic views, was the murderer.[82] A similar (and, as it transpired, erroneous) theory came out about the identity of the Yorkshire Ripper in 1979.

Another theory is that former boxing World Light Heavyweight champion Freddie Mills (1920–65), who was found dead in his car in Soho having been shot, might have been to blame. This is based on gossip by various associates of gangsters. He had been a TV personality and a restaurant owner after his boxing career finished, but was in dire financial straits by the time of his death on 21 July 1965. The official verdict is suicide but some believe this was murder.

A more recent theory, also supported by Professor David Wilson, has been put forward that Harold Jones (1906–71) was responsible. He had killed Freda Burnell and Florence Little, both aged under ten, while he was aged fifteen in Abertilly in 1921. He was found not guilty of the first murder but when he committed the other he was found guilty. Escaping the death sentence due to his youth, he nevertheless spent twenty years in prison. After military service in the Second World War he was known as Harry Stevens and lived at Hestercombe Avenue in Fulham, dying in Hammersmith in 1971. While there is no doubt that he had been a murderer of children when a lad, there is no further evidence against him of any other crime. However, he did live close to at least one of the victims and did live in Hammersmith a few years before the main series of murders began. On the other hand Jones was almost sixty years old at the time of the murders and it is not known whether he could drive or had a van or car (at this time not many elderly working men had cars). Most importantly, there is no direct evidence linking him to the victims. He does not match the description of the man last seen with Frances Brown given by Miss Taylor, though of course this man might not have been her killer. [83]

A newspaper story in 1970 asked 'Was the Maniac Killer a cop?' and the journalist stated that 'My view is shared by certain senior officers'. Elaborating, he alleged that a policeman would have detailed local knowledge, could gain the victims' confidence and would know the police plans to catch the killer and so avoid them.[84] Alone among authors, Seabrooke had unauthorised access to the police files on the case and he did not suggest that any of the previous suspects were guilty. His suspect was a former policeman who had problems with his former colleagues and so wanted to make a mockery of them, hence the killings. A major plank of the 'evidence' for this was that each of the bodies was found in a different division of the police force as it was prior to a divisional reorganisation of 1965. The book did not name the man, who was then (2007) still alive, but provided enough evidence to trace him. Again, as with the other theories, there is nothing to back this up, suggesting that the police files contain no conclusive evidence as to the murderer's identity.[85]

The police files on the case are still closed (meaning the case in theory could be subject to possible further investigation), so access to them for the public is closed for decades to come. Only then will a proper history of the case be written and even then the identity of the perpetrator will probably not be known.

What can we conclude with? The killer was a white male and probably young. He had access to a vehicle and could drive. He lived and/or worked in west London, probably Hammersmith, Fulham, Chiswick, Brentford or Acton, which he clearly knew well. He had access to storage facilities which included paint spraying devices. He had a hatred of prostitutes and probably lived alone as he took their clothes as trophies and to remind himself of his deeds (or had premises to safely store these items). The act of stripping them could have been another facet of his hatred in giving these women a final humiliation, as well as possibly suggesting a knowledge of the forensic axiom that every contact leaves a trace and so removing them lessens the risk of capture. These criteria would fit thousands of men in west London.

It is worth noting that the first three victims were found in or near the Thames, while the next three were found some distance away from it. The last two victims were concealed, unlike the first four, and so were not found until weeks after their deaths.

Why the killer committed these crimes is open to question. Why he stopped is also unknown – perhaps he left London, died, was gaoled for another offence or became too unwell to continue. It is probable, over half a century later, that he is now dead, but this is uncertain.

This was a very difficult case to solve, as with the 1888 killings, especially for serial killings where there is no known prior relationship between victim and killer, no discernible personal motive, no clues and no witnesses.

Superintendent Cherill wrote, of similar crimes:

> It is never an easy matter to solve such a mystery when the victim is a woman of the unfortunate class. Her very mode of living gives rise to many difficulties on account of the number of her haphazard men friends and acquaintances. She picks them up at all hours of the night and day, wherever she may happen upon them, and they represent all sorts and conditions of men. They may or may not be known to her and inevitably there is very little to go upon when checking up as to who was with her at the time of her death, or shortly before.[86]

Partly this is due to the lack of clues; the killer removed all his victims' clothes and so there was no chance of finding any traces between victim and killer. The time lag between finding the corpses also even further reduced the possibility of any physical evidence. There was never anything to connect the location where the corpses were found to the killer, unlike with Haigh and Christie where the location of corpses or their remains was crucial. Lack of DNA or any more recent scientific advance (such as mobile phone records and CCTV) was another factor in the killer escaping justice. Nor were there any victims who survived their attacks and came forward to the police to give descriptions of their attackers (that we know of), as there had been in the case of Cummins. Finally the lack of a lucky break and the ability of the killer to halt after killing Bridget O'Hara worked in his favour. In the case of the Yorkshire Ripper, luck finally turned against Peter Sutcliffe. Continuing his savagery gave the police more opportunities to arrest him, and even then that was only due to good luck at him being stopped for an unrelated offence. This was not, sadly, the case in the London of the 1960s.

We should also remember the victims, whose lives were destroyed at tragically young ages, and also their children who became motherless as a result of the murderer's actions. Their story is generally little known as writers seek to identify the killer, but as with the women killed in 1888, we actually know more about them than their killer. The story is as much about them, the innocents, as about the guilty perpetrator who killed to sate his own selfish desires.

Chapter 10
Other possible serial killings in London, 1881–1948

It is possible that there were other serial murderers operating in London in the period covered by this book. Certainly there were a number of unsolved murders in at least four distinct time periods, which were also in the same locality and which featured the same type of victim. They may have been killed by different men, but they may not. It appears that the motive and means of killing were similar in each of these instances.

West Ham disappearances, 1881–99
Jack the Ripper may not have been the only serial killer operating in late Victorian east London. The rapidly expanding (population doubled between 1881 and 1891) parish of West Ham may seem a long way from the cramped streets of Whitechapel, but it was not so geographically and perhaps not in another way. In this decade a number of young girls disappeared from their homes in West Ham; the body of one was found brutally murdered in an empty house, and two more were killed later in the decade. It is not known if those who disappeared were killed or not, and the absence of any police files on these victims impedes any retrospective investigation as contemporary newspapers are the only source of information open to the historian.

There was a degree of panic in West Ham in the early 1880s on account of two similarly aged girls who disappeared without trace from the same district. Mary Seward was aged fourteen when she left her home at 98 West Road in the early evening of 13 April 1881 to find her nephew. She was four feet six, thin and pale, with dark brown hair and irregular teeth. She did not return. A reward of £35 was set for information leading to her return.[1]

On 4 February 1882 Eliza Carter, aged twelve, of Church Street in West Ham, was playing with a friend. It was beginning to get dark and Eliza was afraid of her trip home, as a man in dark clothes and a high hat had, earlier that day, accosted her asking about her mother. So her friend walked with her to within 50 yards of her home (near West Ham Park), close to where Mary had last been seen ten months previously. Empty premises and lodging houses were searched by the police. There was an alleged sighting of Eliza in Stratford later that night, with a middle-aged woman. Eliza's ripped dress was later found near to where she lived, but of her, alive or dead, there was no trace. Again, a reward was offered. Newspaper reports of a girl assaulted in West Ham and another who fought off her attacker gave rise to much local criticism of inadequate policing. Then everything went quiet for eight years.[2] The police thought that Mary and Eliza had shared the same fate.

There was some discussion about these disappearances in the contemporary press. It was thought that there was a systematic series of kidnappings of young women in the district, and men at Victoria Docks alleged that the girls were being lured away by promises of good jobs abroad. Mary's father was informed that there was a man touting in the locality, well dressed, but looking like a foreign gipsy and accompanied by a woman. Sometimes the girls would be offered a sum of money to deliver a letter to an address and they would never return. Some girls were accosted but managed to escape, but remained fearful in the following days.[3] Possibly, though, they had been murdered and given the amount of building going on locally hiding bodies under housing would not have been difficult. Yet, despite the brief possibility of a corpse found in 1883 in London being one of the missing girls (none of their relatives could make a positive identification), the matter dropped out of public view.

Worst of all, however, was the fate of Welsh-born Amelia Jeffs, and this received a great deal of newspaper coverage. She was nearly fifteen and lived with her working-class parents at 38 West Road, West Ham, the same road that Mary had disappeared from in 1881. On Friday 31 January 1890 Amelia went out at 6.30pm, after dark, to the local fish and chip shop. An hour later she had not returned and her parents became worried. They reported her missing at the police station, where it was immediately taken seriously and all officers were told to make searches for her. Unfortunately she could not be found.[4]

On 14 February, as part of a general search of the district, the police decided to look into the unoccupied new houses on the Portway. There was no key to be found for no.126, so a constable entered the house by the back windows. He then let Sergeant Forth enter by the front door. The latter found that a smell came from a cupboard in the house. It was then recorded:

> The door was forced, and a horrible sight met the eyes of the constables, the body of a decaying girl being discovered lying on the floor. The body was in a partial state of decomposition, and upon it being taken from the cupboard, it was found that a piece of rope had been drawn tightly round the neck, causing strangulation.[5]

Amelia had been found. Nearby were the basket and latchkey that she had taken with her. A post mortem revealed that she had been assaulted and then strangled. Further information revealed that these empty houses were supervised by Samuel Roberts, a watchman and father of the builder, 50-year-old Joseph Roberts, and that he had keys to them all. This was important because the door to the murder house had not been forced; someone had used a key. However, Roberts said his key had been missing since November 1889. He also said that Joseph Hotton had been the locksmith who had made the keys. He had made two per house; Roberts senior had one and another was in a box in each house. In May 1890, rather curiously, the missing keys were found in a box in the attic. It seemed that victim and killer had known each other and footprints in the dust suggested they had entered together by the front door.[6] Oddly, the young son of Joseph Roberts claimed to have entered the house on the day before the corpse was found and he said that nothing was there on that occasion.

The murder remained a mystery and the coroner could only conclude that this was murder by person or persons unknown. There was suspicion against one man, but no proof, and this man was never named. Joseph Roberts (senior) and Hotton are certainly possible suspects as both had access to a house key. Samuel Roberts is also a possibility. Quite possibly one of them was lying. Joseph Roberts is perhaps the more likely of the two as he had been a resident of West Ham since at least 1881, whereas Hotton was a relative newcomer. The killer was certainly a man who knew the victim, as the girl would hardly accompany an unknown man to an empty building, and again it is possible that the thirteen-year-old Roberts was a friend of Amelia's and thus she knew his parents, including the father, Joseph. Child killers often know their victim. Joseph Roberts, builder, remained in West Ham until at least 1911, by which time his son had emigrated to Canada.

Two years later, labourer George Herbert Bush of Walthamstow confessed to the crime, claiming to have chloroformed Amelia first. However, there is no evidence of that and he was in prison at the time, so he was dismissed as a serious suspect.[7]

Unfortunately Amelia's death was not the last unsolved child murder in the vicinity of West Ham in that decade. Florence Ellen Rolph was aged six when she was found murdered in the grounds of Rectory Manor, Walthamstow, on 30 June 1895. She had been sent to a nearby pub for some beer and never returned. As with Amelia, she had been assaulted prior to death. Despite extensive enquiries, no one was ever charged with the murder.[8]

On 31 December 1898 five-year-old Mary Jane Voller was murdered, but not assaulted, at Loxford Brook, Barking, which was close to her home, by person or persons unknown. She had been sent out in the evening by her parents to make a purchase from a nearby shop but never returned. Thomas Pyle, a 17-year-old, was suspected and there was even a question as to whether his parents might have been responsible. Both these theories were dismissed and the murderer and their motive remained unknown.[9]

Finally, there was Bertha Hendricka Russ, aged five, who lived with her family at 29 Byron Avenue, West Ham. She had been at the St Barnabas' Sunday School, Browning Road, at 2pm on 19 February 1899 and on leaving at 4pm had been seen with a man. According to Mrs Alice Morris of 146 Browning Road, she thought he was seventeen and they were standing by the church railings, but she did not take a sufficient look at him to describe him in any detail. The child was crying. She then vanished. She was found dead in a cupboard in a house on Lawrence Avenue, Little Ilford, about a mile from her home, on 5 March. She had been suffocated. It was uncertain whether she had been put there within in a few hours of death or some days after as the police had already searched the premises. The similarity between where she was found and where Amelia was found was perhaps not coincidental, though there was no evidence of assault.[10]

These last three victims were considerably younger than those who were abducted/murdered in 1881–90, but this does not necessarily rule out the same perpetrator, because as the killer aged he would be less physically capable of subduing an older child and so turned his attentions to weaker and younger girls. Bertha was the final victim in this series of killings, if series it was. After all, the murders could have been the work of a copycat killer. Not all of them had been assaulted. There is no reference back to the earlier kidnappings/killings of the girls slain after Amelia Jeffs, so presumably contemporaries did not make any connection between them. The interval between 1882 and 1890 and between 1890 and 1895 is also curious as serial killers rarely leave such gaps between their murders, unless they are elsewhere, ill or in prison, or if there is another reason which frustrates their desires.

It is far from certain whether all these crimes were the work of one man. Mary Seward and Eliza Carter were probably kidnap victims not murder victims, unlike Amelia who was murdered. There seems to have been no link made by contemporaries between the first two girls and Amelia. We are perhaps on more certain grounds with the later murders, but they are considerably spread out in both time and location, though there are of course similarities with the type of victim and in two cases, the place where the corpse was found. This could be a copycat killing, however. It should also be considered that the girls who disappeared may not have been murder victims, and certainly contemporary opinion thought not, so perhaps the killings should be considered as having occurred from 1890–99, rather than beginning in 1881.

The Thames Torso Murders, 1887–89

Parts of women's bodies were found near the Thames in the late 1880s and these murders have been seen as part of a series. Since the perpetrator/s was/were never found it cannot be stated for certain whether this was part of a series. However, we shall briefly survey these deaths, which have also been linked to Jack the Ripper.

On 11 May 1887 a bargeman on the Thames near Rainham, Essex, found the torso of a woman, lacking head, arms, legs and shoulders in the river. It was tied up in canvas, and was later thought to be a young woman who had died two weeks earlier. It was thought that some surgical skill had been required in making the cuts.[11] The leg of a female body was found on the Victoria Embankment a few weeks later and as it was wrapped in the same type of canvas and cord as that found at Rainham the two were probably part of the same woman.[12]

On 2 October 1888, Frederick Wildborn was working on the new Scotland Yard building in Whitehall, which had been originally intended as an opera house. He found a parcel among the foundations and later an employee opened it. It contained part of a human body. A leg and a foot were also found. On 11 September an arm had been found at Millbank on the Thames. The head and lower limbs and arms had been removed by a saw and had been there for several days. There was no indication of who the woman was or how she had been killed, though suffocation was possible. The verdict was 'found dead'.[13]

In the early hours of Tuesday 10 September 1889, PC William Pennett saw, on top of a pile of stones under an archway adjoining Pinchin Street in Whitechapel, the trunk of a human body, lacking legs or a head, partially covered by rags. It had not been there when he last passed at 5pm, and it was now 5.25am. Medical inspections concluded that it belonged to a woman aged between thirty and forty, who had been dead for at least one day before being found. There was no reason to think that whoever had severed the head and legs had any knowledge of anatomy. There had been two sailors asleep in the archways nearby but both attested that they were asleep at the time and knew nothing about the body parts being put there. There was no clue to the identity of the woman or her killer.[14]

Many bodies were found in the Thames on an annual basis and for many the cause of death was never ascertained. It does not seem that those at the inquests in 1888 and 1889 made any connection between these crimes, and the last one was not found in the Thames or even anywhere near it. There may be a link between these three deaths, but the evidence for that seems weak.

The Soho Serial Killings, 1935–36?

The next possible series of linked murders was several decades later. Prostitutes are, sadly, a very vulnerable class of people, as we shall see again in this brief survey of murders in the 1930s, for which the police files fortunately still exist. The first woman to die, Mrs Josephine Martin, whose professional name was 'French Fifi', had been born in Russia and was forty-one years old in 1935. She had lived in a flat at 3–4 Archer Street, Piccadilly, since 1933, paying £4 a week rent. She was not in arrears (ironically she had paid up to the day of her demise). Mrs Martin was described as being of a kindly disposition and rather emotional. She had married Henry Martin, an English waiter, in 1919; he subsequently went to America. Mrs Martin employed Felicitie Plaisant as her housemaid.[15]

On Sunday 3 November, Albert Mechanick, Mrs Martin's brother, visited her. He said that she complained of a little pain in her neck. She gave him some money to help him out. However, she told him nothing about her own affairs. Three weeks previously, one Detective Inspector Edward Warren said that Mrs Martin had complained of being assaulted by a man in her flat. Apparently the man, a foreigner, had seized her by the throat, but she had not been injured and she was not afraid of him. Millicent Warren, her neighbour, had overheard her arguing with a client. Mrs Martin was heard saying, 'Come on, give me the money first, bringing me up on a fool's errand and then saying you've got no money, I've got business to do'. Shortly after the man left, Mrs Martin told her neighbour, 'He was a bilk, coming up here and yet no money. What does he take me for. Did he think I do it for love? He pushed me on the bed and I shouted out. I wasn't afraid of him'.[16]

Martin also had other troubles. She owed 40 guineas for one fur coat and eight guineas for another. These debts were being paid off at the rate of £2 a week. She also owed about £20 to another creditor. Her maid thought her total debts were just over £90. Mrs Martin's own money was apparently put in the dustbin, boxes and between the foot of her stocking and her shoe. Marie Wilson claimed to have seen between £1 and £15 in the flat in the summer of 1935. Vera Barrett thought she had seen several pounds and jewellery in the top drawer.[17]

On Sunday evening of 3 November, Millicent heard Mrs Martin having a row with a man, who had just paid her £6. It was about 9.20pm. One John Salter had seen her with a man on Regent Street about an hour earlier, who was aged between twenty-five and thirty, slim, clean shaven, about five feet six and wearing a grey suit. Charles Burgess had seen her on the previous night on Windmill Street, but the man she was with was about forty, five feet ten in height and wore plus fours (then a fashionable type of men's trousers). Presumably he was correct about the date? Even if he was not, it is not uncommon for two witnesses to give differing descriptions.[18]

At 12.30am the following day, Josephine was seen in the Continental Café. Over an hour later, James Weller, doorman of Mac's Club on Great Windmill Street, recalled seeing her. Afterwards, she went to the Olde Friar's Café on Ham Yard, had a coffee alone, and left sometime after 2am. There was a light in her room from the early hours of the morning, though when Millicent Warren knocked at the door there was no answer.[19]

Later in the morning of Monday 4 November 1935 the maid found her mistress dead on her bed. There was a silk stocking with a yellow tassel attached to her jumper, which had been passed twice around her neck and she had clearly died from asphyxiation. Charles Burton-Ball, manager of the Globe Club, which was below the flat, was called to see the body: 'Missus dead. Missus dead. Come up, come up'. He later summoned help, just after midday. Dr Charles Burney, the police surgeon, noted that the dead woman's left leg was bare, with the shoe and stocking removed. Her clothes had not otherwise been removed.[20]

Spilsbury also examined the corpse and found bruises on her abdomen, shins and neck. A thin dental plate had been removed from her mouth and it lay near her throat, in three pieces. He concluded, 'In my opinion, the deceased was forced down upon the bed where she was strangled by the right hand of an assailant. Consciousness was lost almost immediately and she was unable to struggle'. He also thought that great pressure had been used and the attacker had put his knee on her abdomen during the assault.[21]

But although Spilsbury believed this to be a case of murder, there was an alternative view. Although manual self-strangulation is impossible, self-strangulation with a ligature is not. Some witnesses thought she was tired of life. On 18 October she had said, when being fined for soliciting, 'I'm fed up with this life. I've a good mind to finish with it. No money. Can't get enough to pay the fines when we get taken. I'm sick of it all'. Nor were there any signs of disturbance in the flat, which a struggle would have caused, and there was no evidence that there had been an attacker in the room. Her maid recalled that her mistress told her 'of things being none too good', being in debt. James Orr, an old friend, wrote 'She never made a lot of money at prostitution. She worked hard, but did not get many men and could not have had much money'. Inspector Edwards wrote that there were 'many reasons which point to her having committed suicide'. Yet Spilsbury's reputation, rightly or wrongly, carried all before it and it was his conclusion which was respected.[22]

Albert, Martin's brother, was accused in an anonymous letter. This alleged that he relied on his sister for money and she had cut off his supply. 'Why was Albert so frightened when the police let him go from Vine Street? He is still terrified and he might have a good reason for his fear'. Yet he was apparently playing cards with his cronies on the morning of his sister's death. In any case, if he was used to receiving money from his sister, why should he kill her? However, if she had ceased to give him money, he may have killed her in anger.[23]

There were various theories as to why Martin was killed. One was that she was the victim of gang vengeance, allegedly after having given the police information about the activity of a French crime syndicate. There were talks with the French Sureté about her activities in France. Another explanation is that she was killed for her money; perhaps £150 in total. Yet this theory, which relies on her having accumulated a tidy sum, is contradicted by her having known money worries and debts; perhaps her killer believed she had money. Chief Inspector Sharpe of the Flying Squad wrote in his memoirs, 'I believe "Fifi" was murdered by someone she took to her room on a monetary influence. Who the murderer was has not yet been established [he was writing in 1937] and may well never be'.[24]

The inquest was held on 26 November at Westminster and the question of suicide was raised, but Spilsbury said that it had never been known that someone had strangled themselves with their own hand. The jury brought in a verdict of murder by person or persons unknown, such was Spilsbury's apparent authority on matters relating to forensic science. It is not absolutely certain that Mrs Martin was murdered. There are grounds for believing she committed suicide. However, the subsequent deaths of other women in Soho gave added credence to the theory that she was murdered.[25]

The next possible victim was Marie Jeanet Cotton, born in 1892. In January 1924, she married Louis Cousins in Dartford, Kent. Cousins deserted her the following year and he died in 1929. She went to London, being employed in domestic service. In 1936 she was employed as a servant and lived in a flat at 47 Lexington Street, Soho. This was about two minutes' walk from Mrs Martin's abode. She was not a prostitute. Since 1930 she had lived with Carlo Lanza, an Italian cook, and his 15-year-old son Remo, who also worked in a kitchen.[26]

At 1pm on Thursday 16 April, Mrs Cousins finished her work. She went back to her flat and at 5pm she was talking to Mrs Dorothy Neri, a neighbour. Later that day a shocking discovery was made. Remo recalled, 'I got home about nine o'clock and when I entered the flat I called out Mrs Cotton, but got no reply. Going into the kitchen I switched on the light and then I saw Mrs Cotton lying on the floor. I called out to her, but she did not answer and when I touched her face it was cold'. As with Mrs Martin, she had been strangled and there was a silk stocking round her neck. According to the doctor, death had occurred at 6.30pm or perhaps a little beforehand.[27]

Three hours were spent examining the dead woman's room. The door of the flat was removed for scientific examination, as bloodstains were allegedly found on it. Money was not the motive for this murder. Police found £14 in notes and silver in an open cupboard in the room in which the body was found. Nor had she been subjected to a sexual assault.[28]

Initially there were two men the police wished to locate for questioning. One was her estranged husband, who was not thought to be deceased. The other was Harry Cohen, who allegedly paid occasional visits to the flat. Mrs Neri said that Mrs Cousins was very much afraid of one man, 'a Jew man' who had demanded money from her and that she was in love with another man, though he was never traced. She added that on the evening of 14 April she and Mrs Cousins had gone out together and left a note outside the door, with the following written on the envelope, 'Mr Cohen. Shall not be long. Gone to Marlborough Street'. On their return, they found the note was intact. Could he have been the Harry Cohen who was released from gaol in the autumn of 1934?[29]

Then there was James Allan Hall, who had been a neighbour of Mrs Cousins. Hall had been known to be violent. In 1935 and early 1936 he lived in one of the rooms in Lexington Street. He was homosexual and often invited men back to the flat. Between them, they had damaged a mattress belonging to Mrs Cousins and the latter wanted compensation for this. Hall and Mrs Cousins had arranged to meet on the day before the murder, but it appears they did not do so. Therefore, he had a motive of a kind, and although he claimed that he spent the evening of 16 April in cinemas and pubs in Charing Cross Road, 'it is impossible to verify in every detail the truth of what he says'.[30]

Another suspect was Lanza. According to Neri, he and Mrs Cousins had 'frequent quarrels' and 'did not get on well together'. However, she had seen no sign of physical violence. Yet Josephine Pouliquen, a friend of the deceased, told the police 'I feel certain my friend was murdered by Mr Lanza, he is a brute and often kicked Madame Cotton'. However, he was at work at the time of the murder. Sharpe wrote that many other men were questioned and 'Against one of these persons – to whom I have not previously referred [i.e. not Cohen, Lanza or Hall] – there was a strong suspicion'. Sharpe was convinced that he had spoken to this unnamed man in the course of his investigation. It was 'someone she knew'.[31]

Motive was unclear, since it was neither money nor sexual assault. The police thought that 'It is clear that the crime was committed by some person who knew the woman and had been to the place before'. She had no known male friends and did not go to pubs. The communal door to the flats was locked after six. Either Mrs Cousins let someone in whom she trusted, or perhaps one of Neri's clients killed her.[32]

Finally, we come to Mrs Leah Smith, who was born in the East Ham Infirmary in 1912. She was the daughter of Kathleen Hinds and an engineer. She had been a difficult girl when young and lived with her grandmother, as her mother had tried to help her but had failed. She had left home while in her teens and had lived with a variety of men. She had also had a baby in 1931 (who was soon adopted) and had married, in June 1933, Robert Thomas Smith, a Margate waiter. However, in August 1934 she had left him.[33]

At the beginning of April 1936, she met Stanley King, who had come to London in 1931 and had worked in restaurants and nightclubs. By 1936 he did conjuring tricks for a living. Leah was in love with him and, as a friend declared, 'She didn't intend to give him up as he had been very good to her and she loved him very much'. Yet King, though initially believing Leah was a waitress, was unhappy when he discovered her real profession and wanted her to give it up.[34]

By early May 1936, the couple were living in a flat on the second floor at 66 Old Compton Street. King wanted to move again, in the hope that Smith might discard her old ways, but there was little chance of that. There were arguments between them and King, who worked in the evenings, was unable to supervise her at her most active time and she brought men home as she always had. It was Leah who had the only key between them and so he could not surprise her by arriving unannounced.[35]

On the evening of Friday 8 May, Leah had been with several clients. Later that night she was seen on Old Compton Street, talking to Joan Maymar and another woman. It was about half past eleven. At a quarter to midnight, Leah left her friends, saying 'I must try and get some money, I'm fed up, I haven't been off tonight yet and there is no money coming in'. Leah and Joan walked down Old Compton Street and parted outside the Palace Theatre just before midnight.[36]

Just after midnight on Saturday 9 May, Emilio Piantino saw Leah with a man. He stated, 'I was in the hall looking out into the street when I saw Leah Hinds with a man on the opposite side of the road walking towards Wardour Street. The man was on the inside of the pavement away from me and I do not think I would know him again'. Yet he later said that the man was of fair complexion, slim, clean shaven and with thinning hair. He wore a dark raincoat, but eccentrically enough, was hatless. At half past twelve, two girls saw the two of them enter her flat. One recalled Leah saying 'if you can't get it in the day, you must get it at night'. The man they saw was probably the same man seen by Piantino, described as being aged about thirty, five feet eight inches tall, with long hair and a slouching gait.[37]

Later that morning, King called on her as arranged, but no one answered. He left and soon found himself in a nearby restaurant where he met James Adams. The two went to the flat and Adams broke the door down. The two men soon left and sought a policeman. PC John Davidson was found and Adams said, 'Oh constable, will you come along, I think a girl has been murdered. I have just broken into the flat and I saw her on the bed. Her head was covered with blood. I think her throat is cut. This poor little dog was with her'.[38]

The police investigation was quick to take effect, and as before, Sharpe was in charge. He noticed that the victim was still partially dressed, though her stockings had been rolled down, probably by the woman herself, and she was lying on the bed. She had been strangled by means of a thin wire, but her face had also been battered and there were bruises on the lower jaw and lower lip. The blows had been first, then the strangulation. She had probably met her death at about 12.55am; possibly a little later, but not after 3am. She had not been sexually assaulted. This savage attack led some to believe the attacker was 'a dangerous homicidal maniac'.[39]

Spilsbury examined her. He said that the head injuries were caused by a blunt instrument, such as the flat iron found in the flat. Any one of these several injuries would have rendered her unconscious. Yet it was the electric light wire around her throat which had caused death.[40]

Elsewhere, her handbag was found on the floor, but there was only two pence in it. Sharpe concluded 'Robbery was the most likely motive for this murder, for Leah was known to have had money in her bag that night'. Another clue was found on the edge of the wooden mantelpiece in the room. This was a fingerprint, which was shown not to belong to anyone who normally had access to the room. That part of the mantelpiece with the incriminating mark was sawn off and carried away to the laboratory. However, the print did not match any of those in the police files.[41]

It was thought that six men had seen Mrs Hinds on her last evening. They were asked to report to the police, but unsurprisingly none did. Mr Hinds was questioned, but he had not seen her since she left him two years earlier. As Sharpe noted, 'Soho was turned upside down'. He was pessimistic about the outcome of the case, writing, 'with so little to go on we were pretty well doomed to failure from the word "go"'.[42]

It seems certain that a stranger killed Leah. Joan said 'Leah Hinds has not at any time complained to me of being frightened of any person or anyone ill treating her'. Her mother, who saw her a few days before her death, recalled, 'She seemed perfectly happy and did not complain of being afraid of any person'. The motive was probably the little money she had on her, with the police stating 'It is reasonable to assume that robbery was the motive'. After all, the handbag was empty and only two pence could be found in the room. The police conclusion was as follows:

> The circumstances of the case rather indicate that her assailant was a chance acquaintance who accompanied her home for the purpose of robbery. The ferocity with which he attacked the unfortunate girl suggests he is a dangerous homicidal man.[43]

Leah's estranged husband reported to the police as soon as he knew of the murder. He was resident in Margate and had a strong alibi for the night of the murder as he was with friends and had been seen by tradesmen on the following morning. King, too, can probably be eliminated as a suspect as he was at a night club on Little Denmark Street from 11.15pm to 3.30am. In any case, he seems to have been on excellent terms with Leah, despite disliking her calling.[44]

Soho and the girls and women who worked the streets became increasingly frightened after this murder. Sharpe wrote 'This was Soho's fourth murder within six months, the papers were talking of a new Jack the Ripper'. This was despite the fact that the Ripper's victims had their throats cut and most were mutilated. It is tempting to conclude that a serial strangler was at work here. After all, the women all lived within a short distance of each other and were all killed within six months. All were strangled. Two were prostitutes. All the murders occurred indoors. The press certainly thought this was a series, but it was uncertain whether any of the women knew one another. Mrs Hinds's mother said, 'So far as I know, she was not acquainted with the victims of the previous murders'. On the other hand, some street women, friends of Mrs Hinds, said that she knew the other two victims. Apparently 'Rightly or wrongly, rumour attributed them to some known hand, especially if that hand had already struck more than once'. It was said, 'While some of Scotland Yard's chiefs are inclined to think that the affairs are in no way related, it is pointed out that the possibility of one man being responsible for them all cannot be ruled out'. It was not only the press which thought so, because Detective Inspector Edwards, who had investigated the Martin case, thought that the papers from this case 'might be of assistance in the cases of Jeanett Cousins and Constance May Smith alias Leah Hinds at present under investigation'.[45]

However, in the case of Leah, it was concluded, 'There is nothing to show, however, that there is a connection between any of these cases'. Similarly, Sharpe, who was best placed to know, wrote as follows:

> The murders of French Fifi and Jeannette Cousins remaining unsolved drove us to redouble our efforts to solve the further crime of Soho, but it is unlikely it ever will be solved. I don't think there was any connection between those killings or that they were in any way connected with any vice ring or other organisation. In my opinion: French Fifi was murdered for the money in her flat by someone she had picked up, and Leah Hinds for the same reason. Jeanette Cousins was killed by someone she knew and the motive was one which I believe I know but which I think it best not to mention.[46]

The Soho Murders, 1946–48

Shortly after the end of hostilities in 1945, four prostitutes were slain in Soho in the space of two years. As in 1935–36 two were killed in their own homes, but two were not. They may all have been struck down by the same man. Regrettably the police files for only two of these four murders survive, and one of these is still closed. Thus the account of the last murder is rather fuller than the first three, which rely on scanty newspaper reports.

Margaret Cook, aged thirty, of 30 Devonshire Terrace, was shot dead outside the Blue Lagoon nightclub, Carnaby Street, near Oxford Circus, on the evening of 9 November 1946. To be precise it was in an alleyway between a septic water tank and the night club door. The former yielded cigar butts and bottles but no weapon or ammunition. It was suggested that she had been killed by a man extorting money from her. Divisional Detective R. Higgins and Detective Inspector Burgess interviewed a man who was on good terms with the deceased, but he was soon released. The man wanted for the murder was described as aged between twenty-five and thirty, five feet eight, dark complexion, dressed in a Burberry style rain coat and a pork pie hat.[47]

Margaret had been in borstal and was well known to police. Yet she was known as 'milady'. A woman friend described her as 'an incredible person, so secretive about her mode of living and man friends that we dubbed her Sealed Lips'.[48] She used different names and had twenty different addresses in two years. She arrived in London from Bradford and was known as Margaret Willis until she married a 24-year-old ex-soldier in 1945. She was killed by a .25 bullet from a German automatic pistol, probably taken by a serviceman as a war souvenir.[49] No one was ever charged with her murder.

A year later Soho witnessed another murder. Violet Doris Driver, known as Black Rita, was born in London on 22 January 1917, and was shot and killed on the landing of a flat at 42 Rupert Street in Soho on 7 September 1947. She had married Daniel Green, a silver salesman two years her junior, earlier that year, and her main address was 12 Russell Chambers. On death she had £1,791 to leave her husband, so it would be useful to know where he was at the time of her death.[50]

Violet was six feet tall and described as being handsome. Her father had been a policeman who had died three years earlier. She used to associate with a man called Mr Barratt before her marriage. She was last seen with a man aged between thirty-five and forty, wearing a dark suit, about five feet nine and carrying an instrument or despatch case. The man who killed Margaret was described as being a little younger and a little shorter, but it is perhaps easy for witnesses to err in detail when seeing someone fleetingly and at night time. Scores of people heard the three shots which killed her.[51]

Violet was well off. She regularly carried between £40 and £50 on her person, which she claimed was a day's earnings. She was last fined for streetwalking on 14 August and apparently paid the fines of others to prevent them being imprisoned. She used her maiden name professionally.[52] Again her killing went unsolved. The police file for this case exists but is closed for public inspection until 2050. Whether there was a connection between the two killings: both of prostitutes, both of whom had been shot in the same locality, but nearly a year apart, is again impossible to know.

In the following year there were two killings of women in the same district, but both were stabbings, both took place in the women's flats, and both occurred within weeks. On the night of 5 September 1948 Helen Freedman or Freeman, born on 3 January 1892 and from Lithuania, known as 'Russian Dora', was stabbed to death in her flat at 126 Long Acre, Soho. She had been stabbed repeatedly and it seemed that this was the work of a sadistic maniac rather than someone who knew her. Apparently she fought for her life as the flat was in a state of disorder. The carving knife was left in her body and yielded a fingerprint. She had been seen in Leicester Square that evening with a young man with wavy hair and he was sought.[53]

Helen was a prostitute and allegedly led a double life. By daytime she was innocent Grannie Freedman, a plainly clothed old lady with a wrinkled face, either out doing shopping or playing patience in the afternoon, but by night she was anything but. Apparently by clever use of make-up she was able to transform herself into a younger woman. This hoodwinked a 26-year-old Canadian soldier, whom she met in the war, who asked her to marry him. He ended the romance on finding out her secret. When her body was found, it was that of Grannie Freedman not Russian Dora, as all her make-up had been taken off.[54]

Helen was married to Nathan, a clothing salesman, but allegedly they separated in 1933, and on her death he inherited £165 12s. The fingerprint clue yielded no results because the killer evidently, as with Gordon Cummins, did not have a criminal record. On 22 September an unnamed man was questioned at Bow Street about the murder but was released.[55]

It was believed that Helen Freedman was a friend of Mrs Fennick, who was the last victim. Rachel Annie Fennick had been born as Rachel Hatton in Shoreditch on 19 August 1907. She had been a prostitute since about 1924 and had lived in Soho since about 1928. She had had eighty-four convictions for soliciting, two for larceny and two for keeping a brothel. She married a black American in Holborn in 1930, called Herbert Fennick. They separated in about 1933 and had not met since. He had subsequently lived abroad, but it was uncertain whether he had died in Paris or had gone back to America. The marriage had not produced any children. Her sister did not see much of her and had not seen her since 16 September 1948. She thought that her sister was poor and had recently pawned her two rings. She lived in a first floor flat at 46 Broadwick Street, Soho.[56]

On Sunday 26 September 1948, Edwin Peggs made his way to see Rachel, by appointment. He had known her for two years and had lunched with her on the previous day. The front door was open and so he walked up to the first floor. Although he had a key, he found the door to Mrs Fennick's door locked. It was 12.45. He became alarmed and broke the door down. He then saw his friend's corpse and shouted for the neighbours to call the police.[57]

DS William Bilyard was one of the first officers on the site, arriving at 1.15. He reported thus: 'in the front room of the second floor, I saw the body of a woman. The body was lying on the floor on her back between the table and the divan. It was partially covered with an eiderdown'. She was in state of semi-undress. There were several wounds to the left breast and a stab wound in the stomach. Her fingers were badly cut and bloodied.[58]

DS Eric Shepherd noted, at the scene of the crime, 'She had been savagely attacked with a knife and died as a result of the wounds so inflicted'. There were few clues. Mrs Fennick's identity card and ration book were found. There was also the ration book of one Antonios Ioanou. It was also thought that a few pound notes might have been stolen, as there was no money in the rooms of the dead woman.[59]

Death had occurred between 10pm on 25 September and 2am the following day. The wounds had been inflicted by a two-edged knife, at least seven inches long. Three of the six wounds were particularly severe and death would have followed two or three minutes afterwards. The contents of her stomach revealed that Mrs Fennick had a meal about two or three hours before she died. She had also had a pint of beer or two measures of spirits with the meal. There was blood on her fingers, which evidently had been cut when she had tried to defend herself. There were the dark brown hairs of her killer and the dark blue strands of his jacket. Finally there was some of his blood, but he was blood group A, the commonest type of all.[60]

Mrs Fennick's last hours were described by fellow prostitutes. She had been in the streets that night, soliciting, as usual. Irene Hughes recalled seeing her at between 10.30 and 10.40 in Brewer Street. Thomasina Ingram of Roman Road saw her at 11.15. Alice Nolan was the last known woman to have seen her alive, and this was at 11.25. The police were unconvinced about the accuracy of these statements and they noted, 'These witnesses' accounts vary considerably as to time, and bearing in mind their unreliability and unusual habits, it is fair to assume that they cannot properly assess the actual time when they did, in fact, see the deceased'. However, all three women had known Mrs Fennick for some years and all stood by the truth of their statements.[61]

The women also gave descriptions of the man who was last seen with Mrs Fennick. Thomasina Ingram said that he was wearing a brown striped suit and was well built, but she did not see his face. This might have been the same man who tried to strangle her earlier that evening. This man was six feet tall, aged between thirty and forty, well built, with broad shoulders, had brown hair, wore a brown suit, was deaf, nervous and a foreigner. Alice Nolan's description tallied with hers: 'I would describe this man as being about six feet and very well built, he was wearing a brown suit. I did not see his face. I don't think I have seen him before'. They had been in Lexington Street together at 11.15.[62]

William Yates, a neighbour, recalled that he had not seen Mrs Fennick since 8pm on the Saturday night. On the night of the murder, at 9.45pm, he had heard a scream, but had assumed it was a cry from the nearby pub. On leaving for work at 3.45am next morning he recalled seeing Mrs Fennick's lights were on, though this was usual. His wife thought that she had heard her speak to a man at 9.30.[63]

Those who knew the victim were questioned. Ioanou, whose ration book had been found in her room, had lived with the deceased for a few weeks in 1947. He had known her since 1946, but had not seen her for four weeks prior to the murder. His clothes were tested for bloodstains, but none could be found.[64]

Fred Cribb, a builder from Maida Vale, was another man who once knew Mrs Fennick. He had lived with her from 1939–44. He was still in touch with her in more recent years. In 1947 he had given her money and he still occasionally saw her in the Newcastle pub.[65]

Gerald McDade had once been a client of Mrs Fennick and he had struck her. On 31 August she had agreed to have sex with him for £1. He claimed that she had stolen £5 from him. After an argument, he slapped her in the face.

The police were called, and were aware that Mrs Fennick had been accused of stealing from clients previously. He told them 'I accused her of stealing my money and slapped her across the face. I was mad to think someone had stolen from me'. McDade had an alibi for the night of the murder.[66]

Peggs was perhaps the natural suspect. Yet his movements were checked. He had returned home by midnight and did not leave again until 10.30 the following morning. He told the police that she had once told him that she had previously been in danger from a violent client, 'I was nearly stabbed last night, and the woman upstairs called the police in'. Peggs was not thought to have killed her. Higgins concluded, 'There is no reason to believe he is of a violent nature and no evidence whatever to show that he knows anything further about the circumstances of the murder'.[67]

Recent attacks on other prostitutes were reported at this time in order that the survivors might be able to assist the police in solving the murder of Mrs Fennick. Hermione Hindin had been attacked in July 1948 and helped the police with their enquiries. She said that a man once threatened her in her room with a long knife. Apparently she looked frightened when he threatened her and he said, 'Shut up you little fool. I'm only trying to frighten you'. He then added, 'I've got no time for all you bloody people. I'm going to do all the prostitutes in'. He was about five feet nine, in his mid-thirties, with a sallow complexion, dark hair and dark eyes, clean shaven, with a pointed chin of medium build and 'of the office worker type'.[68]

In the following year, on 5 December, Ada Curran was attacked in her room in Old Compton Street. Francis Shaw tried to assault her with a hammer. However, his would-be victim cried out and her maid appeared. Shaw ran. He was later apprehended and told the police, 'I felt generally mad with all women at that time'. He had recently separated from his wife, was found insane and was sent to Broadmoor.[69]

No one was ever convicted of the murder of Mrs Fennick. Higgins concluded:

> Despite protracted and persistent enquiries into the Soho area no further information has been obtained to assist us in determining the identity of the culprit in this case. I have interviewed many informants and people of the prostitute class, and all seem to be of the opinion that it was the work of a maniacal killer. There has been no suggestion whatever that it was in any way other than this.[70]

As in 1935–36 it cannot be known if these four women's deaths were at the hands of a serial killer, as no one was ever apprehended and no prime suspect emerged. Newspapers certainly linked these murders together because of their geographical proximity and the occupation of the victims. The police may not have done, for there is no reference to Violet or Margaret in the only accessible murder file (that of Rachel Fennick). The deaths of Helen and Rachel have a lot in common: physical and chronological proximity, both had been stabbed and in neither was robbery a motive. Yet Margaret and Violet had been shot one or two years earlier and possibly the latter's relative wealth was a motive, whereas it was not with the two later victims. After Rachel's death there were no further murders thought to be related to these four.

In 2015 a rumour surfaced that a 91-year-old British man living in a nursing home in Canada had confessed to these murders. After military service he had emigrated to Canada in 1951. He was understandably never named and was never extradited. How genuine this was is another question, as it is not uncommon for people to confess to crimes they have not committed, especially if there is little or no danger of punishment. Yet some 'deathbed' confessions are true, as, probably, in the case of the Brighton Trunk murderer and the strangler Harry Loughans. Nothing more was heard of this.[71]

We cannot be sure whether any of these four series of murders were the work of four individual serial killers or several other killers. Police opinion was that the 1935–36 murders were individual crimes (and the first may have been a suicide) and it seems probable that the West Ham cases were kidnappings in 1881–82 and then four murders in the next decade, possibly connected but not necessarily. The 1946–48 killings show possibly two hands at work, with two shootings and then two fatal stabbings. The difficulty in the 1890s and 1940s cases is that there is little material with which to work, for in only one of these murders is the police file open, and no one was ever charged with any of them. All were unsolved and a lack of a solution inevitably leads to uncertainty.

Conclusion

We have looked at a number of serial killings in London and now it is time to draw some conclusions. The following analysis is based on the information from the first nine chapters. The murders outlined in Chapter 10 have been excluded, as it is not certain that they were the work of serial killers. Professor Gee, pathologist in the Yorkshire Ripper cases, was always very careful and deliberate in selecting which crimes were definitely the work of the Ripper in order not to lead the investigation astray and we will follow his principle here.

We turn first to the forty-three victims that we know of (and in the case of Mrs Winters, as with many poisoners, there may well have been more), traditionally downplayed by the media and in many books, as has been noted by Professor David Wilson in 2006, though he does little to correct this as far as individuals are concerned. Being dead they have no voice and as most were very young, sadly they did not have the time to have achieved much with their lives. Yet many were wives and mothers (occasionally husbands and fathers). Several had suffered from marital breakdowns, or were widows, as in the case especially of Cummins', the Ripper's and the Stripper's victims. Most were very ordinary people and would not have attracted much worldly attention had it not been for their terrible fates. When that happened, and when they became of interest to the press, police and others, it was too late for any interview with them or any other verbal examination. And to paraphrase Gordon Burns in his book about Peter Sutcliffe, the Yorkshire Ripper, they were all somebody's wife and somebody's daughter (occasionally husband and son). By their sex, age and occupation they were, in aggregate, as follows:

Sex	Male	Female
Number	7	36
	16%	84%

Age	Child (0-15)	Young (16-39)	Middle-aged (40-60)	Elderly (61+)
Number	2	26	11	4
	5%	58%	28%	9%

Occupation	Prostitute, 'sex worker'	Doctor/ chemist	Other/ None	Retired	Wife (including common-law wife)	Factory worker
Number	20	2	8	3	8	2
	47%	4%	19%	6%	19%	4%

The typical victim of the serial killer is, overwhelmingly, a young female prostitute. This may come as no surprise. However, it is also worth noting that the next most likely category of victim is the 'respectable' woman; wives or those who pass as them. Elderly people and men are rarely victims of serial killers. The majority of victims come from lower income groups; not only prostitutes, but factory workers, people of no regular employment and the elderly poor. Most were English, but six were from Scotland and three from Ireland, one from Austria and one from Sweden.

We now turn to their murderers, who always garner more attention from the media and crime writers. This is partly because there is more information known about them; if arrested they give interviews, are put on trial and are examined by psychiatrists, lawyers and detectives, and where their identity is unknown, speculation knows no bounds. They are not necessarily interesting people themselves, but by their very deeds they are abnormal and thus newsworthy. It is rare to commit murder and the serial killer is even more rare and perhaps, by their actions, of more note. Their personalities are often of little interest; enigmatic or tediously self-centred. They are usually rational and cold-blooded. However, they usually appear respectable and personable, even charming, and so never seem to be obviously dangerous.

Sex	Male	Female
Number	8	1
	89%	11%

Age	Unknown (but probably young)	Young (16-39)	Middle Aged (40-60)	Elderly (61+)
Number	2	3	3	1
	22%	33%	33%	11%

Type	Unknown	Doctor	Publican	RAF	Professional criminal (posing as businessman)	None
Number	2	1	1	1	2	2
	22%	11%	11%	11%	22%	22%

The average serial killer is, again perhaps unsurprisingly, male and young, but there is no typical occupation or social class for such a man. All, however, possess a veneer of respectability, even charm, in order to convince their victims that they are trustworthy and pose no threat. Smith's three doomed 'wives' all adored him and Haigh was deemed remarkably personable. None show any remorse and of those featured in this book, all who were found guilty were hanged, to the regret of few.

Of the seven serial killers we know about, two were born in London; Mrs Winters and Smith, one was Polish, one a Scot raised in Canada and America, and three were born or raised in Yorkshire.

We now come to the terrible interactions between killer and victims.

Relationship	None known	Family member	Friend	Colleague	Acquaintance
Number	15	13	6	1	8
	35%	30%	15%	2%	18%

Although in many cases there is no known prior relationship between killer and victim – this is the case with almost all of the prostitute murders where a man meets a woman on the street for the first and last time (which makes detection all the more difficult) – in most cases the two have met one another previously, and in many cases this relationship has lasted for months or even years. On the other hand, Cream and Christie met all or some of the women they were later to slay prior to the time and place where they did commit the ghastly act.

Method	Poison	Knife	Drowning	Strangulation	Asphyxia	Gun	Cosh
Number	13	6	3	9	6	3	3
	30%	12%	7%	23%	14%	7%	7%

Motive	Mutilation	Money	Sex/power	Unknown
Number	1	5	1	2
	11%	55%	11%	22%

Place	Outdoor	Indoor
Number	5	38
	16%	84%

Method	Unconcealed	Concealed	Passed off as natural
Number	15	12	16
	35%	28%	37%

Number of victims	3	4	5	6
Number	2	2	1	4
	22%	22%	11%	45%

Time between known murders

Number of murders	Jack the Ripper	Mrs Amelia Winters	Dr Cream	George Chapman	George Joseph Smith	Gordon Cummins	John George Haigh	John Christie	Jack the Stripper
1-2	8 days	1 year	1 week	3 years, 2 months	16 months	1 day	10 months	14 months	67 days
2-3	22 days	4 months	6 months	20 months	12 months	2 days	Hours	7 years	13 days
3-4	2 hours	15 months	Hours	-	-	1 day	2 years, 7 months	1 month	82 days
4-5	48 days	10 months	-	-	-	-	Hours	Days	104 days
5-6	-	2 months	-	-	-	-	1 year	c.46 days	80 days

Perhaps surprisingly, the most common weapon used by serial killers in this period is poison, but this was almost wholly a nineteenth-century tool; it was only used in two of the serial murders in the twentieth century. Equally surprising is the lack of use of the knife; our image of Jack the Ripper overshadows reality as he was the only one who used a knife in all his murders. Strangulation and asphyxia (to which we could add the deaths by drowning) were the favoured methods. Only two killers varied their weapons, Haigh switching from cosh to gun once he was able to purloin one belonging to a future victim, and Cummins cut the throat of Evelyn Oatley though he strangled the others.

Motivation may also surprise the reader as the stereotype of the serial killer is that they are motivated by sex and sadism. Yet more of these killers were monetary minded, often because murder was a means to an end for those individuals who wanted more than they possessed; Mrs Winters, Cream, Smith, Cummins and Haigh. However, there seems also to have been an element of sadism in the murders of Cream and Cummins. Hatred of women was behind the sex murders of Christie.

It has been argued that the victims of serial killers are from socially vulnerable groups and that it is to 'structural causes' that we should look to examine the phenomenon of serial killings. However, this is insufficient in itself. Firstly, bad luck in being in the wrong place at the wrong time led to a number of deaths chronicled here. The Ripper did not care who he killed and it was terrible misfortune that led those women he butchered to cross his path. Secondly, incaution led to the deaths of some; but others were more wary. Two of Dr Cream's would-be victims did not accept his poison pills and several women avoided Christie's invitations to 10 Rillington Place, but others were unfortunately more trusting. Decisions made by individuals are just as important as any 'structural causes' of murder. In some cases, the serial killer beguiles their victim into believing that they can help them when no one else can; for example Christie persuading Muriel Eady he could cure her health problems and Haigh convincing the young McSwan he could help him avoid the call-up.

Most of these killers worked indoors so as to conceal their deeds from any witnesses; understandably enough. Yet they were mixed in their attempts to conceal (or not) their grim deeds. Just over a third passed off their victims as having died natural deaths, which was possible if there were no marks on the bodies, as in cases of drowning or poisonings. Christie and Haigh hid their victims' bodies by alternate means, but some killers, such as the Jack the Ripper, Cummins and the Nudes murderer, flaunted their work by exposing their obviously murdered victims in either public places or the victims' homes. This had the short-term risk that they could be spotted or heard in the act of murder, or in the disposal of the corpses, but if not and if they left a minimum of evidence behind, they were relatively safe from a future investigation as there was nothing to tie them to the location of the murder. Passing deaths off as natural ensured there would be no investigation and so the killer could continue their grim deeds.

It has also been argued that killers begin cautiously and slowly and then, as detection does not occur, speed up and become careless and so are caught. This is the case with Haigh; there were two and a half years between his third and fourth murders and then a year between his fifth and sixth; likewise Christie left over a year between his first two killings and then killed three women in the first three months of 1953. However it is not always the case; there was more time between the penultimate and last victims of both Jack the Ripper and Jack the Stripper than between their earlier murders; Mrs Winters killed three people in 1885–86 and three in 1888–89. Cream left many months between his second and third murders and very little time between his first and second. For those who kill for pleasure serial murder can be likened to an addiction that a drug user, alcoholic or gambler might feel; there is an inner compulsion urging them on. Those motivated by money kill when they are broke, putting aside any moral scruples about killing as a means to an end.

Most of the murders took place in a limited geographical district in relation to the murderer, often their home or place of work. When hunting for victims, killers constrained themselves by geography. All of Mrs Winter's victims lived and died within a few streets near to her home in Church Street, Deptford, and all of Cream's lived very near to Waterloo Road in Lambeth. Jack the Ripper was restricted to the East End and Christie to Notting Hill and Paddington. Chapman and Smith killed at home. Cummins killed in central London. After World War Two, with greater access to motor cars, murderers could free themselves of such limits, so the Stripper could deposit his victims throughout west London and Haigh could drive his three last victims to Crawley. Killing in a neighbourhood well known to the killer has obvious advantages as they will know the streets very well and know where they can be seen with and perhaps kill their victims in relative safety. The drawback is that if they know the place well, they may also be well known there.

Detection is very variable. The first and last of these murderers, in chronological order, escaped detection and got away with their crimes. The majority, though, were caught and paid the penalty. However, they got away with their first crimes, and in continuing to do so using the same methods and often in the same locations, increased the risk that someone, whether doctor, relative, friend or detective, would become suspicious, or that they would make sloppy mistakes in inadvertently leaving clues to be found. The power of the press, in reporting 'accidental' deaths and 'disappearances', can also be a powerful tool in detection, as noted with Smith and Haigh. Then it was only a case of painstaking enquiries and dogged pathological examinations, rather than brilliant deduction, that solved the cases.

Serial killings in London in the years under review (1885–1965) were a rare phenomenon. Over the period of eighty years there were nine known serial killers operating in London and they claimed at least forty-three victims. On average, one person fell victim to a serial killer every two years. To provide some context, from 1921–1958 there were 1,674 murders in London, with serial killings (19) a very tiny percentage of these. However, there were periods of higher activity, with two serial killers being active in 1888 and another two in 1943–49. Two people died from serial killers in 1886, seven in 1888, two in both 1891 and 1892, four in 1942, three in both 1944 and 1953, two in 1945 and five in 1964. However, none were active from 1903–11, from 1915–41 and from 1954–63. Some of these murders (Smith's first two and Haigh's last three) took place outside London.

Once a killer has determined their deadly course of action there is usually little to stop them, at least initially. However, their murders can be curtailed sooner rather than later if they are suspected and their crimes recognised for what they are. The best weapon against the serial killer is caution and eternal vigilance; for oneself and one's family, friends and associates. This, combined with the efforts of the police and members of the medical profession, means that most serial killers are brought to justice.

Notes

Chapter 1
1. *Whitechapel Medical Officer of Health Annual Report for 1888*, pp.5-6, 9-10.
2. *Daily Telegraph*, 3 September 1888.
3. Ibid, 3, 4 September 1888.
4. Ibid, 4, 5 September 1888.
5. Ibid, 4 September 1888.
6. Ibid, 3, 4 September 1888.
7. Ibid, 3 September 1888.
8. Ibid, 4 September 1888.
9. Ibid, 3, 4, 18, 24 September 1888.
10. Ibid, 24 September 1888.
11. Ibid.
12. Ibid.
13. Ibid, 13 September 1888.
14. Ibid, 12 September 1888.
15. Ibid.
16. Ibid, 13 September 1888.
17. Ibid, 14 September 1888.
18. Ibid.
19. Ibid.
20. Ibid, 12, 15 September 1888.
21. Ibid, 12 September 1888.
22. Ibid, 12, 15 September 1888.
23. Ibid, 15 September 1888.
24. Ibid, 13 September 1888.
25. Ibid, 15 September 1888.
26. Ibid.
27. TNA, MEPO3/3153.
28. Ibid.
29. *Daily Telegraph*, 2 October 1888.
30. Ibid, 2, 3 October 1888.
31. Ibid.
32. Ibid, 3 October 1888.
33. Ibid.
34. Ibid, 4 October 1888.
35. Ibid.
36. Ibid, 5 October 1888.
37. Ibid, 4 October 1888.
38. Ibid, 5 October 1888.
39. Ibid.
40. Ibid.
41. Ibid.
42. Cited in R. Jones, *The Jack the Ripper Files*, (2014), pp.36-7.
43. *Daily Telegraph*, 4 October 1888.
44. Jones, *Jack the Ripper*, pp.42-43.

45. *Daily Telegraph*, 4 October 1888.
46. Ibid, 2 October 1888.
47. Ibid, 3 October 1888.
48. Ibid, 4 October 1888.
49. Ibid, 5 October 1888.
50. Ibid, 24 October 1888.
51. Ibid, 5, 12 October 1888.
52. Ibid, 5 October 1888.
53. Ibid, 12 October 1888.
54. Ibid, 12 October 1888.
55. Ibid, 5 October 1888.
56. Ibid, 13 October 1888.
57. Ibid, 5, 12 October 1888.
58. Ibid, 5 October 1888.
59. Ibid.
60. Ibid, 12 October 1888.
61. Ibid, 5 October 1888.
62. Ibid, 12 October 1888.
63. Ibid 5 October 1888.
64. Ibid.
65. Ibid.
66. Ibid, 5, 12 October 1888.
67. TNA, MEPO3/3153.
68. *Daily Telegraph*, 13 November 1888.
69. Ibid.
70. Ibid.
71. Ibid.
72. Ibid.
73. Ibid.
74. Ibid.
75. Ibid.
76. Jones, *Jack the Ripper*, pp.98-99.
77. *Daily Telegraph*, 13 November 1888.
78. Ibid.
79. Ibid.
80. Ibid.
81. Ibid.
82. TNA, MEPO3/141.
83. Ibid, MEPO2/140.
84. Ibid, 20/1
85. Ibid, 3/141; M. MacNaghten, *Days of my Years* (1914), p.62.
86. J. Anderson, *The Lighter Side of my Official Life*, (1910), pp.137-138.
87. Quoted in Jones, *Jack the Ripper*, p.100.

Chapter 2
1. *Medical Officer of Health for Greenwich Annual Report for 1894*, Table 1.
2. Ancestry.co.uk, Birth, baptisms and marriage indexes; census, 1881.
3. *Kentish Mercury*, 10 August 1889.
4. Ibid.
5. Ibid.
6. Ibid.
7. *South Wales Echo*, 26 July 1889.

8. Ibid, *Kentish Independent*, 13 July 1889.
9. *Kentish Mercury*, 31 May 1889; *New South Wales Echo*, 26 July 1889.
10. *Kentish Mercury*, 12 July 1889.
11. Ancestry.co.uk, censuses.
12. *Kentish Mercury*, 12 July 1889.
13. Ibid.
14. Ibid.
15. *Kentish Independent*, 13 July 1889.
16. *Kentish Mercury*, 12 July 1889.
17. Ibid.
18. *Kentish Mercury*, 12 July 1889; *Kentish Independent* 13 July 1889.
19. *Kentish Mercury*, 12 July 1889.
20. Ibid, 31 May 1889.
21. Ibid, 7 June 1889.
22. Ibid.
23. Ibid, 12 July 1889.
24. Ibid, 7 June 1889.
25. Ibid.
26. Ibid, 26 July 1889.
27. Ibid, 31 May 1889.
28. Ibid, 26 July 1889.
29. Ibid, 10, 31 May 1889.
30. Ibid, 10 May, 10 August 1889.
31. Ibid, 31 May 1889.
32. Ibid, 26 April, 31 May 1889.
33. Ibid, 31 May, 26 June, 10 August 1889.
34. Ibid, 26 July 1889.
35. Ibid.
36. Ibid.
37. Ibid.
38. Ibid, 26 April 1889.
39. *Luton Reporter*, 7 April 1889.
40. *Kentish Mercury*, 10 May 1889.
41. Ibid.
42. Ibid, 26 April 1889.
43. Ibid, 10 May 1889.
44. Ibid, 17 May 1889.
45. Ibid, 31 May 1889.
46. Ibid, 7 June 1889.
47. Ibid, 19 July 1889.
48. Ibid, 26 July 1889.
49. Ibid, 19 July 1889
50. Ibid, 12 July 1889.
51. Ibid, 26 July 1889
52. Ibid.
53. Ibid, 19 July 1889.
54. *Reynold's Newspaper*, 21 July 1889.
55. Ibid.
56. *Kentish Mercury*, 26 July 1889.
57. Ibid.
58. Ibid.
59. Ibid.
60. Ibid.
61. Old Bailey online.

62. *Kentish Mercury*, 25 October 1889; *Hartlepool Northern Daily Mail*, 23 October 1889; Old Bailey online
63. *Kentish Mercury*, 1 November 1889.
64. Ibid, 10 August 1889.
65. Ibid.
66. Ibid, 12 July 1889.
67. Ibid, 26 July 1889.
68. Ibid, 10 August 1889.

Chapter 3
1. TNA, MEPO3/144.
2. *Western Times*, 24 October 1891; *Dundee Evening Telegraph*, 7 May 1892; Old Bailey online.
3. *Dundee Evening Telegraph*, 7 May 1892.
4. *Western Times*, 24 October 1891; TNA, MEPO3/144.
5. Old Bailey online.
6. *Evening Standard*, 18 October 1892.
7. Old Bailey online.
8. *Evening Standard*, 18 October 1892.
9. Ibid, 24 June, 19 and 29 July 1892; Old Bailey online.
10. *Evening Standard*, 23 June 1892.
11. *Evening Standard*, 23 June 19, 29 July 1892; Old Bailey online.
12. *Evening Standard*, 23 June 1892; Old Bailey online.
13. *Evening Standard*, 19 July 1892; Old Bailey online.
14. *Evening Standard*, 29 July 1892; Old Bailey online.
15. *Evening Standard*, 23 June, 19 July 1892; Old Bailey online.
16. *Evening Standard*, 23 June 1892; Old Bailey online.
17. *Lambeth Medical Officer of Health Annual Report for 1891*.
18. Old Bailey online.
19. Ibid.
20. Ibid.
21. Ibid.
22. Ibid.
23. *Evening Standard*, 14 July 1892.
24. Old Bailey online.
25. Ibid.
26. *Dundee Evening Telegraph*, 7 May 1892.
27. *Evening Standard*, 6 May 1892.
28. *South London Press*, 16 April 1892; *Evening Standard*, 14 April 1892; TNA, MEPO3/144.
29. *South London Press*, 16 April 1892; TNA, MEPO3/144.
30. *South London Press*, 16 April 1892.
31. Old Bailey online.
32. Ibid.
33. *South London Press*, 16 April 1892; Old Bailey online.
34. *South London Press*, 16 April 1892.
35. Old Bailey online.
36. *South London Press*, 16 April 1892.
37. Ibid.
38. Ibid.
39. *Evening Standard*, 6 May 1892.
40. *South London Press*, 16 April 1892.
41. *Dundee Evening Telegraph*, 7 May 1892.
42. *Evening Standard*, 6 May 1892.

43. *Dundee Evening Telegraph*, 7 May 1892.
44. *Evening Standard*, 14 April 1892.
45. Ibid, 14 July, 13 September, 1892.
46. Old Bailey online.
47. Ibid.
48. *Evening Standard*, 25 June 1892.
49. Ibid, 14 July 1892.
50. Ibid, 6 May 1892.
51. Ibid, 23 June 1892; W.T. Shore, *The Trial of Neil Cream* (1922), p.67.
52. Old Bailey online.
53. *Evening Standard*, 19 July 1892.
54. Old Bailey online.
55. Ibid.
56. Ibid.
57. TNA, MEPO1/144
58. Old Bailey online.
59. Ibid.
60. Ibid.
61. Ibid.
62. *Evening Standard*, 19 July 1892.
63. Ibid, 14 July 1892, 29 August 1892.
64. Old Bailey online.
65. *Evening Standard*, 29 August 1892.
66. Ibid, 15 October, 1892.
67. Ibid.
68. Ibid, 18 October 1892.
69. Ibid, 19 October 1892.
70. Ibid, 22, 25 October 1892.
71. Ibid, 12 November 1892.
72. Ibid, 16 November 1892.
73. *Newcastle Evening Chronicle*, 15 November 1892.
74. Angus McLaren, *A Prescription for Murder: The Victorian Serial Killings of Dr Thomas Neill Cream* (1990).
75. Ibid, p.60.
76. A.C. Doyle, *The Adventure of the Speckled Band* (1891).

Chapter 4
1. Old Bailey online; *South London Press*, 17 January 1903; H.L. Adam, *Trial of George Chapman*, (1930), pp.201-2.
2. Old Bailey online, ancestry.co.uk, census 1891.
3. Adam, *Trial*, pp.100-101.
4. Adam, *Trial*, pp.204, 101, 203.
5. Ancestry.co.uk
6. *South London Press*, 3 January 1903; Old Bailey online; Adam, *Trial*, p.203.
7. *South London Press*, 17 January 1903, Adam, *Trial*, pp.205, 208.
8. Ibid and *Evening Standard*, 18 December 1902, Adam, *Trial*, p.208.
9. *South London Press*, 17 January 1903; Adam, *Trial*, p.208.
10. *South London Press*, 17 January 1903.
11. Ibid, 24 January 1903.
12. Adam, *Trial*, p.210.
13. *South London Press*, 17, 24, January 1903.
14. Adam, *Trial*, p.209

15. Adam, *Trial*, pp.210-211.
16. *South London Press*, 17 24, January 1903.
17. Old Bailey online.
18. *South London Press*, 24 January 1903.
19. *South London Press*, 3, 24 January, Adam, *Trial*, p.203.
20. Ancestry.co.uk, census and baptism registers.
21. *South London Press*, 31 January 1903; TNA, HO144/680.
22. *South London Press*, 7 February 1903.
23. Old Bailey online.
24. *South London Press*, 7 February 1903; Old Bailey online.
25. Old Bailey online; Adam, *Trial*, pp.134, 137.
26. Adam, *Trial*, p.135.
27. Old Bailey online.
28. Adam, *Trial*, p.138.
29. *South London Press*, 3 January, 7 February 1903.
30. Old Bailey online.
31. *South London Press*, 31 January 1903.
32. Ibid.
33. Adam, *Trial*, p.142.
34. *South London Press*, 1 November 1902.
35. Old Bailey online.
36. Ancestry.co.uk, census returns and baptism register.
37. Old Bailey online; *South London Chronicle*, 15 November 1902.
38. *South London Chronicle*, 15 November 1903.
39. Old Bailey online.
40. Adam, *Trial*, pp.42-43
41. Ibid, pp.40-41.
42. *South London Press*, 22 November 1902.
43. *Evening Standard*, 19 November 1902.
44. Ibid.
45. Ibid; TNA, CRIM1/84.
46. *South London Chronicle*, 15 November 1902.
47. Ibid, 29 November 1902.
48. *South London Press*, 20 December 1902; Old Bailey online.
49. *South London Chronicle*, 29 November 1902.
50. *Evening Standard*, 19 November 1902, Old Bailey online; *South London Chronicle*, 15 November 1902.
51. *Evening Standard*, 19 November 1902.
52. Old Bailey online.
53. Ibid.
54. *South London Press*, 15 November 1902.
55. *South London Chronicle*; 22 November 1902.
56. Old Bailey online.
57. Ibid.
58. *Evening Standard*, 19 November 1902.
59. *South London Press*, 13 December 1902.
60. Old Bailey online.
61. *South London Chronicle*, 29 November 1902.
62. *South London Press*, 15 November 1902.
63. Ibid.
64. *South London Press*, 1 November 1902.
65. *Evening Standard*, 13 December 1902.
66. *South London Press*, 1 November 1902.
67. Ibid.

68. Arthur Neil, *Forty Years of Man-Hunting* (1932), p.23.
69. *South London Press*, 1 November 1902.
70. *Evening Standard*, 13 December 1902.
71. *South London Press*, 8 November 1902.
72. *South London Chronicle*, 29 November 1902.
73. *South London Press*, 13 December 1902.
74. *South London Press* 31 January 1903, *South London Chronicle*, 7 February 1903.
75. *South London Chronicle*, 14 February 1903.
76. Adam, *Trial*.
77. Ibid, pp.151-165.
78. TNA, HO144/680.
79. *Western Mail*, 8 April 1903.
80. *Londonderry Sentinel*, 11 April 1903
81. *Northern Times*, 2 April 1915.
82. Helen Wojtczak, *Jack the Ripper at last: The Mysterious Murders of George Chapman* (2014), pp.183-185.
83. *Dundee Courier* 23 March 1903.
84. *Worcestershire Chronicle*, 28 March 1903.
85. Neil, *Forty Years*, p.26.
86. Adam, *Trial*, pp.45-52.
87. Wojtczak, *Jack the Ripper*, pp.197-234.
88. Ibid, p.151.

Chapter 5

1. Eric R. Watson, *Trial of George Joseph Smith* (1922), p.316.
2. Ibid, pp.75, 59; *Witney Gazette and West Oxfordshire Advertiser*, 16 December 1899; TNA, MEPO3/225B.
3. *Eastbourne Gazette*, 21 November 1900.
4. Old Bailey online; *Witney Gazette and West Oxfordshire Advertiser*, 16 December 1899; Watson, *Trial*, p.315.
5. *Hastings and St. Leonard's Observer*, 12 January 1901, census 1901.
6. TNA, MEP3/225B.
7. Watson, *Trial*, pp.311-312.
8. Ibid, pp.253-255.
9. Ibid, pp.312-3.
10. Ibid, pp.76, 81.
11. A.C. Doyle, 'The Disappearance of Lady Frances Carfax', *Strand Magazine* (1911).
12. Watson, *Trial*, pp.77, 88; TNA, MEPO3/225B.
13. Watson, *Trial*, p.77.
14. Ibid, p.89.
15. Ibid, pp.77, 90, 87.
16. Ibid, pp.82, 92; census 1911; TNA, MEPO3/225B.
17. Watson, *Trial*, pp.77, 92.
18. Ibid, p.79.
19. Ibid, p.95.
20. TNA, MEPO3/225B; CRIM1/155.
21. Watson, *Trial*, pp.105, 108, 113,
22. Ibid, pp.116-117.
23. Ibid, p.125.
24. Ibid, pp.124, 80, 126, 82.
25. Ibid, pp.96, 114.
26. Ibid, pp.326, 135.
27. TNA, MEP3/225B.

28. Ancestry.co.uk
29. Watson, *Trial*, p.140.
30. Ibid, p.141.
31. Ibid, pp.142-143.
32. TNA, MEPO3/225B.
33. Watson, *Trial*, pp.140, 136.
34. Ibid, pp.151-152.
35. Ibid, p.166.
36. Ibid, p.143.
37. Ibid, pp.165, 153
38. Ibid, pp.169-170.
39. Ibid, p.171.
40. Ibid, p.172.
41. Ancestry.co.uk, census returns, 1881-1911.
42. Watson, *Trial*, pp.317-8.
43. Ibid, p.182.
44. Ibid, pp.313-4.
45. Ibid, pp.183-4.
46. Ibid, pp.176, 177.
47. Ibid, pp.176, 318-320.
48. Ibid, pp.176-7.
49. Ibid, pp.177-8.
50. Ibid, p.184.
51. Ibid, p.319.
52. Ibid, p.187.
53. Ibid pp.184, 195.
54. Ibid, pp.184, 178-9, 200.
55. Ibid, pp.192-193.
56. Ibid, pp.189, 196.
57. Ibid, pp.200, 318.
58. Ibid, pp.202, 255, 317.
59. Ibid, pp.192-199, 323.
60. Ibid, pp.200-201.
61. Ibid, p.323.
62. Neil, *Forty Years*, p.32-37.
63. Watson, *Trial*, p.257.
64. Ibid, pp.257-258.
65. *Manchester Evening News*, 4 February 1915.
66. TNA, CRIM1/155.
67. *Daily Citizen*, 5 February 1915.
68. Neil, *Forty Years*, pp.47-48.
69. Watson, *Trial*, p.204.
70. Ibid, pp.263, 289-290.
71. Ibid, p.309.
72. *Leeds Mercury*, 14 August 1915.
73. TNA, PCOM8/138.
74. *Dundee People's Journal*, 14 August 1915; *Londonderry Sentinel*, 14 August 1915.
75. *Larne Times*, 21 August 1915.
76. *Dundee People's Journal*, 5 August 1915.
77. *Western Mail*, 2 August 1915.
78. *Larne Times*, 21 August 1915.
79. Watson, Trial, pp.44-46; Neil, *Forty Years*, p.38.
80. David Wilson, *British Serial Killings* (2006), pp.55-57; *Daily Mail*, 31 July 2020.
81. Jane Robins, *The Magnificent Spilsbury and the Brides in the Bath* (2014), pp.153-154.

Chapter 6
1. TNA, MEPO3/2206.
2. *Shields Daily News*, 13 February 1942; *Daily Herald*, 10 February 1942; Frederick Cherrill, *Cherrill of the Yard*, (1954), p.177.
3. TNA, MEPO3/2206.
4. Cherrill, *Cherrill*, p.179.
5. *Daily Herald*, 10 February 1942.
6. *Newcastle Evening Chronicle*, 12 February 1942; *Shields Daily News*, 13 February 1942; TNA, MEPO3/2206.
7. *Liverpool Echo*, October 1960.
8. TNA, MEPO3/2206.
9. Ibid.
10. *Shields Daily News*, 13 February. 1942.
11. *Daily Mirror* 11 February; ancestry.co.uk, census 1911, 1939 register; London Metropolitan Archives, COR/LN/1942/044.
12. *West London Observer*, 20 February 1942; *Daily Mirror* 11 February 1942; *Gloucester Citizen*, 11 February 1942; MEPO3/2206.
13. TNA, MEPO3/2206.
14. Ibid.
15. Ibid.
16. Cherrill, *Cherrill*, pp.178-179.
17. TNA, MEPO3/2206.
18. *Daily Mirror* 12 February 1942; TNA, MEPO3/2206.
19. Islington Local Studies Centre, Diary of Gladys Langford, 1942.
20. Cherill, *Cherrill*, pp.183-184, *Liverpool Evening Express*, 13 March 1942; *Derby Daily Telegraph*, 13 March 1942; TNA, MEPO3/2206.
21. *Liverpool Echo*, 13 February 1942; Cherrill, *Cherrill*, p.184; TNA, MEPO3/2206.
22. *Daily Mirror*, 14 February 1942.
23. Cherrill, *Cherrill*, p. 185.
24. TNA, MEPO3/2206.
25. Ibid.
26. *Daily Mirror*, 14 February 1942.
27. *Derby Daily Telegraph*, 13 March 1942.
28. TNA, MEPO3/2206.
29. *West London Observer*, 19 February 1942.
30. TNA, MEPO3/2206.
31. Cherrill, *Cherrill*, p.180.
32. TNA, MEPO3/2206.
33. Cherill, *Cherill*, pp.180-181.
34. TNA, MEPO3/2206.
35. *Liverpool Echo*, 4 October 1960
36. Ibid.
37. TNA, MEPO3/2206.
38. Ancestry.co.uk, 1939 register TNA, MEPO3/2206; *Eastbourne Chronicle*, 21 February 1942.
39. TNA, MEPO3/2206.
40. Ibid.
41. Cherrill, *Cherrill*, p.182.
42. TNA, MEPO3/2206.
43. Ibid.
44. Cherrill, *Cherrill*, p.182.
45. TNA, MEPO3/2206.
46. Cherrill, *Cherrill*, pp.182-183.
47. *Liverpool Echo*, 4 October 1960.

48. Cherrill, *Cherrill*, p.183.
49. *Liverpool Echo*, 4 October 1960.
50. Ibid.
51. Ibid.
52. *Lincolnshire Echo*, 14 February 1942.
53. *Stirling Observer* 24 February 1942.
54. Oates, *Unsolved London Murders, 1940s/1950*, (2009), pp.29-36.
55. *Daily Herald*, 20 October 1941; *Gloucestershire Echo*, 31 October 1942.
56. TNA, MEPO3/2206; LMA, COR/LN/1941/217-218.
57. *West London Observer*, 20 February 1942.
58. *Belfast Telegraph*, 7 April 1942.
59. TNA, MEPO3/2206
60. Ibid.
61. Ibid.
62. Cherrill, *Cherrill*, p.186.
63. *Gloucester Echo*, 27 April 1942; *Manchester Evening News*, 24 April 1942.
64. *Aberdeen Press and Journal*, 25 April 1942.
65. Cherrill, *Cherrill*, p. 187.
66. *Aberdeen Press and Journal*, 29 April 1942; *Dundee Courier*, 29 April 1942.
67. Cherrill, *Cherrill*, pp.187-188.
68. TNA, MEPO3/2206.
69. Ibid.
70. TNA, PCOM9/919, MEPO3/2206.
71. TNA, MEPO3/2206.
72. Ibid.
73. Ibid.
74. *Hartlepool Northern Daily Mail*, 9 June 1942.
75. Cherrill, *Cherrill*, p.188-189.
76. TNA, PCOM9/919.
77. TNA, MEPO3/2206.
78. TNA, CRIM1/1397.
79. TNA, PCOM9/919.
80. *Liverpool Daily Post*, 25 June 1942.
81. *Liverpool Echo*, 4 October 1960.
82. *The People*, 15 February 1942.
83. TNA, MEPO3/2206.

Chapter 7
1. TNA, HO45/23636.
2. Lord Dunboyne, *Trial of John Haigh*, (1953) pp.110-111.
3. Dunboyne, *Trial*, pp.110-111.
4. TNA, HO45/23636; MEPO3/3128; John DuRose, *Murder was my Business* (1971), p.22.
5. J. Oates, *John George Haigh: A Portrait of a serial killer and his victims* (2014), pp.94-100.
6. TNA, MEPO3/3128.
7. TNA, MEPO3/3128; DuRose, *Murder*, p.21.
8. *The Leeds Mercury*, 4 December 1934.
9. *Surrey Advertiser*, 23 November 1937.
10. LMA, Acc.2385/199.
11. Dunboyne, *Trial*, pp.120-122.
12. Ibid, pp.122-124.
13. DuRose, *Murder*, p.23.
14. Ibid, pp.23-24.

15. Dunboyne, *Trial*, p.118.
16. Dunboyne, *Trial*, pp.118-119.
17. TNA, MEPO3/3128.
18. Dunboyne, *Trial*, pp.118-119, 124.
19. Ibid, p.131.
20. Dunboyne, *Trial*, p.131.
21. Dunboyne, *Trial*, p.88.
22. Dunboyne, *Trial*, pp.126-128.
23. Ibid, pp.129-130.
24. Oates, *John Haigh*, pp.50-56.
25. Ibid, pp.57-61.
26. Dunboyne, *Trial*, p.130.
27. Oates, John Haigh, pp.68-73.
28. Ibid, pp.74-76.
29. Dunboyne, *Trial*, pp.128-130.
30. Keith Simpson, *Forty Years of Murder* (1980), p.197.
31. Ibid, pp.197-198.
32. Ibid, pp.198-199.
33. Dunboyne, *Trial*, p.133.
34. Ibid, p.133.
35. Ibid, pp.133-134.
36. Ibid, p.80.
37. Ibid, p.165.
38. Ibid, p.228.
39. Islington Local Studies Library, Diary of Gladys Langford, 1949.
40. Oates, *John Haigh*, pp.1-19.
41. TNA, HO45/23636.
42. TNA, HO45/23635, 23636.
43. TNA, HO45/23636.
44. TNA, HO45/23634.
45. Tales from the Black Museum, John George Haigh, Discovery Channel, 1999.
46. *Sunday Pictorial*, 6 March 1949.
47. TNA, MEPO3/3128.
48. Dunboyne, *Trial*, pp.104-106.
49. TNA, PCOM 9/818; *News of the World*, 7 August 1949.

Chapter 8
1. TNA, MEPO2/9535, 1798.
2. *News of the World*, 29 March 1953.
3. TNA, MEPO2/9535.
4. TNA, MEPO2/9353.
5. *The Times*, 25 March 1953.
6. D. Brabin, *Rillington Place* (1966), pp.189-190.
7. J. Oates, *John Christie: Biography of a Serial Killer* (2012), pp.109-113.
8. Ibid, pp.114-117.
9. Ibid, pp.117-122.
10. Ibid, pp.10-12.
11. Brabin, *Rillington Pla*ce, pp.192-193.
12. F. Camps, *Medical and Scientific Investigations in the Christie Case*, (1953), pp.174-175.
13. TNA, MEPO2/9535.
14. *The Daily Mirror*, 25, 26 March 1953; *Sunday Pictorial*, 29 March 1953; *The News of the World*, 29 March 1953.

15. *Sunday Pictorial*, 29 March 1953.
16. TNA, MEPO2/9535.
17. TNA, MEPO3/9535.
18. Ibid.
19. Ibid.
20. Ibid.
21. Ibid.
22. *Sunday Pictorial*, 28 June 1953; *The Halifax Daily Courier and Guardian*, 26 March 1953.
23. Oates, *John Christie*, pp.6-7; J. Maxwell, *The Christie Case* (1953), p.20.
24. Oates, *John Christie*, pp.7-9.
25. *Halifax Guardian*, 16 April 1921; *Halifax Daily Courier and Guardian*, 15 January 1923.
26. *West Middlesex Gazette*, 27 September 1924
27. *The South Western Star*, 17 May 1929.
28. *Middlesex Advertiser and Gazette*, 3 November 1933.
29. Oates, John Christie, pp.25-29.
30. Ibid, pp.30-33, 41-42, 93, 103.
31. Ibid, pp.38-39.
32. Ibid, pp.33-35.
33. F. Tennyson-Jesse, *The Trials of Evans and Christie* (1957), pp.157-158.
34. Ibid, p.158.
35. Ibid, p.161.
36. Peter Thorley, *Inside 10 Rillington Place* (2020); J. Eddowes, *The Two Killers of Rillington Place* (1994); John Curnow, *The Murders, Myths and Reality of 10 Rillington Place* (2016); Oates, *John Christie*.
37. Islington Local Studies Centre, Diary of Gladys Langford, 1953.
38. Tennyson-Jesse, *The Trials of Evans and Christie* Ibid, p.209.
39. TNA, PCOM9/1668.
40. *Sunday Pictorial*, 28 June 1953.
41. Ibid.
42. Ibid.
43. Ibid, 5 and 12 July 1953.
44. TNA, HO227/291.
45. TNA, PCOM9/1668.
46. *Sunday Pictorial*, 26 July 1953.
47. *Sunday Pictorial*, 12 July 1953.
48. TNA, MEPO2/9535.
49. *Sunday Pictorial*, 28 June 1953.
50. TNA, MEPO2/9535.
51. TNA, MEPO3/9535; CAB143/21.
52. TNA, MEPO2/9535.

Chapter 9
1. *Hammersmith and Shepherd's Bush Gazette*, 6 February 1964; Wandsworth Local Studies Centre, Dairy of Barbara Robinson, 1964.
2. *Hammersmith and Shepherd's Bush Gazette*, 6 February 1964.
3. *Torbay Express*, 5 February 1964.
4. *Hammersmith and Shepherd's Bush Gazette*, 30 April 1964, *Liverpool Echo* 24 April 1964, *Newcastle Journal* 6 February 1964, *Daily Mirror* 5 February 1964.
5. *Newcastle Journal*, 6 February 1964.
6. *Hammersmith and Shepherd's Bush Gazette*, 30 April 1964.
7. *Newcastle Journal*, 6 February 1964.
8. P. Hoskins, *Sound of Murder*, (1971), p.146.
9. *Newcastle Journal*, 6 February, 1964.

10. *Hammersmith and Shepherd's Bush Gazette*, 30 April 1964.
11. *Daily Mirror*, 11 February 1964.
12. Simpson, *Forty Years*, p.191.
13. *Hammersmith and Shepherd's Bush Gazette* 23 April 1964; *Daily Mirror*, 11 April 1964.
14. *Daily Mirror*, 10 April 1964.
15. Ibid.
16. *Daily Mirror* 12 April 1964.
17. *Hammersmith and Shepherd's Bush Gazette*, 23 April 1964.
18. Ibid.
19. *Acton Gazette*, 7 May 1964.
20. Ibid, 14 May 1964.
21. Ibid, 21 May 1964.
22. Ibid, 28 May 1964.
23. Ibid, 25 June 1964
24. *Middlesex County Times*, 2 May 1964.
25. Ibid; *Daily Mirror*, 27 April 1964.
26. *Coventry Evening Telegraph*, 25 April 1964 *Birmingham Daily Post* 28 April 1964.
27. *Daily Herald* 25 April 1964.
28. *Liverpool Echo*, 25 April 1964.
29. *Daily Mirror*, 25 April 1964. *Belfast Telegraph*, 27 April 1964.
30. *Liverpool Echo*, 25 April 1964.
31. Ibid, 18 February 1965.
32. *Daily Mirror*, 24-25 April 1964.
33. *Belfast Telegraph*, 27 April 1964.
34. *Liverpool Echo*, 28 April 1964.
35. *The People*, 12 April 1964.
36. *Daily Herald*, 25 April 1964, *Daily Mirror*, 27 April 1964, *The People*, 12 April 1964.
37. J. Oates, *Unsolved London Murders: 1940s and 1950s* (2009), pp.160-166.
38. *Daily Mirror*, 4 December 1963; *Daily Herald*, 27 November 1963; *Liverpool Daily Echo*, 26 November 1963.
39. *Acton Gazette*, 16 July 1964.
40. Ibid.
41. *Aberdeen Press and Journal*, 15 July 1964.
42. *Daily Herald*, 15 July 1964.
43. *Liverpool Echo*, 18 February 1965.
44. *Hammersmith and Shepherd's Bush Gazette*, 4 June 1964.
45. *Daily Mirror*, 27 November 1964.
46. *Daily Mirror*, 27 and 28 November 1964.
47. *Kensington Post*, 26 February 1965.
48. *Kensington Post*, 26 February 1965.
49. *Coventry Evening Telegraph*, 24 February 1965.
50. *Liverpool Echo*, 18 February 1965.
51. *Daily Mirror*, 3 December 1964.
52. *Middlesex County Times*, 26 February 1965, *Torbay Express*, 19 February 1965, *Liverpool Echo*, 18 February 1965, *Hammersmith and Shepherd's Bush Gazette*, 17 February 1966.
53. *Daily Mirror*, 3 December 1965.
54. *Daily Mirror*, 17 February 1965.
55. *Hammersmith and Shepherd's Bush Gazette*, 12 October 1980.
56. *Acton Gazette*, 18 February 1965, *Hammersmith and Shepherd's Bush Gazette*, 17 February 1966.
57. *Daily Mirror*, 19 February 1965.
58. *Liverpool Echo*, 18 February 1965.
59. *Acton Gazette*, 25 February 1965.
60. *Middlesex County Times*, 26 February 1965.

61. *Coventry Evening Telegraph*, 19 February 1965.
62. *Liverpool Echo*, 18 February 1965.
63. *Daily Mirror*, 23 February 1965.
64. *The People*, 21 February 1965.
65. *Newcastle Journal*, 27 February 1965.
66. David Bowen, *Body of Evidence* (2003).
67. Hoskins, *Sound*, pp.148-150.
68. Michael Bilton, *Wicked beyond belief* (2012), p.94.
69. Hoskins, *Sound*, pp.150-152.
70. Ibid, p.152.
71. DuRose, *Murder*, pp.106-107.
72. *Hammersmith and Shepherd's Bush Gazette*, 17 February 1966.
73. Ibid.
74. TNA, MEPO2/10321.
75. *Hammersmith and Shepherd's Bush Gazette*, 17 February 1966.
76. Ibid.
77. TNA, MEPO26/26.
78. David Seabrooke, *Jack of Jumps* (2007), pp.310, 321-322.
79. DuRose, *Murder*, p.107.
80. Richard Jackson, *Occupied with Crime* (1966), p.94n.
81. *Hammersmith and Shepherd's Bush Gazette*, 9 February 1978.
82. Brian McConnell, *Found Naked and Dead* (1975).
83. Neil Milkins, *Who was Jack the Stripper?* (2011).
84. MEPO26/171.
85. Seabrooke, *Jack*, pp.354-363.
86. Cherill, *Cherill*, p.128.

Chapter 10
1. *Penny Illustrated Paper*, 18 June 1881.
2. *Worcester Journal*, 11 February 1882.
3. *Reynold's News*, 5 June 1881.
4. *The Times*, 15 February 1890.
5. Ibid.
6. Ibid, 18 February, 4 March and 17 May 1890.
7. Ibid, 12 August 1892.
8. *Hampshire Telegraph*, 20 July 1895 *Coventry Evening Telegraph*, 18 July 1895.
9. *Essex Herald*, 10 January and 7 February 1899.
10. *North Devon Gazette*, 28 March 1899; *Bury and Norwich Post*, 28 March 1895.
11. *Essex Newsman*, 14 May 1887.
12. *Western Times*, 7 June 1887.
13. *Times*, 9 October 1888; *Daily Telegraph*, 23 October 1888.
14. *Times*, 11 and 25 September 1889.
15. TNA, MEPO3/1702.
16. Ibid.
17. Ibid.
18. Ibid.
19. Ibid.
20. Ibid.
21. Ibid.
22. Ibid.
23. Ibid.
24. F.D. Sharpe, *Sharpe of the Flying Squad* (1938), p.125.
25. TNA, MEPO3/1706.
26. Ibid.

27. Ibid.
28. Ibid.
29. Ibid.
30. Ibid.
31. Ibid.
32. Ibid, 1707.
33. Ibid.
34. Ibid.
35. Ibid.
36. Ibid.
37. Ibid.
38. Ibid.
39. Ibid.
40. Ibid.
41. Sharpe, *Sharpe,* p.117.
42. TNA, MEPO3/1707.
43. Ibid.
44. Ibid.
45. Sharpe, *Sharpe,* p.117.
46. *Daily Herald*, 11 November 1946
47. Ibid, 12 November 1946.
48. *Daily Herald*, 11 November 1946.
49. Ancestry.co.uk, wills index.
50. *Liverpool Echo*, 9 September 1947
51. Ibid.
52. *Hull Daily Mail*, 7 September 1948.
53. *Daily Mirror*, 7 September 1948
54. *Daily Herald*, 22 September 1948
55. TNA, MEPO3/3026.
56. Ibid.
57. Ibid.
58. Ibid.
59. Ibid.
60. Ibid.
61. Ibid.
62. Ibid.
63. Ibid.
64. Ibid.
65. Ibid.
66. Ibid.
67. Ibid.
68. Ibid.
69. Ibid.
70. Ibid.
71. *The Sun*, 15 July 2015.

Bibliography

Manuscripts

The National Archives
CAB143/21
CRIM1/155
CRIM1/1397
HO45/23634
HO45/23635
HO45/23636
HO227/291
MEPO2/140
MEPO2/9535, 1798
MEPO2/10321
MEPO3/141, 3153
MEPO3/225B
MEPO3/1702
MEPO3/1706
MEPO3/1707
MEPO2/2206
MEPO3/3026
MEPO3/3128
MEPO20/1
MEPO26/26
MEPO26/171
PCOM8/138
PCOM9/919
PCOM9/1668

London Metropolitan Archives
COR/LN/1941/217-218
COR/LN/1942/044

Islington Local Studies Centre
Diaries of Gladys Langford, 1942, 1949, 1953

Wandsworth Local Studies Centre
Diary of Barbara Robinson, 1964

Printed

H.L. Adam, *Trial of George Chapman*, (1930).
Robert Anderson, *The Lighter Side of my Official Life* (1910).
David Bowen, *Body of Evidence* (2003).
Daniel Brabin, *Rillington Place* (1966).
Francis Camps, *Medical and Scientific Investigations in the Christie Case*, (1953).
Fred Cherrill, *Cherrill of the Yard*, (1954).
A.C. Doyle, 'The Adventure of the Speckled Band' and 'The Disappearance of Lady Frances Carfax'.
Lord Dunboyne, *Trial of John Haigh*, (1953).
John DuRose, *Murder was my Business* (1971).
Percy Hoskins, *Sound of Murder*, (1971).
Melville MacNaghten, *Days of my Years* (1914).
James Maxwell, *The Christie Case* (1953).
Medical Officer of Health for Greenwich Annual Report for 1894.
Lambeth Medical Officer of Health Annual Report for 1891.
Whitechapel Medical Officer of Health Annual Report for 1888.
Arthur Fowler Neil, *Forty Years of Man-Hunting* (1932).
F.D. Sharpe, *Sharpe of the Flying Squad* (1938).
W.T. Shore, *The Trial of Neil Cream* (1922).
Keith Simpson, *Forty Years of Murder* (1980).
F. Tennyson-Jesse, *The Trials of Evans and Christie* (1957).
Peter Thorley, *Inside 10 Rillington Place* (2020).
Eric R. Watson, *Trial of George Joseph Smith* (1930).

Newspapers

Aberdeen Press and Journal, 1964.
Acton Gazette, 1964, 1965.
Belfast Telegraph, 1964.
Birmingham Daily Post, 1964.
Bury and Norwich Post, 1895.
Coventry Evening Telegraph, 1895, 1964, 1965.
Daily Citizen, 1915.
Daily Herald 1946, 1948, 1963-1964.
Daily Mail, 2020.
Daily Mirror, 1948, 1953, 1964, 1965.
Daily Telegraph, 1888.
Dundee Courier, 1903.
Dundee Evening Telegraph, 1892.
Dundee People's Journal, 1915.
Eastbourne Chronicle, 1942.
Evening Standard, 1892, 1902.
Halifax Daily Courier and Guardian, 1923, 1953.
Halifax Guardian, 1921.
Hammersmith and Shepherd's Bush Gazette, 1964, 1966, 1978, 1980.
Hampshire Telegraph, 1895.
Hartlepool Northern Daily Mail, 1889.
Hastings and St. Leonard's Observer, 1901.
Hull Daily Mail, 1948.
Kensington Post, 1965.
Kentish Independent, 1889.
Kentish Mercury, 1889.
Larne Times, 1915.

Leeds Mercury, 1915, 1934.
Liverpool Echo, 1947, 1964, 1965.
Londonderry Sentinel 1903, 1915.
Luton Reporter, 1889.
Manchester Evening News, 1915.
Middlesex Advertiser and Gazette, 1933.
Middlesex County Times, 1964, 1965.
Newcastle Evening Chronicle, 1892.
Newcastle Journal, 1964, 1965.
News of the World, 1953.
North Devon Gazette, 1899.
Northern Times, 1915.
Penny Illustrated Paper, 1881.
People, 1964, 1965.
Reynold's Newspaper, 1881, 1889.
South London Chronicle, 1902-1903.
South London Press, 1892, 1902-1903.
South Wales Echo, 1889.
South Western Star, 1929.
Sun, 2015.
Sunday Pictorial, 1949, 1953.
Surrey Advertiser, 1937.
Times, 1890, 1892, 1953.
Torbay Express, 1964, 1965.
West Middlesex Gazette, 1924.
Western Mail 1903, 1915.
Western Times, 1891.
Worcester Journal, 1882.
Worcestershire Chronicle, 1903.

Books

Michael Bilton, *Wicked beyond belief: The Hunt for the Yorkshire Ripper* (2012).
Jan Bondeson, *Murder Houses of London* (2015).
Jan Bondeson, *Murder Houses of South London* (2015).
John Curnow, *The Murders, Myths and Reality of 10 Rillington Place* (2016).
John Eddowes, *The Two Killers of Rillington Place* (1993).
Richard Jones, *The Jack the Ripper Files*, (2014).
Brian McConnell, *Found Naked and Dead* (1975).
Angus McLaren, *A Prescription for Murder: The Victorian Serial Killings of Dr Thomas Neill Cream* (1990).
Neil Milkins, *Who was Jack the Stripper?* (2011).
Jonathan Oates, *Foul Deeds and Suspicious Deaths in Lewisham and Deptford* (2007).
Jonathan Oates, *Unsolved London Murders: 1940s and 1950s* (2009).
Jonathan Oates, *John Christie: Biography of a Serial Killer* (2012).
Jonathan Oates, *John George Haigh: A Portrait of a serial killer and his victims* (2014).
Jane Robins, *The Magnificent Spilsbury and the Brides in the Bath* (2014).
David Seabrooke, *Jack of Jumps* (2007)
David Wilson, *British Serial Killings* (2006).
Helen Wojtczak, *Jack the Ripper at last: The Mysterious Murders of George Chapman*, (2014).

Electronic sources

Ancestry.co.uk; census returns, baptism and marriage registers, indexes to civil registration records; wills.
Old Bailey online.
Tales from the Black Museum, John George Haigh, Discovery Channel, 1999.

Index

Acton 146, 160, 163-164, 166-167, 169, 172
Adams, Dr John Bodkin 43, 62, 79

Barthelemy, Helen 160-162, 168, 170
Bolton, Sidney 34-38, 40-42, 45
Bond, Dr Thomas 22, 37
Brentford 160, 162, 172
Brown, Frances 164-166, 172
Burnham, Alice 88-91, 95

Camps, Dr Francis 2, 137-138
Carter, Eliza 174
Chapman, Annie 6-10
Chapman, George 64-81, 94-95, 97, 118, 194
Cherrill, Superintendent Frederick 102-103, 105, 108, 110, 114-115, 117-118, 173
Chiswick 158-160, 163-164, 172
Christie, Agatha 1, 81, 133
Christie, Ethel 139, 141-142, 145-152, 154
Christie, John 1, 115, 138, 156-162, 167, 173, 193-195
Clover, Matilda 48-51, 55-56, 58-62
Coles, Frances 23
Cook, Margaret 185-186, 189-190
Coroners 5-6, 8-9, 14, 17-18, 21, 37, 44, 47, 54-56, 58, 77, 94, 158, 169
Cotton, Marie 181-182, 185
Cream, Dr Thomas Neill 56-63, 73, 80, 97, 118, 193-195
Cummins, Gordon 106, 111-118, 140, 173, 187, 191, 194-195

Deptford 1, 28-29, 30-45, 54, 195
Doctors 3-5, 7-8, 11, 13-14, 16-17, 21, 23, 30-37, 44, 48, 51, 54, 58,67-70, 73-78, 87-91, 93-96, 158, 169
Donworth, Ellen 46-47, 54, 59, 62
Druitt, Montague 24-25
Durand-Deacon, Henrietta 119-126, 129, 131, 135-136
DuRose, John 120-122, 168-171

Eady, Muriel 146, 148-149, 152-154, 195
Ealing 160, 163
Eddowes, Catherine 14-18
Executions 45, 61, 78, 98, 118, 132, 151

Fennick, Rachel 187-190
Figg, Elizabeth 163-164
Fleming, Mary 163-165, 168, 170
Freedman, Helen 186-187, 189
Frost, Elizabeth 29-32, 34-45
Frost, Elizabeth Jane 30-32, 37, 39-42
Fuerst, Ruth 147-148, 151-154

Green, Violet 186, 189-190

Haigh, John 1, 80, 114, 119-136, 140, 150-151, 154-156, 168, 173, 193-196
Hamilton, Evelyn 101-103, 105, 108, 111, 113, 118
Hammersmith 129, 144, 146, 157-158, 165, 168-169, 171-172
Harvey, Louisa 49-50, 57, 59, 61
Henderson, Dr Archibald 122-123, 126-128, 134-136
Henderson, Rose 122-123, 126-128, 134, 136
Hinds, Leah 182-185
Hospitals 3, 26, 35, 37, 46, 49-50, 53-56, 72-73, 76
Huckle, Emily
Humphreys, Sir Travers 97, 117, 131

Inquests 5-8, 11, 14, 17-18, 21-22, 38-40, 44, 47, 54-55, 58-59, 77-78, 87, 90, 94-95, 158, 165, 167, 169, 181

Jack the Ripper 1, 10, 23, 27-28, 37, 40, 51, 59, 62-63, 65, 79-80, 101, 112, 116, 118, 163, 170-171, 174, 177, 184, 194-195
Jeffs, Amelia 174-177
Joaunnet, Doris 108-111, 118

Kelly, Marie 19-22, 37
Kensington 82, 164
Kosminski, Aaron 24-25

Lambeth 46-47, 49, 52, 61, 81
Langford, Gladys 105
Lockwood, Irene 159-160, 164
Lofty, Margaret Elizabeth 90-95, 99
Lowe, Margaret 105-108, 114, 118

MacKenzie, Alice 23
Maclennan, Hectorina 139, 144, 154
MacSwan, Amy 122-123, 126-127, 134-135

215

McSwan, Donald 122-123, 126-127, 134-135
McSwan, William 122-123, 126-127, 130, 134-135, 195
Madam Tuassaud's Waxworks 27, 63, 80, 100, 132, 151
Maloney, Katherine 138-139, 143-144, 152-154
Marsh, Alice 52-55, 57-58, 61-62
Marsh, Maud 71-78
Martin, Josephine 178-181, 185
Mundy, Bessie 84-88, 90-91, 97

Neil, Arthur 76, 79, 95-96, 98
Nelson, Rita 139, 143-144, 153-154
Newgate Prison 60
Newspapers 1, 28, 41-42, 51, 54, 56, 71, 88, 90, 95, 98, 112, 118, 132, 136, 140, 145, 150-151, 156, 158, 162, 170
Nichols, Mary Ann 4-8, 10
Notting Hill 137, 140, 146, 159-160, 162-166, 171, 195

Oatley, Evelyn 103-105, 108, 113-114, 118, 194
O'Hara, Bridget 166-167, 169-170, 173
Old Bailey 41-42, 60, 78, 82, 97-98, 113-114, 145, 160
Ostrog, Michael 24-25

Pegler, Edith 83-84, 88, 90-91, 94, 98-100
Phillips, Dr 7-8, 13-14, 21, 23
Pentonville Prison 151
Poison 28-30, 38, 43-44, 46, 48, 51, 53, 55-56, 58-59, 61, 63, 66, 76-77, 80-81
Prostitutes 4, 9, 46-47, 52, 57-58, 60, 101, 106-107, 109, 111, 113, 118, 138-139, 154, 156-157, 161-162, 164-165, 168, 178, 184-189, 192-193
Pubs 4, 8, 12, 46, 48, 50, 64, 66-74, 76, 126, 130, 160, 165-166, 188

Rees, Gwyneth 161, 163, 169
Russ, Bertha 177

Seward, Mary 174-175, 177
Shepherd's Bush 95, 139, 158, 166, 168
Shipman, Dr Harold 43, 62, 79
Shrivell, Emma 52-55, 57-58, 61-62
Simpson, Dr Keith 2, 128-129
Smith, George Joseph 81-100, 115, 136, 140, 193-194, 196
Soho 1, 104, 111, 113, 181, 184-187
Southwark 15, 48, 69, 76-77
Spilsbury, Sir Bernard 2, 96-97, 108, 114, 180-181, 183
Spink, Mary 65-68, 77, 79
Spitalfields 3, 6, 8-9, 13, 15
Stevenson, Sir John 37-38, 54-56, 60, 77
Stride, Elizabeth 12-14, 25
Sutton, John 30, 32-34, 37-42

Tabram, Martha, 4, 6
Tailford, Hannah 157-159
Taylor, Bessie 68-71, 77
Teare, Dr Donald 159-160, 162, 167
Thames, River 25, 29, 46, 156, 160, 162-163, 171, 177-178
Trials 41-42, 60, 78, 97-98, 131-132, 150-151
Tumblety, Dr Francis 25-26

Upper Holloway

Wandsworth Prison 78, 118, 132, 146
West Ham 45, 174-177, 190
Whitechapel 3-4, 9-10, 22, 24-26, 64-65, 79-80, 164, 178
Winters, Amelia 29-46, 80-81, 191, 193-195
Workhouses 4-5, 7, 15, 30, 33, 38, 43, 68

Yorkshire Ripper 18, 26, 157, 166, 168, 170-171, 173, 191